D1249383

Macromedia®
Dreamweaver® MX

fast&easy®
web development

Annesha Bakharia

Premier
Press

Publisher: Stacy L. Hiquet

Marketing Manager: Heather Buzzingham

Managing Editor: Sandy Doell

Acquisitions Editor: Kevin Harreld

Project Editor: Kim V. Benbow

Editorial Assistant: Margaret Bauer

Marketing Coordinator: Kelly Poffenbarger

Technical Reviewer: Greg Perry

Copy Editor: Howard Jones

Interior Layout: Marian Hartsough

Cover Design: Mike Tanamachi

Indexer: Kelly Talbot

Proofreader: Elizabeth Agostinelli

ISBN: 1-931841-88-8

Library of Congress Catalog Card Number: 2002104491

Printed in the United States of America

02 03 04 05 RI 10 9 8 7 6 5 4 3 2 1

This book is dedicated to my family.

Without their love, support,
and encouragement,
this book would not have been completed.

Acknowledgments

I would like to thank the following people:

- My Grandmother who took care of me before I started school.

- My Mum for taking care of me even though I'm all grown up now.

- My Dad for forcing me to attend a computer course 12 years ago. That is where my career began.

- Kevin Harrald (acquisitions editor) for his enthusiasm and support throughout the whole project.

- Kim Benbow (project editor) for her patience, understanding and close attention to detail. Kim is an excellent editor and really made this book happen!

- Greg Perry (technical editor) and Howard Jones (copy editor) for providing valuable suggestions and comments.

- The entire Premier Press team for a job well done. Marian Hartsough (interior layout), Kelly Talbot (indexer), and Elizabeth Agostinelli (proofreader).

- My family (Kulsum, Hajira, Shaida, Julie, Celine, Tess, Zaeem, Ebrahem, Rashid, Cassim, Anne & Judy).

- Everybody who worked on the first and second edition of this book, especially the previous project editors Heather Talbot and Lori Swan.

- Emi Smith for her continued support and encouragement.

- Tracy Willaims for giving me the opportunity to write the first edition of this book.

- And Madonna for making excellent *MUSIC*.

About the Author

ANEESHA BAKHARIA is a Web developer and author. She is fluent in C#, Java, JavaScript, ASP, JSP, HTML, XML, and VB.NET. Aneesha specializes in creating dynamic database-driven Web sites. She has a Bachelor of Engineering degree in Microelectronic Engineering and various postgraduate qualifications in multimedia, online course development, and Web design. In her spare time, she is a keen Madonna fan. She can be reached via e-mail at aneesha@iprimus.com.au.

Contents at a Glance

Contents

Introduction

While the Web was still in its infancy, the technologies used to deliver it were always changing. I remember a time when I had to hand-code every page in a Web site. At that time, a Web site was just a couple of static pages. Still, dealing with raw HTML tags was not very pleasant. A few WYSIWYG (What You See Is What You Get) tools began to appear, but nothing really impressed me. Most tools did not produce clean HTML that looked identical in popular Web browsers like Microsoft Internet Explorer and Netscape Navigator. Static content seemed to rule. But the size of the Web sites that I was developing grew beyond the point where I could hand-code every page.

I dreamed of a tool that could answer all my prayers, a tool that would allow me to create Web sites visually and still allow me to tweak the code. In 1997, Macromedia made my dream come true when they released Dreamweaver. It certainly answered the prayers of Web developers all over the world. Dreamweaver is currently one of the most popular Web site design tools.

Today, static pages no longer rule the Web, though technologies are still always changing. The trend has once again shifted, and database-driven Web sites are now the norm. Once again, you have to acquire new skills—this time in database design and server-side scripting.

All this required knowledge can be overwhelming unless you have a sound programming background or the time to leverage your existing skills to create dynamic database-driven applications. Until recently, you had a steep learning curve ahead.

Enter Dreamweaver MX, an amazing upgrade to Dreamweaver. Dreamweaver MX allows you to create a Web-enabled database in a snap. You can simply design your database without having to worry about writing code to perform standard tasks such as displaying, inserting, updating, and deleting records. So even if you're an expert at hand-coding dynamic Web sites, Dreamweaver MX can vastly improve your productivity. Probably the best feature is that Dreamweaver MX supports five of the most popular application servers available: ASP (Active Server Pages), ASP.NET, JSP (JavaServer Pages), PHP, and ColdFusion. Using a single tool to develop for multiple application servers is now a reality. As a Web developer who is comfortable with using Dreamweaver MX, you can now develop applications that will run just about anywhere.

Dreamweaver MX still incorporates all those features that made Dreamweaver great in the first place:

- **WYSIWYG Web page design**. Dreamweaver MX has an array of visual tools to help you build flawless HTML. Tables, image maps, links, frames, and layers can all be created by clicking a few buttons.

- **Round-trip HTML**. You can configure Dreamweaver MX to generate HTML exactly the way you want. All code can be edited without any interference from Dreamweaver MX.

- **Web site management**. The Site window provides a central location from which you can manage your entire Web site in terms of structure and links.

- **A built-in FTP (File Transfer Protocol) client** that enables you to transfer files to a remote Web server. You don't need to use another application just to upload and download files to a remote server.

- **Templates**. You can easily create templates for your Web site. Templates allow you to concentrate on content rather than layout

- **Collaboration tools**. Design Notes and File Check-in/Check-out make it a pleasure to work in a team environment. You don't need to worry about overwriting files or miscommunicating with other team members.

- **Automation**. Almost everything that you do in Dreamweaver MX is recorded in the History panel. Your actions can be edited and stored for later use. There is no reason why you should have to do repetitive tasks over and over.

- **Behaviors**. Behaviors allow you to create image rollovers, play sounds, open browser windows, and animate layers. Behaviors do all the hard work and insert the required client-side JavaScript into your Web page.

- **Extensibility**. You have full access to the Dreamweaver MX JavaScript API (Application Programming Interface) and DOM. With a working knowledge of JavaScript you can create new extensions (objects, commands, and behaviors). You can also download extensions from Dreamweaver MX Exchange (http://www.macromedia.com/exchange).

Dreamweaver versus Dreamweaver MX

The following additions make creating dynamic database-driven Web sites possible in Dreamweaver MX:

- The Bindings panel simplifies the process normally used to retrieve and display data from a database. You can now query your database and bind the returned data to a Web page in a totally visual manner. You can also retrieve and display posted form data, cookies, and session variables.

- Server behaviors are the key to Dreamweaver MX's success. Server behaviors generate server-side code to provide the database functionality you require. They can be used to create multi-paged search results with intuitive navigation. Server behaviors also enable you to create a Web-based interface for your database. Web site visitors can insert, update, and delete records in a database. All of this functionality can be implemented on any of the five application servers that Dreamweaver MX supports.

- Dreamweaver MX is the first Web development tool to allow server-side data (including data retrieved from a database) to be viewed and edited in the same environment. There is no need to switch repeatedly between your Web browser and Dreamweaver MX. You can bind data to a Web page, instantly view the results, and apply formatting in Live Data View.

- Application objects facilitate the creation of common features found in database-driven Web sites. A wizard-driven interface will guide you though the process of creating customized master-detail page sets, inserting new records, updating existing records, displaying recordset statistics, and navigating search results that span multiple pages. The resulting Web pages are completely editable in Dreamweaver MX.

- Password protection is now easier than ever to implement with the introduction of Authentication server behaviors. You can now build login pages, validate users against a database, and restrict access to pages in your Web site. It is also possible to require Web site visitors to register before they are allowed to access your Web site.

- The Server Behavior Builder has tremendously simplified the creation of server behaviors. You don't need to spend any time learning about the Dreamweaver MX API or reading through the lengthy Dreamweaver MX reference manual. The Server Behavior Builder transforms your server-side code into a reusable server behavior. This leaves you with more time to concentrate on building dynamic Web applications.

What You Need to Get Started

The source code for this book is available for download from http://www.premier pressbooks.com/downloads.asp.

To follow the instructions in this book, you will also need

- Dreamweaver MX

- Internet Information Server (IIS)

- Access 2000/XP

Developing Web applications will never be the same again. Let the fun begin . . .

Conventions Used in This Book

Many Dreamweaver MX commands can be selected with either a mouse or the keyboard, so menu commands in this book are written in a way that enable you to choose the method you prefer. For example, if the instruction says "Choose File, Open," click on the File menu to open the menu, and then click on the Open option. Alternatively, you can press the Alt key and the letter F to open the File menu, and then press the letter O to select Open.

When you need to hold down the first key while you press a second key, a plus sign (+) is used to show this combination (such as Alt+f or Ctrl+z). When two keys are pressed in sequence, they are separated with a comma. For example, the hot-key sequence for opening a file would be written as "Alt+f,o."

You will also find several special elements that will make using this book easier as you read each chapter.

- **Tips** tell you about new and faster ways to accomplish a goal.

- **Notes** delve into background information regarding a given topic.

- **Cautions** warn about pitfalls and glitches in the application or procedures.

1

Introducing Dreamweaver MX

You'll be pleased to know that the Dreamweaver interface has had a major makeover. Dreamweaver has always had a relatively simple interface, but Macromedia obviously decided that it was time to take Web development to the next level. Dreamweaver MX delivers a truly user-friendly, intuitive, and customizable interface. In this chapter, you'll learn how to do the following:

- Identify the main interface windows and panels
- Manage panels and Panel Groups

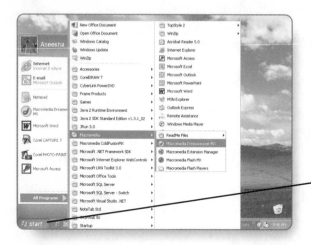

Exploring the Dreamweaver MX Interface

In this section you will learn how to open Dreamweaver MX and learn about the integral interface elements.

1. Click on the Start button. The Start menu appears.

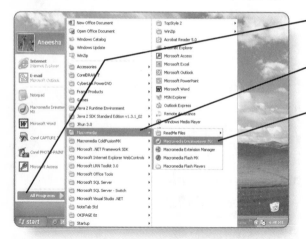

2. Click on All Programs. The Programs menu appears.

3. Click on Macromedia. A submenu appears.

4. Click on Macromedia Dreamweaver MX. Dreamweaver MX opens and displays a blank Web page in the Document window.

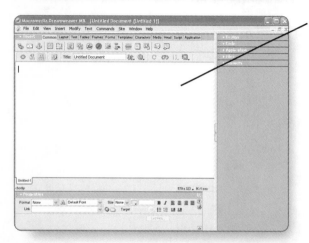

5. The Document window displays the current Web page. All Web page editing is done within the Document window.

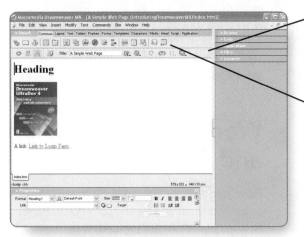

6. The Document toolbar contains buttons that enable you to view the HTML source code and enter a title, as well as preview the current Web page.

7. The Insert bar contains objects that help you visually create a Web page. Objects are really just wizards that generate HTML code. Related objects are grouped together within a tab. The Common tab includes objects that insert tables, links, and images.

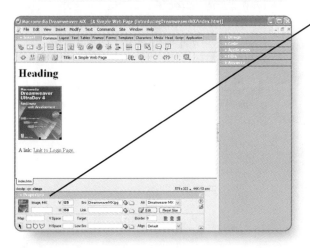

8. The Properties Inspector reflects the properties that belong to the currently selected item in the Document window.

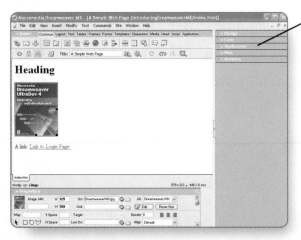

9. Panel Groups contain related panels that have been docked together.

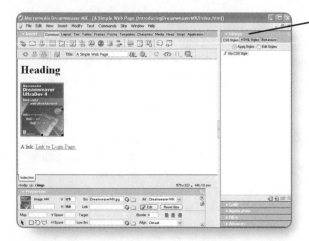

10. The Design Panel Group contains the CSS Styles, HTML Styles, and Behaviors tabs. A docked panel becomes a tab within the Panel Group.

Working with Panels and Panel Groups

Panels and Panel Groups enable you to make the most of screen real estate. Panel Groups can easily be expanded or contracted as required. You can even choose to hide the Panel Groups when you require more space for the Document window.

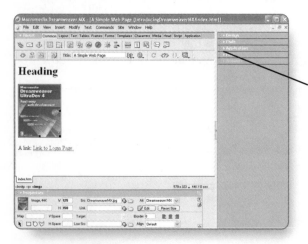

1. Click on an Expander arrow to expand a Panel Group. The docked panels are displayed as tabs on the Panel Group.

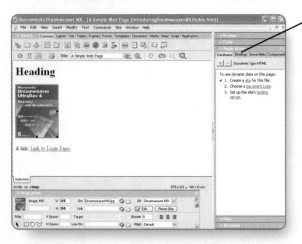

2. Click on a tab. The panel is displayed.

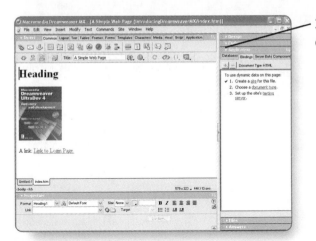

3. Click again on the arrow. The Panel Group is collapsed.

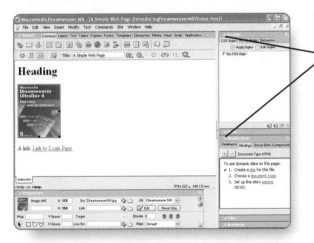

NOTE

Multiple Panel Groups can be expanded at the same time.

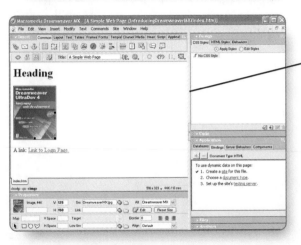

TIP

You can drag the splitter bar to give the Document window or Panel Groups more space as required.

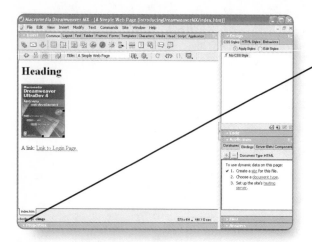

NOTE

The Properties Inspector can also be collapsed if you require more space while editing.

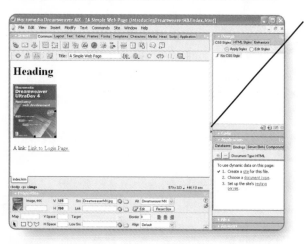

4. Click on the Hide Panel Groups button. The Document window expands to fill the screen.

5. Click on the Show Panel Groups button. The Panel Group is displayed again.

2

Dreamweaver MX Basics

Before you can master creating dynamic, database-driven Web sites, you need to be comfortable with using Dreamweaver MX as an HTML editor. Dreamweaver MX is an excellent WYSIWYG (What You See Is What You Get) editor that enables you to build complex HTML layouts in a matter of minutes. The flexibility that Dreamweaver MX brings to HTML editing is unmatched. In this chapter, you'll learn how to do the following:

- Open Dreamweaver MX
- Create, save, open, and close Web pages
- Format text
- Create hyperlinks
- Incorporate images in your Web pages
- Create and modify tables

Working with Web Pages

The most basic tasks in Dreamweaver MX are opening, saving, and closing files. You will always be performing these tasks, no matter what you are doing in Dreamweaver MX. They are simple to master and, after a while, will no doubt become second nature.

Opening Dreamweaver MX

After Dreamweaver MX has been installed, you can launch it from the Start menu.

1. Click on the Start button. The Start menu appears.

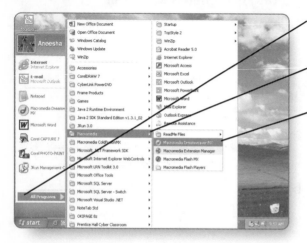

2. Click on All Programs. The Programs menu appears.

3. Click on Macromedia. A submenu appears.

4. Click on Macromedia Dreamweaver MX. Dreamweaver MX opens and displays a blank Web page in the Document window.

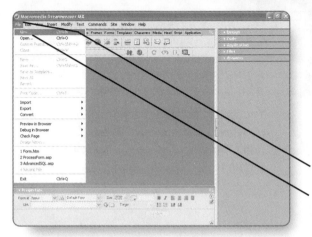

Creating a New Web Page

Before you can start work on your award-winning Web site, you first need to create a blank page. This is easily done in Dreamweaver MX.

1. Click on File. The File menu appears.

2. Click on New. The New Document dialog box opens.

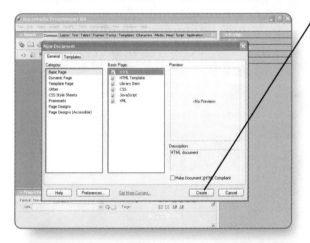

3. Click on Create. A blank Web page is displayed in the document window.

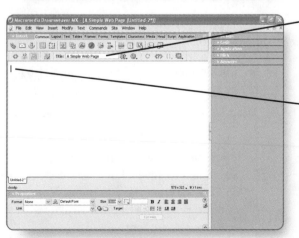

4. Enter a title for the Web page. The title describes the purpose of the page. The title is displayed in the Web browser's title bar.

5. Click inside the Document window. The cursor appears where you click.

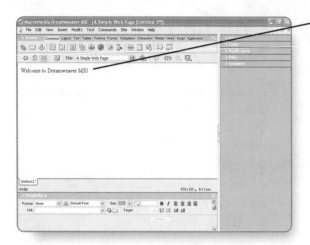

6. Type some text. The text appears in the Document window.

Saving a Web Page

You've just created the world's best Web page ever, but nobody will see it if you don't remember to save it. Luckily this is a simple task in Dreamweaver MX.

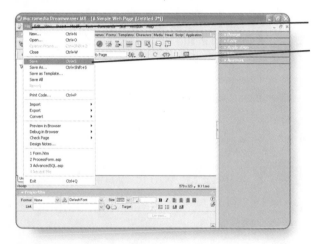

1. Click on File. The File menu appears.

2. Click on Save. The Save As dialog box opens.

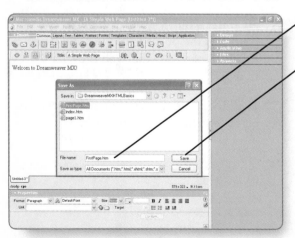

3. Type the name of the file in the File name field.

4. Click on Save. The Save As dialog box closes and the file is saved.

NOTE

If you have many files open and would like to save all of them, click on Save All from the File menu. You can also press Ctrl+s periodically to save your document.

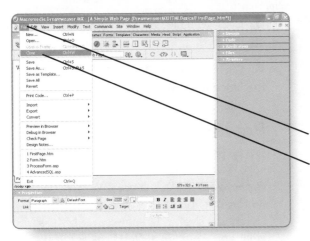

Closing a Web Page

It is a good idea to close files that are not currently in use. This prevents you from accidentally editing the Web pages and conserves precious memory.

1. Click on File. The File menu appears.

2. Click on Close. If your file has changed since the last time it was saved, you are prompted to save the file.

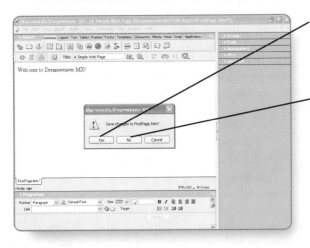

3a. Click on Yes. The Web page is saved and then closed.

OR

3b. Click on No. The Web page closes without saving new content.

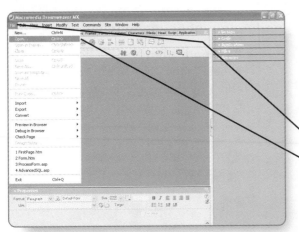

Opening a Web Page

Most Web developers spend more time editing then they do creating Web pages. But before pages can be edited, they must first be opened.

1. Click on File. The File menu appears.

2. Click on Open. The Open dialog box opens.

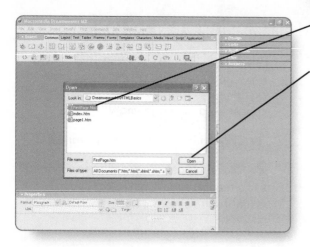

3. Click on a file. The file name is highlighted.

4. Click on Open. The file is displayed in the Document window.

Previewing a Web Page in a Browser

Dreamweaver MX is a great WYSIWYG editor, but you can't always trust that "what you see" in Dreamweaver MX "is what you'll get" in a Web browser. It is always wise to test your Web pages in popular browsers such as Netscape and Internet Explorer.

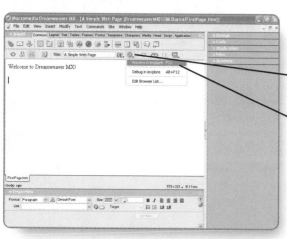

1. Click on the Preview/Debug button. A submenu appears.

2. Click on the browser you would like use to preview the Web page. The browser of your choice opens and the current Web page is displayed.

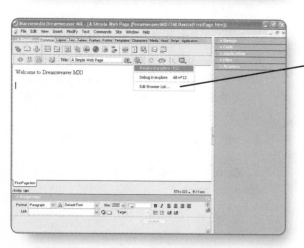

NOTE

If your preferred browser does not appear in the list, you can manually add it by choosing Edit Browser List from the submenu shown here.

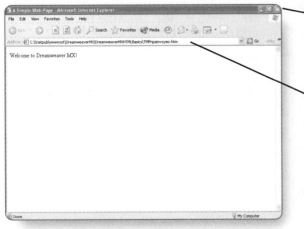

3. Click on the Close icon. The Web browser closes.

Quitting Dreamweaver MX

When you have completed your Web site, you will want to quit Dreamweaver MX. This is not a lengthy process, but Dreamweaver MX first makes sure that you have saved all your files before it exits.

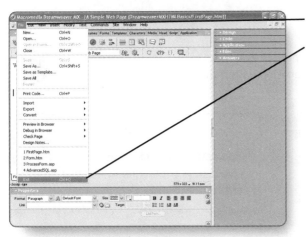

1. Click on File. The File menu appears.

2. Click on Exit. Dreamweaver MX closes.

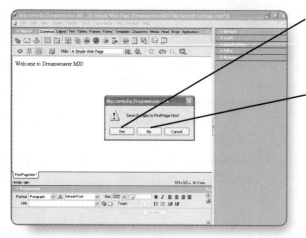

3a. Click on Yes. The Web page is saved and Dreamweaver MX exits.

OR

3b. Click on No. Dreamweaver MX exits without saving the Web page.

Working with Text

Creating, editing, and formatting text is no longer a chore. Dreamweaver MX incorporates functionality that used to be available only in word processing software. Master the following simple techniques, and working with text will always be a breeze.

Selecting Text

Text can be selected by using the mouse. You must select text before you can apply formatting or move text to a new location within the Document window.

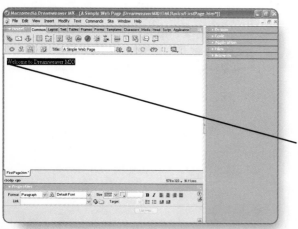

TIP

You can double-click on a word to select it. A triple-click will select an entire paragraph.

1. Click and hold the mouse button within the Document window. The cursor appears where you click.

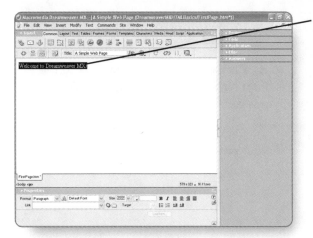

2. Drag the pointer across a line of text. The text is highlighted as you move the mouse. Release the mouse button. The selected text is highlighted on the screen.

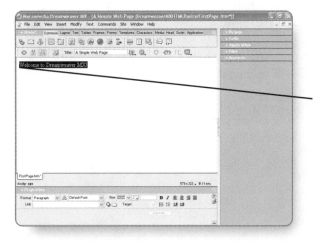

Deleting Text

The Delete key is used to remove selected text from the Web page.

1. Select the text you wish to delete. The text is highlighted.

2. Press the Delete key. The text is removed from the Web page.

Formatting Text

Dreamweaver MX enables you to format text in an extremely intuitive manner. You can easily change the font, size, and color of the currently selected text. All the changes to formatting are immediately reflected in the Document window because Dreamweaver MX is a WYSIWYG editor.

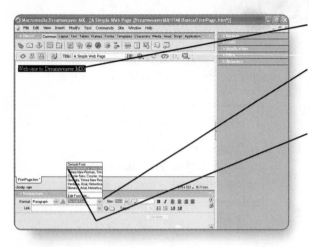

1. Select some text. The text is highlighted.

2. Click on the down arrow next to the Font Name list on the menu bar. A list of available fonts appears.

3. Click on a font name. The font style in your selected text changes accordingly.

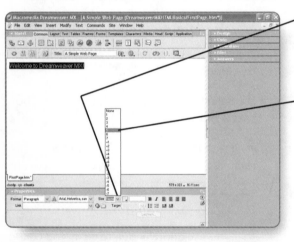

4. With the text still selected, click on the down arrow next to the Font Size list on the menu bar. A list of available font sizes appears.

5. Click on an appropriate size. The size of the selected text changes.

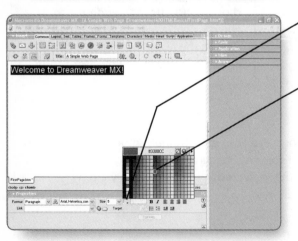

6. With the text still selected, click on the Text Color down arrow on the menu bar. The Colors palette appears.

7. Click on a color with the eyedropper cursor to select it. The color of the text changes.

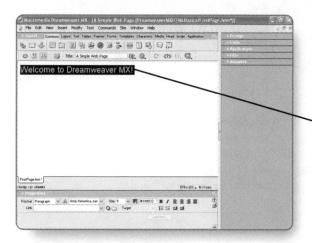

Moving Text

You can easily cut text from a page, move it to another location, or remove the text from the current Web page entirely.

1. Select the text you would like to move. The text is highlighted.

2. Press Ctrl+x. The selected text is removed from the document but still stored on the Clipboard for easy retrieval.

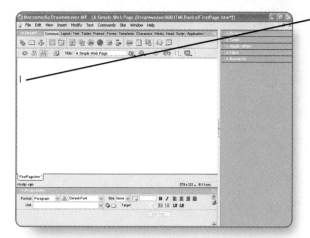

3. Click inside the Document window where you would like to insert the text. The cursor appears where you click.

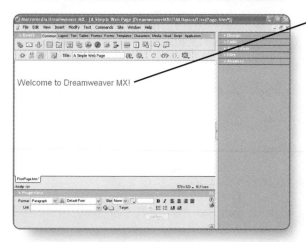

4. Press Ctrl+v. The text appears at the new location. All the formatting that has been applied to the text is retained.

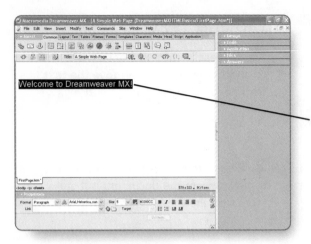

Copying and Pasting Text

You can copy text to a new location in the current Web page or to another page using keyboard shortcuts.

1. Select the text you would like to copy to a new location. The text is highlighted.

2. Press Ctrl+c. The selected text is copied to the Clipboard.

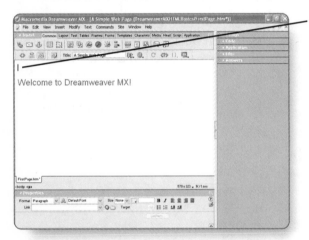

3. Click the mouse pointer at the new location where you would like to insert the text. The cursor appears where you clicked.

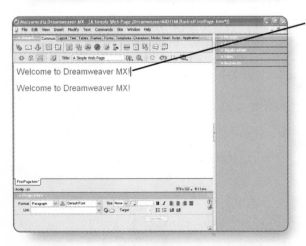

4. Press Ctrl+v. The copied text appears at the new location.

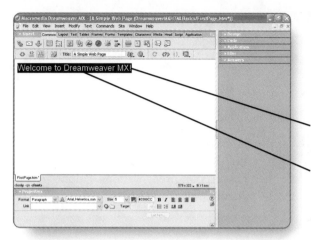

Drag-and-Drop Text Editing

In Dreamweaver MX, you can drag text around your Web page using the mouse.

1. Select the text you want to move. The text is highlighted.

2. Click and hold the selected text. The mouse pointer changes to the drag pointer.

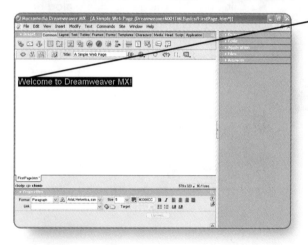

3. Drag the selected text to another location in the Document window. The drag pointer moves to the new location.

4. Release the mouse button. The selected text appears at the new location in the Document window.

Creating Links

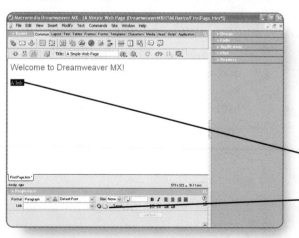

The World Wide Web is really just a series of documents held together by hyperlinks. Links may seem mysterious and complex if you have never created one before. Fear not, because you can't go wrong with Dreamweaver MX leading the way. Both text and images can be hyperlinked.

1. Select the text you want to link to another Web page. The text is highlighted.

2. Click on the Folder icon. The Select File dialog box opens.

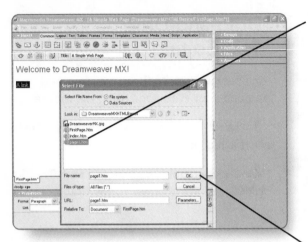

3. Click on the file to be linked. The file name is highlighted.

NOTE

The file that you are linking to may not always be another Web page. You can also link to Word documents, Excel spreadsheets, PowerPoint presentations, Adobe Acrobat files, and more.

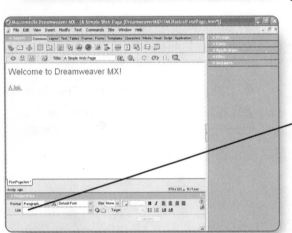

4. Click on OK. The Select File dialog box closes, and the linked text appears underlined onscreen.

TIP

Assuming you know the complete URL, you can skip the preceding steps and type the Web page address directly in the Link field.

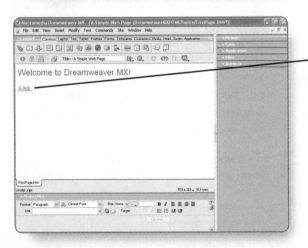

NOTE

The linked text is now underlined and appears in a different color. You will need to view the page in a browser to test the link.

Working with Images

Web sites that only contain text can be pretty dull and boring. Images help to make Web sites visually appealing. Inserting and positioning images in a Web page has never been easier.

Inserting Images

The two most common image file formats are GIF (Graphics Interchange Format) and JPEG (Joint Photographic Experts Group). You may need to use an image editor (such as Macromedia Fireworks, Adobe Photoshop, or JASC Paintshop Pro) to convert your graphics to either of these formats before you can insert them into a Web page.

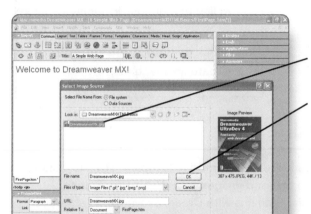

1. Click in the Document window where you would like the image to appear. The cursor appears where you click.

2. Click on the Image button on the Common tab. The Select Image Source dialog box opens.

> ### TIP
>
> As a general rule, convert all line art graphics to the GIF format and all photographs to the JPEG format.

3. Click on the image file to be opened. The file name is highlighted.

4. Click on OK. The image is inserted into the Web page.

Aligning Images

By default, an inserted image is aligned with the left margin of a Web page. Use the Properties Inspector to change the alignment of an image.

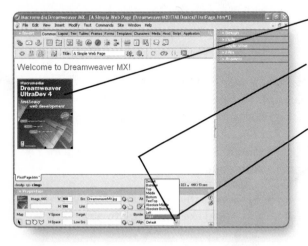

1. Select the image by clicking on it. The image is highlighted.

2. Click on the down arrow of the Align drop-down list. A list of alignment options is displayed.

3. Click on an alignment option. The image is repositioned accordingly.

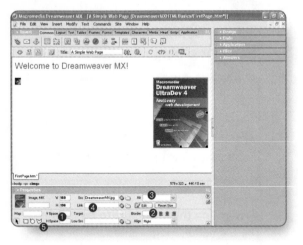

NOTE

Using the Properties Inspector, you can also

❶ Set the vertical and horizontal space around an image.

❷ Add a border to the image.

❸ Enter alternate text, which appears in lieu of a graphic in some browsers.

❹ Link the image to another page.

❺ Create an image map.

Working with Tables

With the help of tables, you can easily create and modify complex HTML layouts. Without tables, it is difficult to align text and images on a Web page. Editing complex tables has never been easier than it is with Dreamweaver MX. Tables are also particularly important in building database-driven Web sites where they are used to format and display search results.

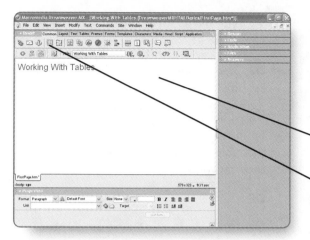

Inserting a Table

When you create a table, you need to specify the number of rows and columns your table requires. This is the first step to creating interesting layouts.

1. Click within your Document window. The cursor appears where you click.

2. Click on Insert Table. The Insert Table dialog box opens.

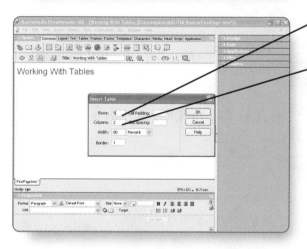

3. Type the number of rows required in the table row field.

4. Type the number of columns required in the table column field.

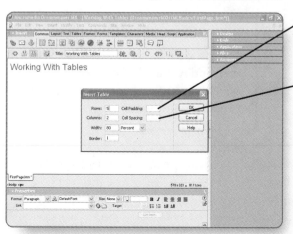

5. Type the number of pixels required between the contents of a cell and the cell border. This is known as *cell padding*.

6. Type the number of pixels required between the cells in a table. This is known as *cell spacing*.

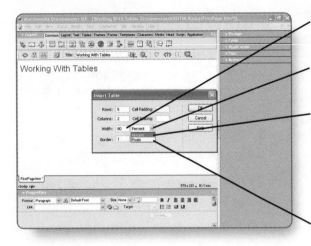

7. Type the width of the table in the Width field.

8. Click on the down arrow of the Percent list box.

9a. Click on Percent. The percentage option is selected. This makes the width of the table vary according to the size of the browser window.

OR

9b. Click on Pixels. The absolute pixel option is selected. This makes the width of the table a fixed size.

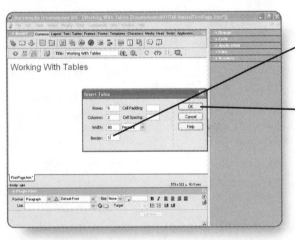

10. Type the size of the table border in pixels. A zero (0) value means that the table has no border.

11. Click on OK. The table is created.

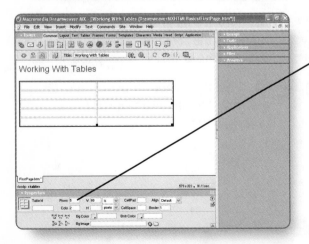

NOTE

Once a table has been inserted, you can modify it at any time by adjusting the table properties in the Properties Inspector.

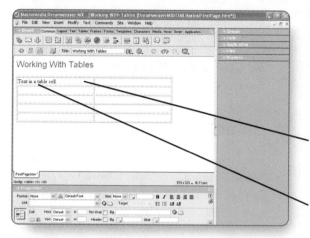

Adding Text to a Table Cell

Tables are used to display and organize tabular data. Each cell in a table can hold text.

1. Click in a cell where you would like to insert text. The cursor appears where you click.

2. Type some text. The text appears within the cell.

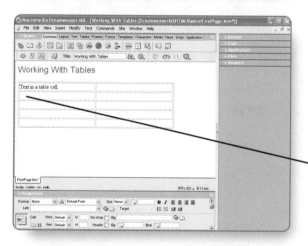

Adding Images to a Table Cell

Tables provide a practical way to display complex layouts involving both text and images. Inserting an image into a cell is as easy as inserting text into a cell.

1. Click in a cell where you would like to insert an image. The cursor appears where you click.

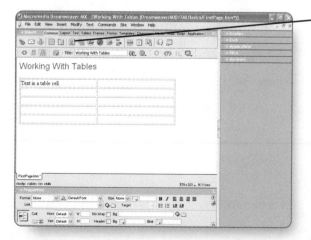

2. Click on the Image button on the Common tab. The Select Image Source dialog box opens.

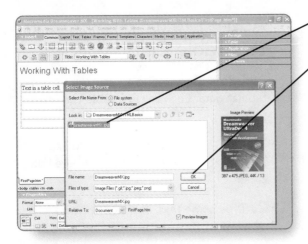

3. Select the image to be inserted. The file name is highlighted.

4. Click on OK. The image is inserted in the table cell.

Selecting Table Elements

You need to select table elements such as rows, columns, and cells before you can format them. Select a table if you want to change its background color or width, for example. Dreamweaver MX enables you to select and format individual rows and columns as well.

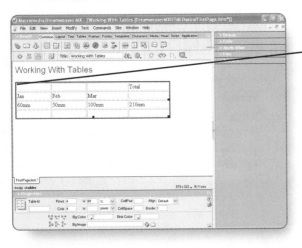

1. Click on the upper-left corner of the table. The cursor changes to a four-pointed arrow and selection handles appear around the selected table.

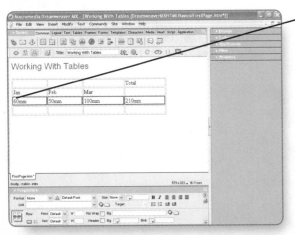

2. To select a row, place the cursor next to the left margin of the table. The cursor changes to an arrow.

3. Click to select the row. The table row is highlighted.

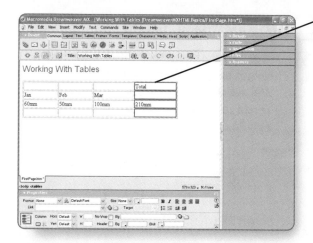

4. To select a column, place the cursor above the top table margin. The cursor changes to an arrow.

5. Click to select the column. The table column is highlighted.

Adding Color to a Table

You can change the background color of a table, cell, row, or column. Color can make your table easier to read. You can also use it to draw attention to certain values.

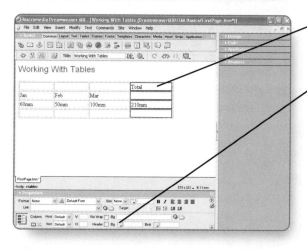

1. Select the table, row, or column where you would like to change the background color. The selected item is highlighted.

2. Click on the down arrow. The Colors palette appears.

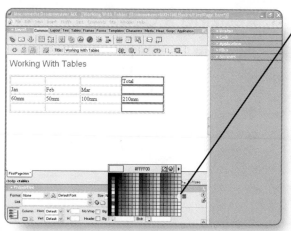

3. Click on a color with the eyedropper cursor. The background color of the selected item changes.

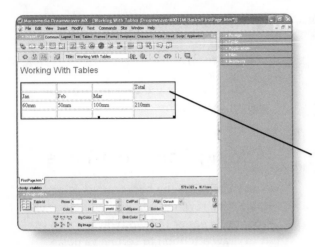

Resizing a Table

It will take a while to create the perfect layout for your Web page. Dreamweaver MX assists in the process, enabling you to resize tables by simply dragging selection handles.

1. Select the table. The table will be highlighted.

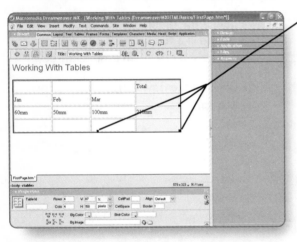

2. Click and drag the selection handles to resize the table. The size of the table changes.

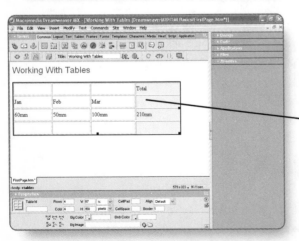

Resizing a Column or Row

The easiest way to adjust row height and column width is to drag the row or column border.

1. Move the mouse pointer over a row or column border. The cursor changes to a double-arrow.

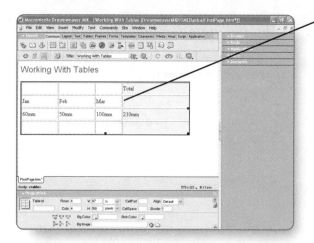

2. Drag the cell border to resize the row or column. The size of the row or column changes.

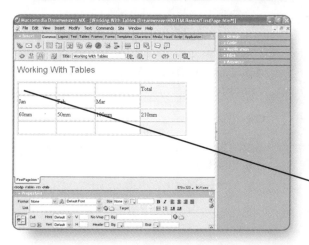

Adding Rows and Columns

When you create a table you need to enter the number of rows and columns that your table should contain. However, as you design your Web page, you may decide that you need additional rows and columns.

1. Right-click in a cell. A shortcut menu appears.

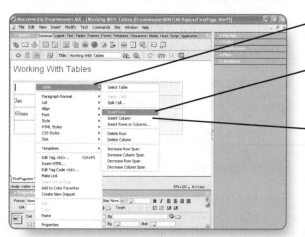

2. Click on Table. The Table submenu appears.

3a. Click on Insert Row. A row is inserted.

OR

3b. Click on Insert Column. A column is inserted.

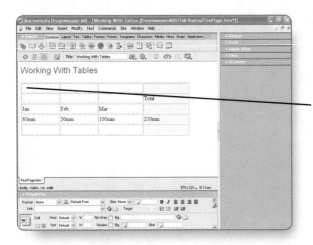

Deleting a Row or Column

You can easily delete rows and columns that you no longer need.

1. Right-click in any cell within the row or column you want to delete. A shortcut menu appears.

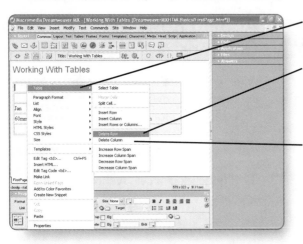

2. Click on Table. The Table submenu appears.

3a. Click on Delete Row. The row is deleted.

OR

3b. Click on Delete Column. The column is deleted.

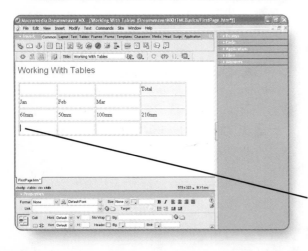

Inserting Tables within Tables

It may not always be possible to create the layout you want using a single table. You can, however, insert tables within tables. This is known as *nesting*. Nesting tables may be the only way that you can create a complex layout in HTML.

1. Click within a table cell. The cursor appears where you click.

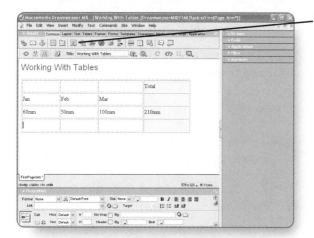

2. Click on the Table button on the Common tab. The Insert Table dialog box opens.

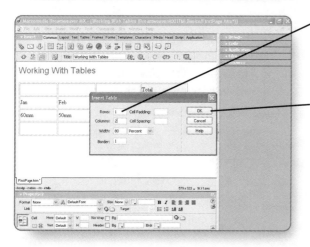

3. Type the number of columns and rows required. You can also specify values for cell padding, cell spacing, table width, and border.

4. Click on OK. A nested table is created.

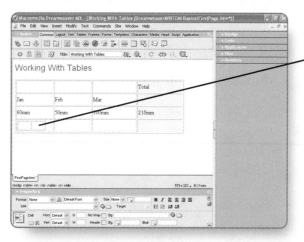

NOTE

Nested tables can each have their own properties. You can specify the size, border width, spacing, color, and background image of each nested table. This allows you great flexibility when laying out a Web page.

Merging Table Cells

Each row in a table has the same number of columns, and all cells in a column are the same size. Sometimes, however, you will need to create a table that is not a perfect grid. In Dreamweaver MX, you can easily create a table in which some of the cells are wider than others. This is known as *merging cells*.

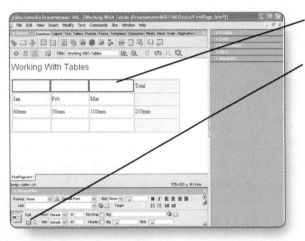

1. Select the cells to be merged. The cells are highlighted.

2. Click on the Merge Cells button in the Properties Inspector. The cells are merged.

NOTE

You can select multiple cells by dragging across the cells you want to select. Hold down the Shift key while clicking on each cell to add to the selection.

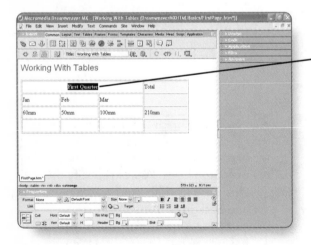

NOTE

The same technique can be used to merge cells that span multiple rows.

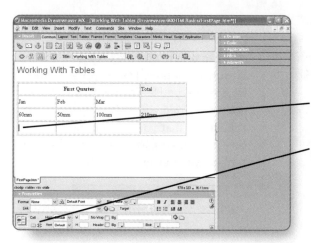

Splitting Table Cells

A cell can also be split into either rows or columns.

1. Click inside the cell to be split. The cursor appears in the cell.

2. Click on the Split Cell button in the Properties Inspector. The Split Cell dialog box opens.

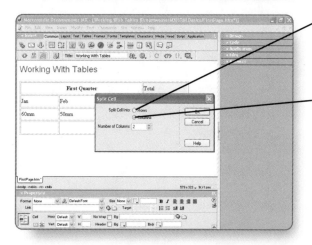

3a. Click on the Split Cell Into Rows option button. The option is selected.

OR

3b. Click on the Split Cell Into Columns option button. The option is selected.

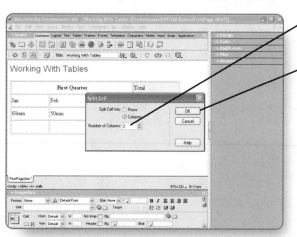

4. Enter the number of rows or columns into which the cell should split.

5. Click on OK. The cell is split.

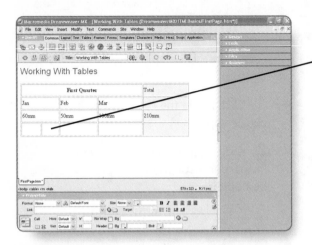

NOTE

You can create complex table layouts by applying the simple techniques you learned in this chapter. When you are designing, remember that you can add or delete rows and columns, nest tables, and merge or split cells.

3

Managing Web Sites with Dreamweaver MX

Dreamweaver MX has many features that make managing Web sites a breeze. In particular, it can keep track of all your Web site links and publish your Web site to a Web server using FTP (File Transfer Protocol). Dreamweaver MX can also synchronize local and remote files. In this chapter, you'll learn how to do the following:

- Create a site
- Create files and folders
- Validate links
- Change links globally
- Use Dreamweaver MX to FTP files to and from a remote server
- Synchronize local and remote files

Working with Sites

A site consists of a set of pages on your local hard disk that make up a Web site. A site helps you manage the files in your Web site by making it easier for you to locate pages, check links, and transfer files to and from a remote server. Within the Files panel, you can manage all the files and folders in your Web site.

Creating a Site

It is a good idea to create a site for each Web site that you work on. As your project grows, Dreamweaver MX can automatically update links when you move or rename

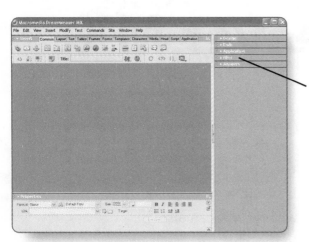

files. Every database-driven Web site that you create must be in a site. A site can be created for a new Web site or an existing one.

1. Expand the Files Panel Group. The Site and Assets tabs are displayed.

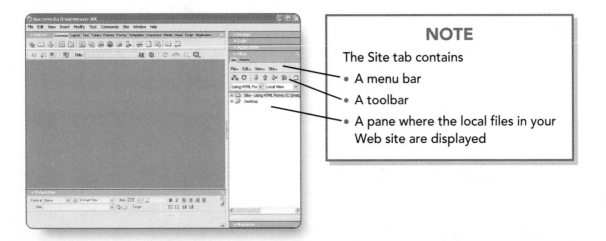

NOTE

The Site tab contains

- A menu bar
- A toolbar
- A pane where the local files in your Web site are displayed

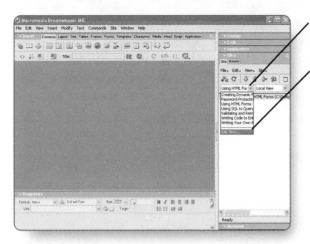

2. Click on the down arrow next to the Sites list box.

3. Click on Edit Sites. The Edit Sites dialog box opens.

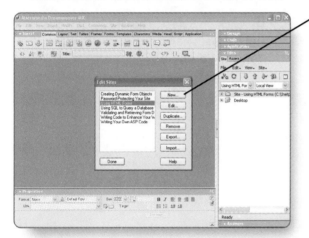

4. Click on New. The Site Definition dialog box opens.

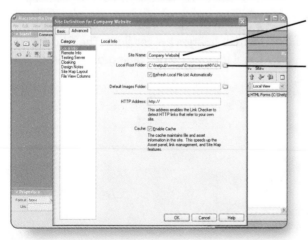

5. Type the name of your site into the Site Name field.

6. Click on the Folder icon next to the Local Root field. The Choose Local Root Folder dialog box opens.

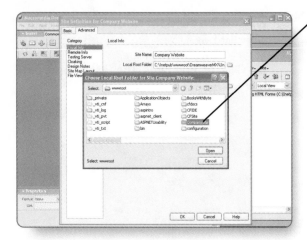

7. Double-click on a folder to open the directory. The folders within this subdirectory are displayed. No files are displayed in the Choose Local Root Folder because a folder must be specified before a site can be created.

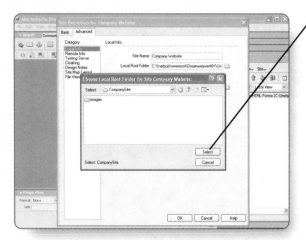

8. Click on Select. The dialog box closes and the path name appears in the Site Definition dialog box.

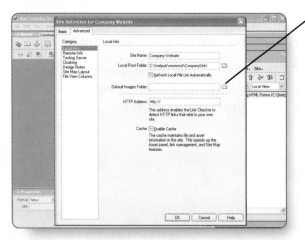

9. Click on the Folder icon next to the Default Images Folder field. The Choose Local Images Folder dialog box opens.

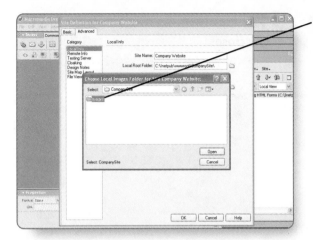

10. Double-click on a folder to open the directory. The folders within this subdirectory are displayed.

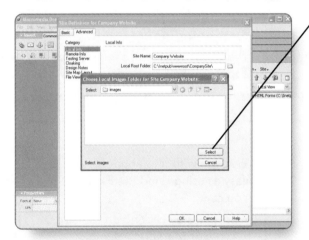

11. Click on Select. The dialog box closes and the path name appears in the Site Definition dialog box.

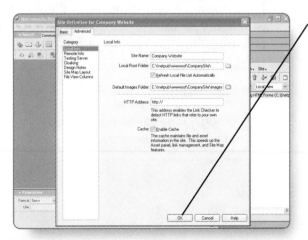

12. Click on OK. The Site Definition dialog box closes, and Dreamweaver MX asks if you would like to create a cache file.

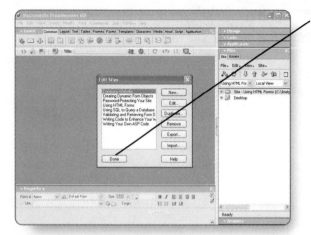

13. Click on Done. The Edit Sites dialog box closes.

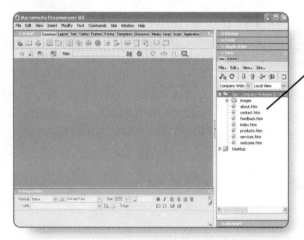

NOTE

The contents of your Web site now appear in the Local View pane.

NOTE

Working with files and folders is as easy as using Windows Explorer. You can

- Sort files by clicking on the Size, Type, or Modified column headings found at the top of the folder panes.

- Move files and folders using drag-and-drop techniques.

- Expand column headings to display the file names in full by dragging the bar on the right side of the column description.

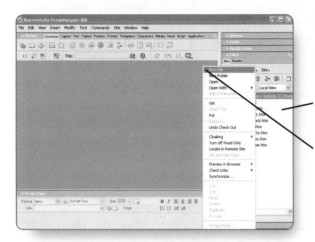

Creating Files

Within the Site window, you can create new files using a few simple steps.

1. Right-click on a blank area of the Local View pane. A shortcut menu appears.

2. Click on New File. A new file appears and is highlighted in the Local View pane.

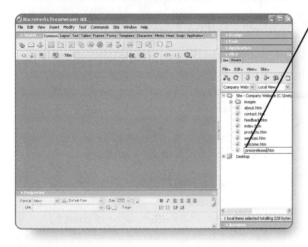

3. Type in a name (with an appropriate extension) for the file that has just been created. The file name is already selected.

4. Press Enter when finished. The new file is created.

NOTE

The following file extensions can be used:

- .asp if you're creating an ASP (Active Server Pages) file
- .aspx if you're creating an ASP.NET file
- .php if you're creating a PHP file
- .jsp if you're creating a JSP (Java Server Pages) file
- .cfm if you're creating a ColdFusion file.
- .htm or .html if you're creating an HTML-only Web page.

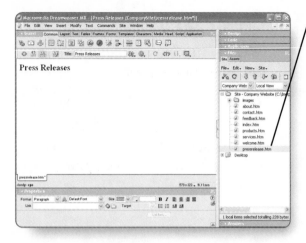

5. Double-click on the file name to open it. The file opens in the Document window.

You can now use Dreamweaver MX to create and format the Web page visually. Please refer to Chapter 2, "Dreamweaver MX Basics," if you are not familiar with using Dreamweaver MX to create a Web page.

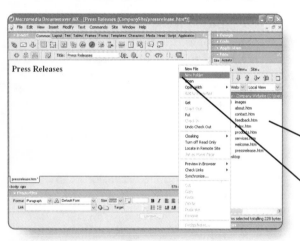

Creating Folders

Folders enable you to organize your files in a logical manner. Creating a new folder in Dreamweaver MX is as simple as creating a new file.

1. Right-click on a blank area of the Local View pane. A shortcut menu appears.

2. Click on New Folder. A new folder called untitled.htm is created in the Local View pane. The folder name is already selected.

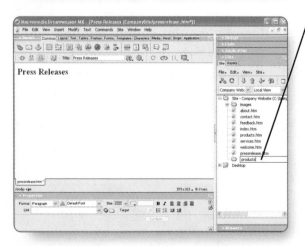

3. Type a name for the folder that has just been created.

4. Press Enter when finished. The new folder is created.

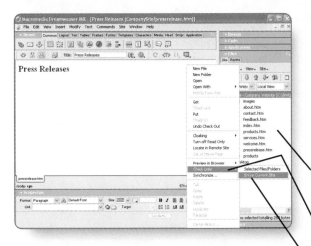

Checking Links

Broken links can be really annoying to Web site visitors. A few years ago it used to be a tedious and time-consuming task to test every link in your Web site. Dreamweaver MX makes finding and repairing broken links a snap.

1. Right-click on a blank area of the Local View pane. A shortcut menu appears.

2. Click on Check Links. A submenu appears.

3. Click on Entire Current Site.

4. Click on a file that is listed in the Broken Links column. A field and folder icon are displayed next to the file.

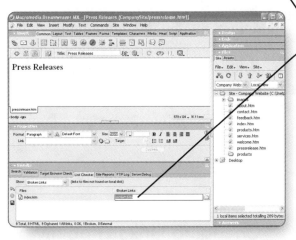

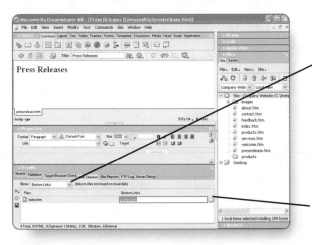

NOTE

You can also view external links and orphaned files by selecting the corresponding option from the Show drop-down box on the Link Checker tab. Orphaned files are files that are not linked to any file in your Web site.

5. Click on the Folder icon. The Select File dialog box opens.

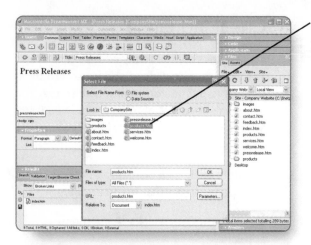

6. Double-click on the file you want to link. The dialog box closes and the desired file and path names are added to the Links field.

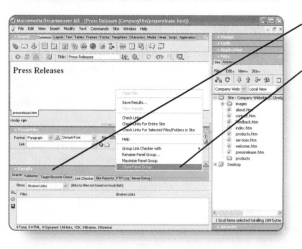

7. Click on the Results panel options icon. A submenu appears.

8. Click on Close Panel Group. The Results panel closes.

Changing Links Globally

If the location of a file that you often link to has changed, Dreamweaver MX can help you update all occurrences of that link. This comes in handy when you're dealing with large Web sites that multiple people have worked on.

1. Click on a file. The file name is editable.

2. Change the name of the file. The Update Files dialog box opens and displays all the pages that contain links to the specified file.

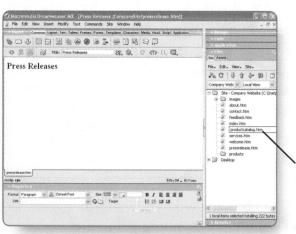

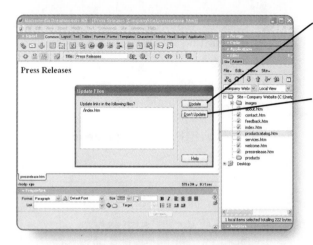

3a. Click on Update. All links are updated and you are returned to the Site window.

OR

3b. Click on Don't Update. The Update is cancelled and you are returned to the Site window.

Setting Up a Remote FTP Site

FTP (File Transfer Protocol) is used to publish your Web site to a Web server. There is no need to use a standalone FTP client because the Site window has built-in FTP features. You can upload files from your local folder to a remote Web server as well as download files from your remote Web server. The details of the remote server must first be entered.

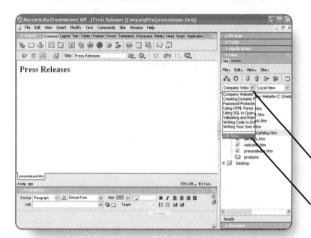

1. Click on the down arrow of the Sites drop-down box. A list of sites appears.

2. Click on Edit Sites. The Edit Sites dialog box opens.

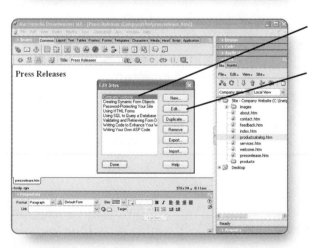

3. Click on a site name. The site is selected.

4. Click on the Edit button. The Site Definition dialog box opens.

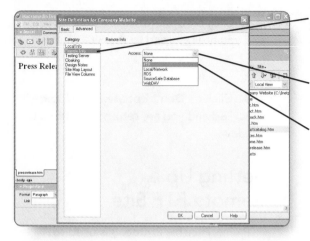

5. Click on Remote Info in the Category list. The setting for Remote Info is displayed.

6. Click on the down arrow of the Access drop-down list.

7. Click on FTP. Fields for entering FTP details are displayed.

TIP

Your FTP details, such as host location, user name, and password can all be obtained from your server administrator. Usually, these details are supplied to you when an FTP account is created.

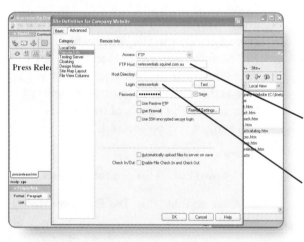

8. Enter the FTP host location. The host location is an alphanumeric address for the Web server.

9. Enter your username into the Login field.

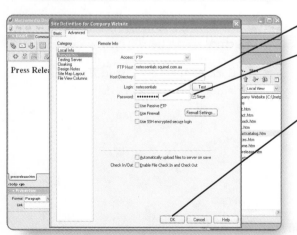

10. Enter your password.

11. Click in the Save check box if you want to save your password. A check appears in the box.

12. Click on OK to save your settings and close the Site Definition dialog box.

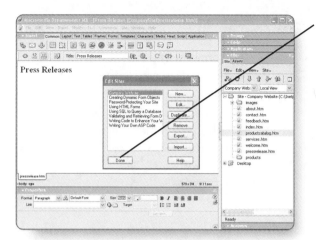

13. Click on Done. The Edit Sites dialog box closes.

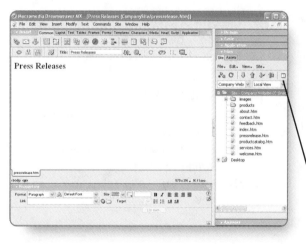

Connecting to and Disconnecting from a Remote Server

Within Dreamweaver MX you can connect and disconnect from a remote server with a single click.

1. Click on the Expand Site window icon. The Site window is displayed.

2. Click on the Connect button. Once clicked, the text on the button changes to Disconnect.

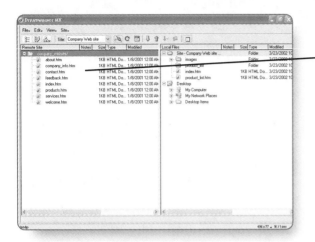

NOTE

The contents of the remote Web server are displayed in the Remote Site pane.

You can move, rename, and create new files on a remote site using the same techniques you learned when working with local files.

3. Click on Disconnect. The FTP connection is disconnected, and the text on the button changes to Connect.

Uploading Files

Uploading files involves transferring files from your local folder to a remote server. The uploading process enables you to publish your Web site or selected pages on the World Wide Web.

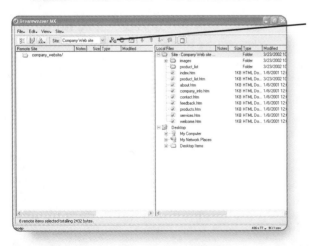

1. Click on Connect. A connection is made to your FTP server.

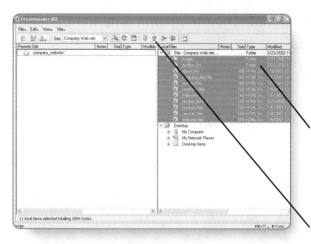

NOTE

The remote Web site is displayed in the Remote Site pane.

2. Select the files you want to upload from your local folder to the remote site. To select more than one file, hold down the Ctrl key and then click on the files you want to include.

3. Click on the Put button. The selected files are uploaded.

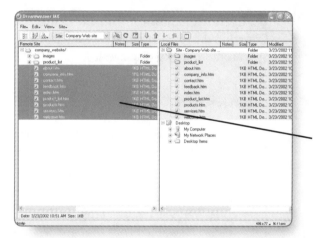

Downloading Files

Downloading files involves transferring files from a remote Web server to your local folder.

1. Select the files on the remote site that you would like to download to your local folder. To select more than one file, hold down the Ctrl key, and then click on the files you want to include.

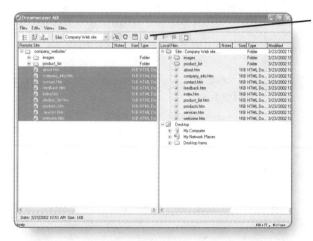

2. Click on the Get button. The selected files are downloaded.

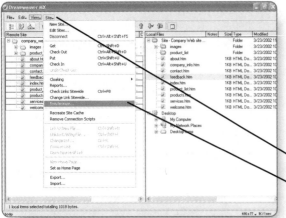

Synchronizing Files

File synchronization basically compares the files on the remote site with those in your local folder and only keeps the newest versions of the files. File synchronization involves uploading and downloading files from both remote and local sites.

1. Click on Site. The Site menu appears.

2. Click on Synchronize. The Synchronize Files dialog box opens.

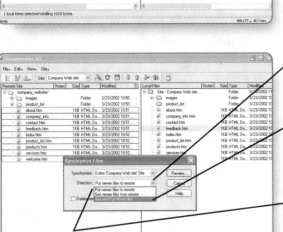

3. Click on the down arrow next to the Direction drop-down list. The types of synchronization are displayed.

4. Click on Get and Put newer files. The option is selected.

NOTE

- **Put newer files to remote**. Files on the remote site will be compared with those in the local folder. Newer versions that are found in the local folder will be uploaded to the remote site.

- **Get newer files from remote**. Files on the remote site will be compared with those in the local folder.

- **Get and Put newer files**. Files on the remote site will be compared with those in the local folder. Only the newest versions of the files found on either the local or remote sites are kept.

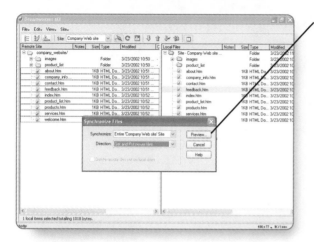

5. Click on Preview. The Synchronize Files dialog box closes and the Site dialog box opens.

NOTE

The list of files to be synchronized is displayed.

- Files that are uploaded to the remote site have a Put action.
- Files that are downloaded to the local site have a Get action.

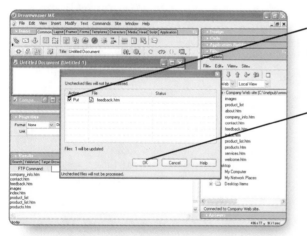

6. Click in the check box next to the action of a file if you do not want the file to be synchronized. The check is removed from the Action check box.

7. Click on OK. The synchronization process begins. The OK button changes to a Save Log button when synchronization is complete.

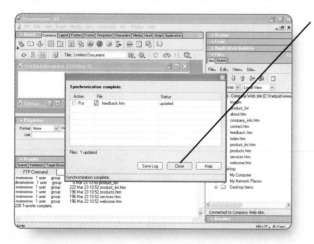

8. Click on Close. The Site dialog box closes.

CAUTION

It is a good idea to back up files before they are synchronized. You can sometimes accidentally delete files because the file with the latest date may not be the correct version.

4

Using Style Sheets

A Cascading Style Sheet (CSS) contains a group of formatting attributes that describe how a Web browser should display your Web page. A style sheet can be made up of many styles. Dreamweaver MX is a visual environment in which you can create, modify, and apply style sheets. With Dreamweaver MX there is no need to waste valuable time hand-coding style attributes. Styles make it easier for you to maintain consistency across your Web site. You can update your entire Web site in just a few seconds. In this chapter, you learn how to do the following:

- Create an embedded style sheet
- Apply an embedded style sheet
- Create an external style sheet
- Link to an external style sheet

Creating an Embedded Style Sheet

An embedded style sheet is stored in the header of a Web page. The embedded styles can only be used on the page where they were created. Modifying the embedded style sheet will only change the formatting of the current page. The Edit Style Sheet dialog box enables you to manage the styles that you create. You can create new styles or edit existing ones.

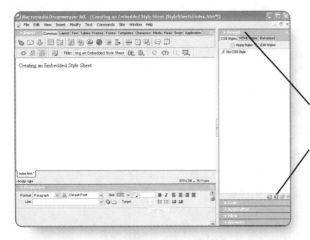

1. Expand the Design panel. The CSS Styles tab is displayed.

2. Click on the New Style icon. The New CSS Style dialog box opens.

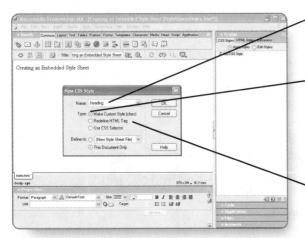

3. Type the style name into the Name field. Custom CSS style names must begin with a period.

4. Click on the Make Custom Style (class) option button. The option is selected. The Make Custom Style (class) option creates a style that can be applied to a block of text as a class attribute.

NOTE

- **Redefine HTML Tag** changes the default formatting of standard HTML tags.
- **Use CSS Selector** creates a style that can be applied to tags containing a specific ID.

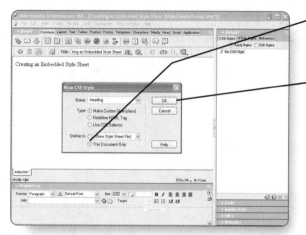

5. Select the This Document Only option. The style sheet will be embedded within the current Web page.

6. Click on OK. A blank style is created, and the CSS Style Definition dialog box opens.

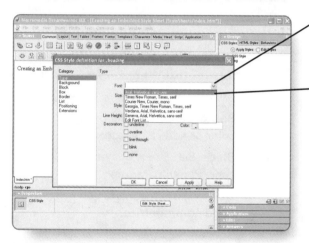

7. Click on the down arrow of the Font drop-down list. A list of available fonts is displayed.

8. Click on a font. The option is selected.

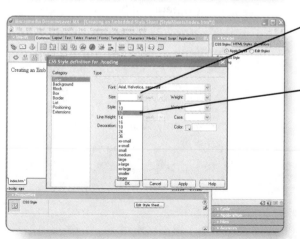

9. Click on the down arrow of the Size drop-down list. A list of available font sizes is displayed.

10. Click on a font size. The option is selected.

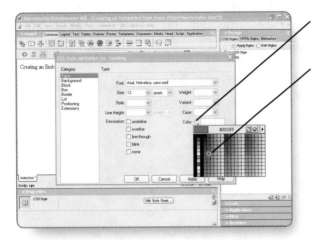

11. Click on the Color button. The Color palette appears.

12. Click on a color. The color is selected.

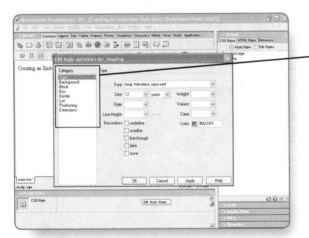

NOTE

CSS has a rich set of formatting attributes that are not all available in HTML.

- **Background.** Sets the background color or adds a background.
- **Block.** Sets the alignment and line spacing of a paragraph.
- **Box.** Adjusts the margin and padding properties.
- **Border.** Sets the border properties of a paragraph.
- **List.** Specifies bullet point images.
- **Positioning.** Positions images and text exactly where you want them on the page.
- **Extensions.** Views CSS properties that are only supported in Internet Explorer.

NOTE

Some CSS attributes may only work in Internet Explorer. Netscape and Internet Explorer don't implement all of the attributes. The best way to become familiar with all of the attributes is to experiment. You should, however, be aware that Dreamweaver MX does not display some CSS properties in the Document window. You must preview the Web page in a Web browser.

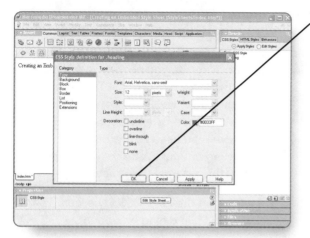

13. Click on OK. The style attributes are saved and the new style appears in the CSS Styles tab.

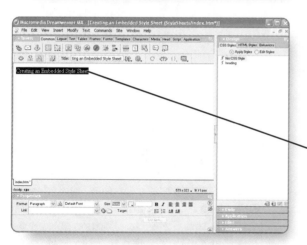

Applying an Embedded Style

Once you have created a custom style, it can easily be used to format your current Web page.

1. Select the text you would like format with a style. The text is highlighted.

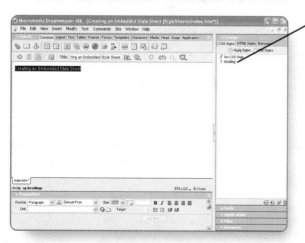

2. Click on a style name. The name of the style is highlighted and the formatting of the selected text changes to match that of the chosen style.

Creating an External CSS Style Sheet

The CSS styles that you create are stored in the header of the currently open Web page. However, when you are working on a large Web site you need to make your styles available to all pages. This is achieved by storing your styles in a separate file that can be accessed by all Web pages. Whenever you need to change the formatting of your Web site, you simply modify the external style sheet.

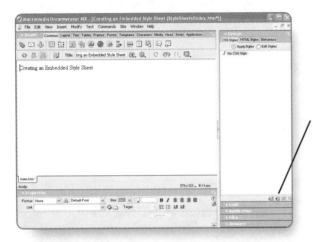

1. Click on the New CSS Style icon. The New CSS Style dialog box opens.

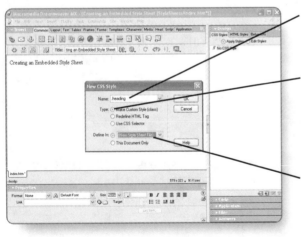

2. Type the style name into the Name field. Custom CSS style names must begin with a period.

3. Click on the Make Custom Style (class) option button. The option is selected. The Make Custom Style (class) option creates a style that can be applied to a block of text as a class attribute.

4. Select the New Style Sheet File option.

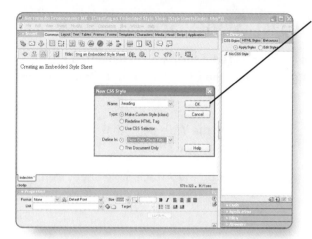

5. Click on OK. The Save Style Sheet File As dialog box opens.

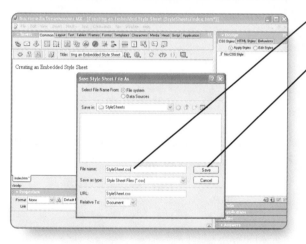

6. Enter a name for the file. The file must have a .css extension.

7. Click on Save. The CSS Style Definition dialog box opens.

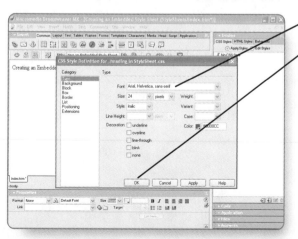

8. Set the attributes of the style.

9. Click on OK. The style is added to the external style sheet.

Linking to an Existing Style Sheet

The awesome power of style sheets is only realized if they are implemented across whole Web sites. This involves linking each Web page to a style sheet. Dreamweaver makes a seemingly tedious task somewhat trivial.

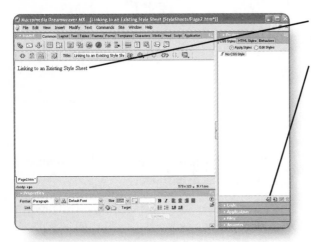

1. Open the Web page that you would like to link to a style sheet.

2. Click on the Attach Style Sheet icon. The Link External Style Sheet dialog box opens.

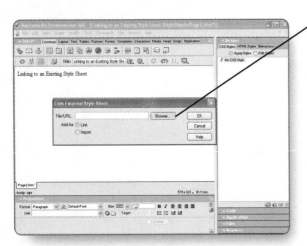

3. Click on Browse. The Select Style Sheet File dialog box opens.

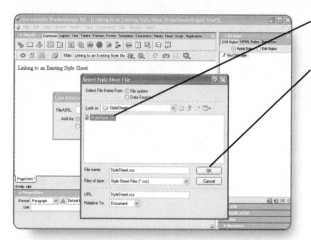

4. Click on the style sheet file. It will have a .css extension. The file name is selected.

5. Click on OK. The Select Style Sheet File dialog box closes.

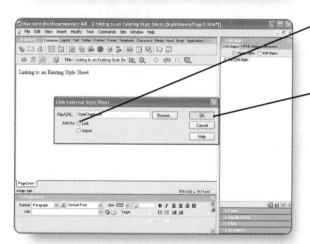

6. Click on the Link option button. The option is selected. The style sheet is used as a linked style sheet.

7. Click on OK. The Link External Style Sheet dialog box closes and the style sheet is linked to the current page.

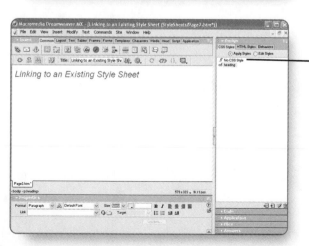

NOTE

All of the styles that are stored in the external style sheet will be listed in the CSS Styles tab.

5

Editing HTML

Dreamweaver MX is one of the few tools that aims to satisfy the needs of visual and code-centric developers. You are already familiar with its intuitive visual editing abilities, but you may not be aware that Dreamweaver MX has evolved into a full-featured HTML code editor. In this chapter, you'll learn how to do the following:

- View the HTML code of a page being edited
- Use code hints, the Tag Chooser, and Tag Editor to insert and edit tags
- Create and reuse Code Snippets

Viewing HTML

It is important for all Web developers to have a basic understanding of HTML. This section shows you how to view and edit the HTML source code of a Web page in Dreamweaver MX.

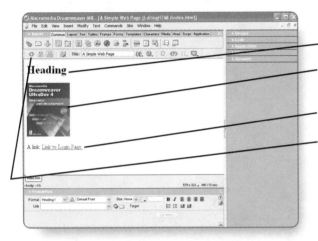

1. Create a new Web page.

● Insert a heading that uses the H1 style.

● Use the Insert Image object to insert an image.

● Create a link.

2. Click on Code View. The HTML Source code is displayed.

NOTE

A Web page must contain opening and closing `<html>`, `<head>`, and `<body>` tags. The `<title>` tag is placed within the `<head>` tag.

A tag is placed within the `<` and `>` delimiters. Some tags have a matching closing tag. Closing tags include a `/` after the `<` delimiter. Tags also have attributes to set their properties. You use

● Opening and closing `<h1>` tags to format text as a heading.

● The `<p>` tag to line a paragraph break.

● The `<img>` tag to insert an image. The `<img>` tag has attributes. The `src` attribute specifies the location of the image that is being displayed.

● The `<a>` tag to create a link. The `href` attribute specifies the page to which you are linking.

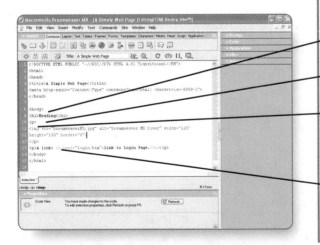

3. Click on the `<img>` tag. The Properties Inspector is updated to display the properties of the currently selected image. The properties that are displayed match the tag attributes.

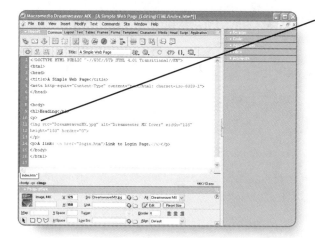

NOTE

You can still use the Properties Inspector while editing in Code View.

---

4. Click on the Code View options icon. A submenu appears.

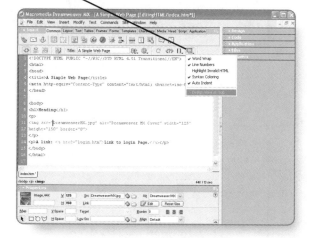

NOTE

You can configure the code editor by enabling

- **Word Wrap**. This will wrap the code in the HTML Source window and free you from scrolling to read lengthy lines of HTML code.

- **Line Numbers**. Each line of code on the Web page will be numbered. This will help you when you need to debug server-side script such as ASP, JSP, ColdFusion, or PHP. Error messages always display the line number on which the error occurred.

- **Highlight Invalid HTML**. Invalid HTML will be detected and high-lighted in yellow.

- **Syntax coloring**. Allows you to eas-ily differentiate HTML, JavaScript, and server-side code. This feature makes editing and debugging much easier.

- **Auto Indent**. This will automatically indent certain tags. Indentation is a handy way to make your code more readable.

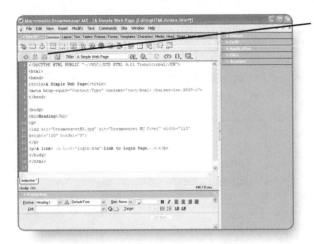

5. Click on Design View. The Web page is displayed.

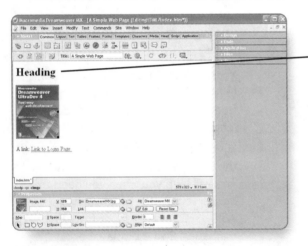

NOTE
Viewing a page in Design View is just like previewing a page in a Web browser.

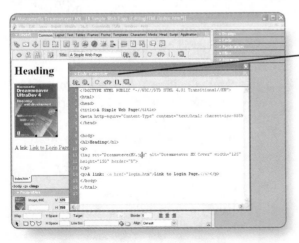

TIP
Press F10 to open the HTML code editor (called the Code Inspector) in its own window.

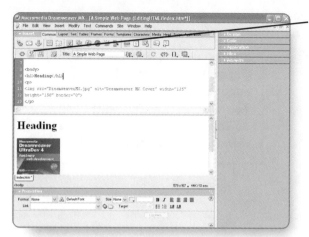

6. Click on Show Code and Design View. You are able to see the Web page and view its HTML source code at the same time.

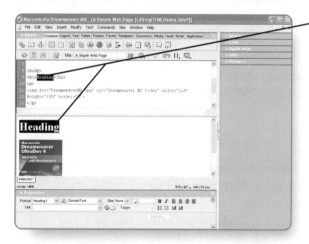

7. Select the Heading text in Code View. The text is selected in Design View as well.

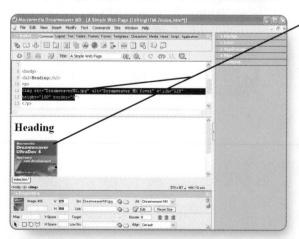

8. Select the image in Design View. The cursor is placed within the `<img>` tag in Code View.

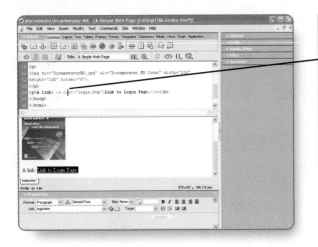

Writing HTML

Dreamweaver MX offers multiple ways to author error-free HTML. You can use either a keyboard or a mouse to insert and edit HTML tags.

Using Code Hints

Code hints offer context-sensitive assistance while HTML is being typed. Code hints are drop-down lists populated with either a list of available tags or attributes applicable to the tag you are currently editing. You simply select the tag or attribute that you require instead of having to type it. Code hints are also helpful if you can't remember the title of a tag or attribute. Dreamweaver MX automatically adds a closing tag after an opening tag has been typed.

1. Type <. A drop-down list of HTML tags in alphabetical order is displayed.

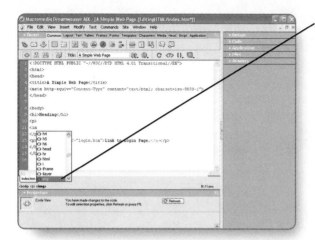

2. You can choose a tag by

- Typing the first character of the tag name
- Selecting it with a mouse
- Using the arrow keys

NOTE

In this example we will insert an `<img>` tag.

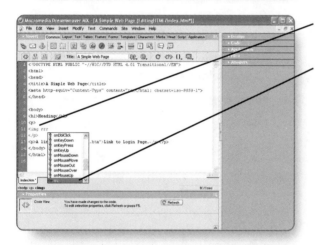

3. Press the spacebar. A drop-down list of tag attributes is displayed.

4. You can choose a tag attribute by

- Typing the first character of the tag name
- Selecting it with a mouse
- Using the arrow keys

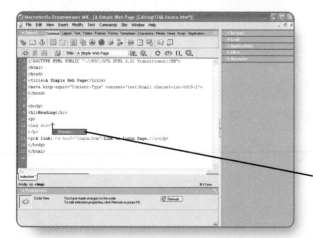

NOTE

We have selected the `src` attribute, which is used to specify the path to the image file. The Browse option is displayed because a file needs to be specified.

5. Press Enter to select the Browse option. The Select File dialog box appears.

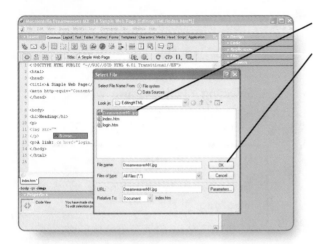

6. Select the file.

7. Click on OK. The Select File dialog box closes.

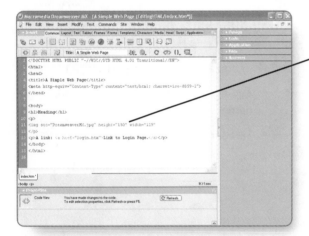

NOTE

Press the spacebar to insert width and height attributes.

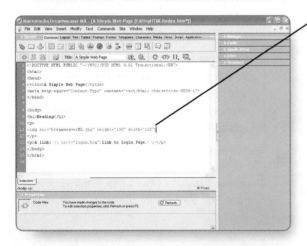

8. Type > to close the tag.

Using the Tag Chooser

The Tag Chooser is a library that contains all of the tags supported by Dreamweaver MX. Tags are arranged by category and stored in appropriately named folders. Once a tag is selected you can view syntax and usage guidelines to help you use the tag correctly. The Tag Editor opens when you insert a tag. The Tag Editor is a dialog box that enables you to set tag properties. The Tag Editor also appears when you edit a tag.

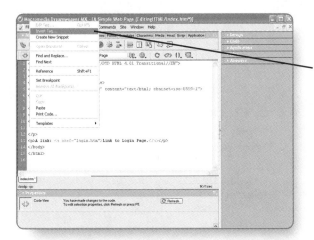

1. Right-click where you want to insert a tag. A shortcut menu appears.

2. Click on Insert Tag. The Tag Chooser dialog box opens.

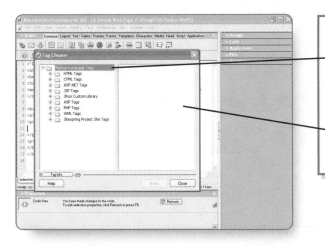

NOTE

- The left pane displays a list of supported tags. Tags are grouped in folders and categorized in terms of functionality.

- The right pane displays all the tags found in the selected folder.

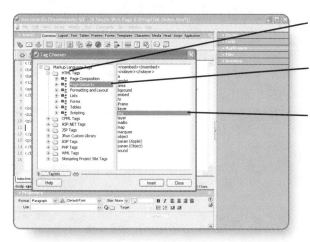

3. Click on a folder. Subcategories are displayed.

4. Click on a subcategory. The tags within the selected subcategory are displayed.

5. Click on a tag. The tag is selected.

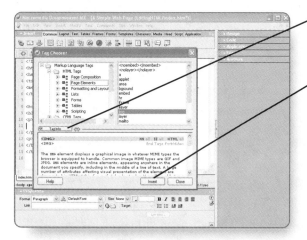

6. Click on Tag Info. Tag-specific help is displayed. This includes tag syntax and usage guidelines.

7. Click on Insert. The Tag Editor for the selected tag is displayed.

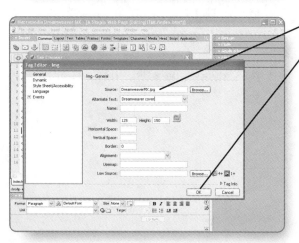

8. Set the tag attributes.

9. Click on OK. The Tag Editor closes and inserts the tag source code.

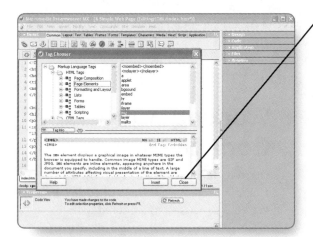

10. Click on Close. The Tag Chooser dialog box closes.

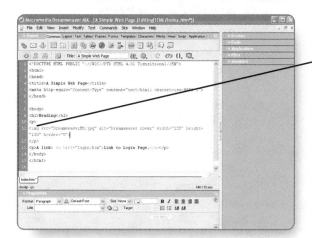

NOTE

The HTML source code for the tag is inserted with the appropriate attributes set.

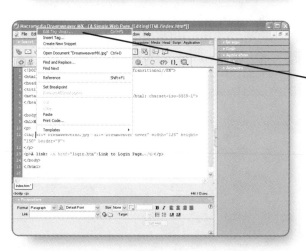

11. Right-click within a tag. A shortcut menu appears.

12. Click on Edit Tag. The Tag Editor dialog box opens.

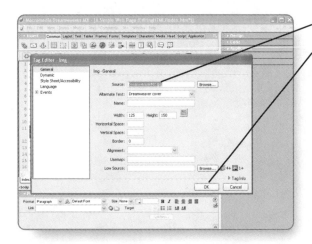

13. Edit the Tag properties.

14. Click on OK. The tag source code is updated.

Working with Code Snippets

Snippets facilitate code reuse across multiple projects. Sections of code can be stored and reused at a later stage.

Creating Snippets

Any selection of code can be made into a Snippet. Use folders to organize your Snippets. Code should always be tested before it is made into a Snippet. A Snippet can be made up of a single block of code or start and end blocks that wrap around a selection when inserted.

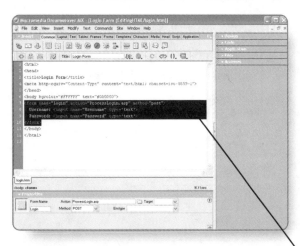

1. Create the code you want to save as a Snippet. The code could include HTML, JavaScript, Styles, or server-side code written in ASP, ASP.NET, JSP, ColdFusion, or PHP.

2. Select and copy the code.

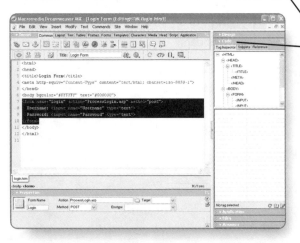

3. Expand the Code panel. The Tag Inspector, Snippets, and Reference tabs are displayed.

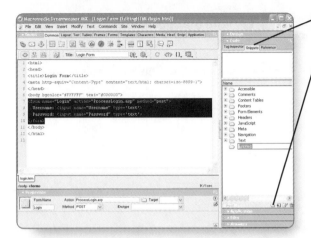

4. Click on the Snippets tab. The Snippets tab is displayed.

5. Click on New Folder. A new untitled folder is created. You will store your Snippets in this folder.

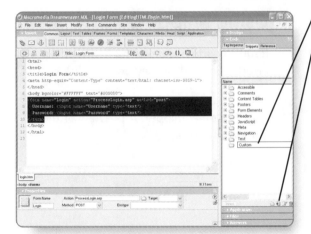

6. Enter a descriptive folder name.

7. Click on the Add Snippet icon. The Snippet dialog box appears.

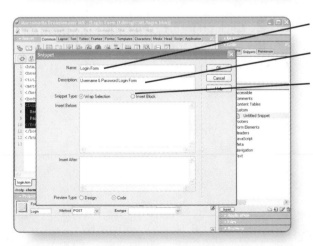

8. Enter the Snippet name.

9. Enter a description.

10. Select the Insert Block option.

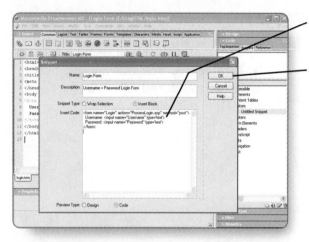

11. Paste the code into the Insert Code text area.

12. Click on OK. The Snippet is created.

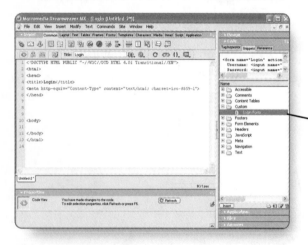

Using Snippets

Reusing code has never been easier. To insert a Snippet, simply double-click on the Snippet.

1. Click on a Snippet. A preview of the Snippet is displayed.

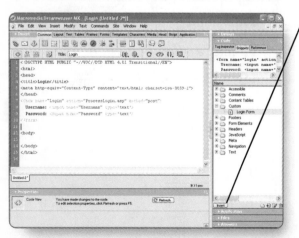

2. Click on Insert. The code is inserted into the currently open Web page.

6

Planning a Database-Driven Web Site

Dreamweaver MX can generate code for five of the most popular application servers available. These include ASP, ASP.NET, JSP, PHP, and ColdFusion. Dreamweaver MX has totally revolutionized the way in which database-driven Web sites are created. Once you're familiar with Dreamweaver MX, you can use your skills to build dynamic Web sites for any of the supported application servers. This has drastically lowered the learning curve for implementing a Web site in an unfamiliar technology. You will still, however, need to make an informed decision when selecting an appropriate application server and back end. In this chapter, you'll learn how to do the following:

- Select an application server for your dynamic Web site
- Select a database for your Web site
- Specify an application server for your Dreamweaver MX project

Selecting an Application Server

Dreamweaver MX has made it much easier to develop Web sites for multiple application servers, but you still need to make a decision about whether you will implement your dynamic site in ASP, ASP.NET, JSP, PHP, or ColdFusion. There is no definitive answer. You will have to make a decision based upon the functionality required, where the site will be hosted, and your development expertise. Here are some possible scenarios that may dictate which you will have to use.

- **The application server that you choose will depend upon where the site is hosted.** Sometimes your client may already have a Web server or one that is externally hosted. If this is the case, you will need to find out whether the server is Unix- or Windows-based, what Web server is being used, and what server-side scripting languages are available. In a situation like this, the solution you develop needs to be compatible with the current technology and still implement the required functionality. This may be very difficult in some situations, but you will be in luck if at least one of the application servers that Dreamweaver MX supports is available. Dreamweaver MX enables you to utilize your existing skills and achieve instant results.

- **The application server must support specific functionality.** There are times when the required functionality is only available on a particular application server. If this is the case, your decision is obvious. However, if the features that the Web site requires are available on multiple application servers, you'll need to compare the cost and time to implement each solution. You should also make sure that the application server can handle the traffic that the site will attract. There is nothing worse than having a site crash because heaps of visitors are making requests to the server.

- **You and your development team must have the required expertise.** It often makes sense to stick to what you know. This reduces the project duration and maximizes your profit. The possibility of encountering technical difficulties is also greatly reduced.

Using ASP

ASP takes a template-based approach to server-side scripting. Code is embedded in a Web page. ASP can be scripted in either VBScript or JScript. Both of these scripting languages are easy to learn, even if you have no programming experience. The script on the Web page is processed, and only HTML is sent to the Web browser.

The Advantages of Using ASP

- It is relatively cheap and easy to find a host for an ASP-driven Web site.

- There is a large ASP community, and it is easy to find resources (books and Web sites).

- ASP is stable and mature in the Windows environment.

- ASP is free. It is bundled with IIS (Internet Information Server) on Windows NT.

- ASP can interface to ODBC-compliant databases (Access and SQL Server) through ADO (ActiveX Data Objects).

- ASP can be extended by third-party components. You can also build your own components so that code can be reused and execution speed is improved.

- ASP has built-in objects that aid Web development, such as the `Request` object (retrieves posted form data), and the `Session` object (handles user sessions).

- Microsoft is committed to improving ASP and the supporting scripting languages. ASP.NET is a major upgrade to ASP.

The Disadvantages of Using ASP

- ASP is not totally cross-platform. You will need to purchase plug-ins (Chillisoft or InstantASP) to run ASP on a Unix platform. These plug-ins are not free. Many third-party components only function on the Windows NT/2000 platform.

- Third-party components can be expensive. If your Web-based application requires many components, you should look to either ColdFusion or JSP.

- Not all Web hosting companies allow third-party components to be installed.

- VBScript and JScript are only scripting languages.

Recommended Servers

The following servers are recommended for running ASP-driven Web sites:

- Microsoft PWS (Personal Web Server). This can be downloaded from the Microsoft Web site or installed from the Windows 98 CD.

- Internet Information Server (IIS). This Web server comes with Windows NT/2000 and Windows XP Professional.

Using ASP.NET

ASP.NET represents the next step in Web development and is much more than just an upgrade to ASP. ASP.NET uses an event-driven programming model that is similar to the way Visual Basic currently works. Basically, code that resides on the server can respond to events that occur within a Web browser.

The Advantages of Using ASP.NET

- ASP.Net lets you separate code, content, and layout. This allows programming logic to change without affecting the layout of a site, and vice versa.

- ASP.NET is language independent. VB.NET, C#, and Jscript.NET can be used to program Web applications.

- ASP.NET applications are compiled. This offers a major performance boost over interpreted ASP applications.

- Simplified application configuration and deployment.

- Enhanced functionality. It is possible to send e-mail, upload files, generate images, and password-protect your Web site using built-in functionality.

The Disadvantages of Using ASP.NET

- ASP.NET is only available for Windows-platforms at the moment. ASP.NET is, however, designed to be operating system neutral. There are plans to port ASP.NET to FreeBSD, which will eventually see ASP.NET running on an Apache Web Server.

Recommended Server

The following server is recommended for running ASP.NET–driven Web sites:

- Internet Information Server (IIS). This Web server comes with Windows NT/2000 and Windows XP Professional.

Using JSP

JSP is modeled after ASP and has many similar objects to aid Web development. JSP is powerful because it enables developers to leverage the power of Java, a cross-platform, object-oriented programming language.

The Advantages of Using JSP

- Although JSP is similar to ASP and ColdFusion, it is much more powerful because Java code is embedded in a Web page.

- JSP is a cross-platform, server-side technology.

- Web applications built with JSP are highly scalable.

- JSP uses JDBC as an interface to databases.

- You can build your own tag libraries to extend JSP.

- JSP is a key component of J2EE (Java 2 Enterprise Edition) and has a bright future.

- Many Web server vendors already support JSP.

- JSP can be extended through Javabeans. Javabeans are very similar to components in ASP. You can purchase them or build your own. It is very easy to build a Javabean with a basic grasp of the Java language.

- JSP is free and can be downloaded from Sun's Web site. Both J2EE and JSWDK (JavaServer Web Development Kit) 1.1 are available.

The Disadvantages of Using JSP

- JSP has a steep learning curve if you don't have a good programming background.

- The back-end database must have a JDBC driver.

- Web site hosting may be harder to find and slightly more expensive.

- JSP is not as popular as ASP.

- While the JSP community is substantial, there are a limited number of JSP-specific resources available.

Recommended Servers

The following servers are recommended for running JSP-driven Web applications:

- IBM's WebSphere Server

- Macromedia JRun

- Netscape's iPlanet Enterprise Server

Using ColdFusion

ColdFusion uses a tag-based scripting language that cleanly interfaces with HTML. The tag-based language is known as CFML (ColdFusion Markup Language) and includes more than 70 tags.

The Advantages of Using ColdFusion

- ColdFusion is simple to learn.
- ColdFusion is very powerful. It has tags to access databases, send e-mail messages, transfer files through FTP (File Transfer Protocol), and programming constructs. These include loops and conditional statements.
- ColdFusion is cross-platform. There are versions for Windows NT, Linux, and Solaris.
- ColdFusion has a large developer community.
- You can build your own tags.

The Disadvantages of Using ColdFusion

- ColdFusion is not free. You will have to purchase a ColdFusion server from Macromedia.
- Hosting ColdFusion–based applications can be quite expensive.
- It is sometimes hard to follow and debug nested tags. This should only be a concern if the logic that you're building into a page is complex.

Recommended Server

The following server is recommended for running ColdFusion:

- Macromedia's ColdFusion Server

Using PHP

PHP is an open source server-side scripting language that has been developed specifically for Web applications. PHP mixes code that gets processed on the server with HTML.

The Advantages of Using PHP

- PHP is open source. This means that it is free to use and extend.
- PHP is cross-platform. There are versions for Windows, Linux, and Unix.
- PHP has a large and active developer community.
- PHP integrates well with MySQL, an open source relational database server.
- Short learning curve for C, C++, and Java programmers.

The Disadvantages of Using PHP

- PHP has a steep learning curve if you are not familiar with C programming syntax.
- ASP is more popular.
- There are a limited number of PHP-specific books available.

Recommended Server

PHP can be downloaded from http://www.php.net/downloads.php.

Selecting a Database

Although Dreamweaver MX enables you to connect to most commercially available databases, the database you select needs to be compatible with the application server. The chosen database needs an ODBC- (Open DataBase Connectivity) compliant driver to interface to ASP, and a JDBC- (Java DataBase Connectivity) compliant driver to interface to JSP. It is also important that the database can handle the amount of data you wish to store and the traffic that your site could receive.

Microsoft Access is a low-end database that can be Web-enabled through ODBC. Access is not a client/server database and will not handle a large number of requests in an efficient manner. It should only be used on small-scale Web sites. If you have no prior experience with relational databases, then I would recommend learning Access. It is very easy to learn and might already be installed on your computer if you have Microsoft Office. All the concepts you learn also apply to other databases.

Dreamweaver MX makes light work of binding the actual data to a Web page, but you're probably wondering how to create a database in the first place. Chapter 9, "Designing a Database," will answer all your questions. It explains relational database theory in a practical manner and takes you step by step through creating your first Access database.

If your Web site needs to handle a great number of simultaneous users, you need to consider using an enterprise database. Enterprise databases are powerful and complicated but can also be quite expensive. Here are some of the most popular enterprise databases:

- Oracle
- Microsoft SQL Server
- IBM DB2
- MySQL

These are all true client/server databases. Databases that run in a client/server environment can handle gigabytes of data and a large number of users. Client/server databases can also store and run powerful scripts. This removes complex code from your Web page and improves performance. Enterprise databases can usually run on a wide variety of platforms and offer enhanced security, data locking, scalability, and data replication capabilities.

Specifying an Application Server for a Site

Dreamweaver MX needs to know where all the pages on your Web server are stored. You need to specify the physical path to your Web site and the URL of your Web server. This enables you to view and edit the dynamic content generated by your application server within the Live Data window. All Web pages that you preview through your browser will be served from your local Web server.

1. Click on Start. A menu appears.

2. Click on All Programs. A submenu appears.

3. Click on Control Panel. The Control Panel is displayed.

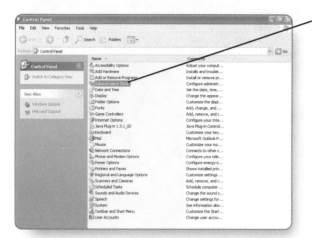

4. Double-click on Administrative Tools. The Administrative Tools window opens.

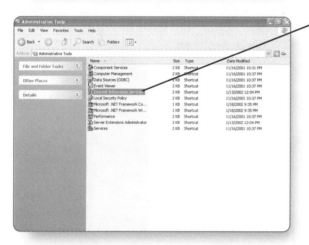

5. Double-click on Internet Information Services. The Internet Information Services window opens.

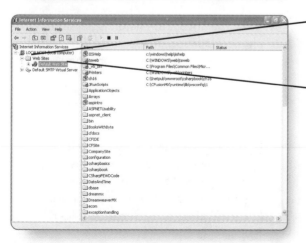

6. Expand the LOCALHOST and Web Sites folders. The Default Web Site node is displayed.

7. Right-click on the Default Web Site node. A shortcut menu appears.

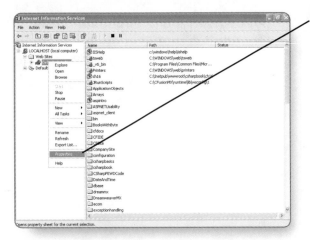

8. Click on Properties. The Default Web Site Properties dialog box opens.

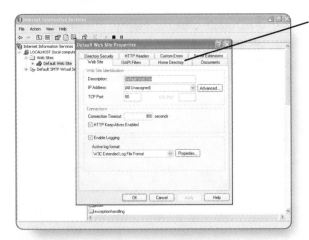

9. Click on the Home Directory tab. The tab is displayed.

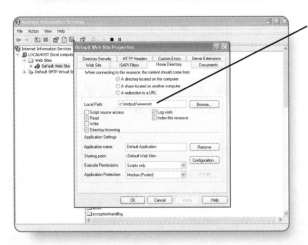

10. The Local Path field displays the physical location of your local Web server. This is the home directory on your Web server.

NOTE

You will need to create a new folder within the home directory. This folder will be used to store a Web site on your Web server. You should store each Web site in a separate folder.

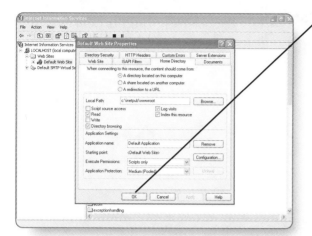

11. Click on OK. The Default Web Site Properties dialog box closes.

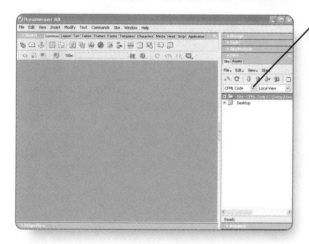

12. Click on the down arrow of the Sites drop-down list. All the sites in Dreamweaver MX are displayed.

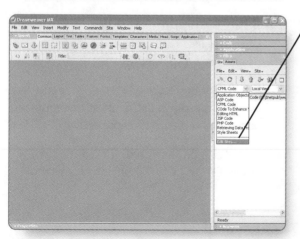

13. Click on Edit Sites. The Edit Sites dialog box opens.

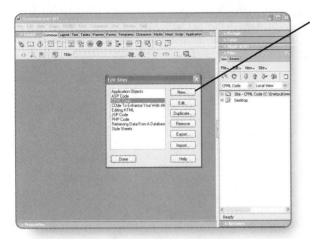

14. Click on New. The Site Definition dialog box opens.

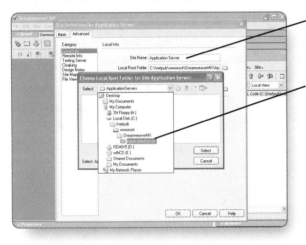

15. Enter a name for the site in the Site Name field. This name will be used to identify your Web site in Dreamweaver MX.

16. Enter the physical path to the folder that you created within the home directory of your local Web server.

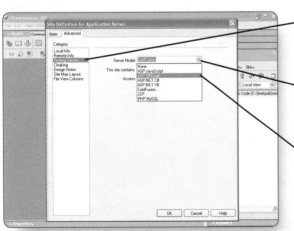

17. Click on Testing Server in the Category list. The application server options are displayed.

18. Click on the down arrow of the Server Model drop-down list. The list of supported application servers is displayed.

19. Click on the server model that you would like to use. The option is selected.

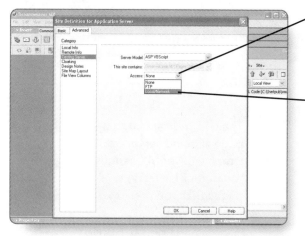

20. Click on the down arrow of the Access drop-down list. The list of supported options for accessing your application server is displayed.

21. Click on Local/Network. The option is selected.

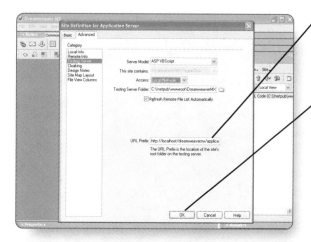

22. Enter the URL Prefix for your Web site. The prefix is made up of the URL of your Web server and the folder that will store your Web site.

23. Click on OK. The Site Definition dialog box closes.

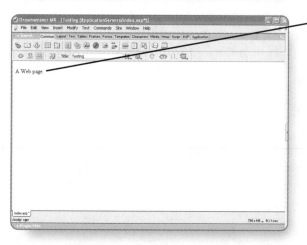

24. Type some text to create a simple Web page.

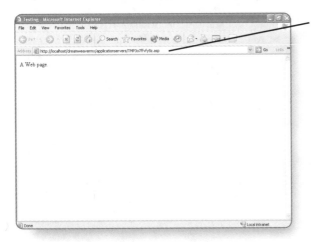

25. Press F12 to preview the Web page. The browser opens and loads the Web page

NOTE

The URL indicates that the Web page is being served by IIS. Dreamweaver MX assigns a temporary file name to all Web pages that you preview in a browser.

Introducing Server Behaviors

Behaviors enable you to achieve complex tasks without having to write a single line of code. Behaviors make Dreamweaver MX the powerful Web site development tool that it is. Dreamweaver MX has both client and server behaviors. It is essential that you know the difference between the two and are familiar with the functionality that can be achieved with each.

Server-Side versus Client-Side Behaviors

Client-side behaviors insert JavaScript code into a Web page. The script is only processed when the Web page is displayed in a Web browser. A client-side behavior is interpreted on a user's own computer (the client). Client-side scripting is dependent upon the type of browser that the user has installed. This is perhaps the biggest disadvantage in using client-side behaviors. Browsers implement JavaScript differently, so it is important that the behaviors you insert function without errors in popular browsers such as Microsoft Internet Explorer and Netscape Navigator. Luckily, Dreamweaver MX takes care of inserting compatible code once you have decided upon your target browsers. This makes life much easier.

A server-side behavior, on the other hand, inserts JSP, ASP, or ColdFusion script into a Web page. Server-side scripts are interpreted in the server. Once the script is processed, only HTML is sent to the browser. You have total control over the environment in which your script will be executed and don't have to worry about the capabilities of a Web browser.

Client and server behaviors are by no means competing technologies. There are features that you can use from both to make your Web site more compelling and dynamic. Client-side behaviors will help you create a visually appealing Web site. You can create image rollovers, play sounds, and use layers to create complex timeline animations. Server-side behaviors enable you to create dynamic database-driven Web sites. There are behaviors that will generate code to display, insert, update, and delete records from a database.

The Behaviors Tab

The Behaviors tab contains all the available client-side behaviors. Before you insert a behavior you need to select the browsers you wish to target.

NOTE

It is beyond the scope of this book to explain how to implement all the available behaviors. This section only highlights the functionality that can be achieved.

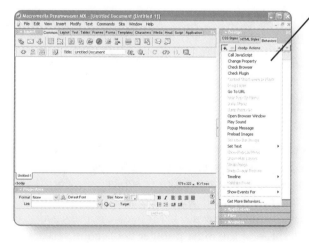

You can utilize behaviors to

- **Swap images**. This enables you to swap images by moving a mouse over or clicking on an image.

- **Preload images**. You should preload images that are being swapped. This reduces the time it takes for an image to be displayed.

- **Play sounds**. You can play a sound once a button is clicked on or when the page loads.

- **Display a message on the status bar**. The status bar can be used to provide feedback and guidance to your users.

- **Open a URL**. You can use an event other than a mouse click to open a new Web page.

- **Display a pop-up alert message**. This can be used to confirm users' actions.

- **Open a new browser window**. You can display a Web page in a new browser. Both the size and attributes of the new window are configurable.

- **Detect whether a user's browser has a plug-in installed**. This is important if your Web site is using either Shockwave or Flash. You can redirect a user without the required plug-in to a low bandwidth HTML version of the page.

- **Check browser type and function**. Sometimes you may implement functionality that only works in a specific browser and version. If your script is displayed in the incorrect browser, an error message will appear. You need to detect the browser being used and redirect the user to a page that their browser can view.

- **Control Shockwave or Flash movies**. You can enable users to play, stop, or rewind interactive movies.

- **Control layers**. Layers enable you to create DHTML (Dynamic HTML) applications. The Behaviors tab contains a set of behaviors that enable you to hide or show layers and create timeline-based animations.

- **Validate forms**. You can ensure that a user has filled out all of the mandatory fields on an HTML form. You can also check the format (text, numeric, or e-mail address) of the data entered. Using the Validate Form behavior is fully explained in Chapter 8, "Validating and Retrieving Form Data."

Some behaviors are grayed out. This means that they are disabled until your Web page contains the required elements. You need to have layers before you can use the behaviors that control layers. You also need a form before you can use the Validate Form behavior.

The Server Behaviors Tab

Server behaviors are new additions to Dreamweaver MX that enable you to create dynamic database-driven Web sites. Server behaviors do all the hard work by inserting all the required code. Perhaps the greatest feature of server behaviors is that you can target multiple application servers (ASP, ASP.NET, JSP, PHP and ColdFusion). Thus after you are familiar with Dreamweaver MX, you can use your skills to build Web applications for all three of the most popular application servers.

While server behaviors are very easy to use, you still need to have a clear understanding of what each server behavior can achieve and where it can be used. As a new user, you may find the names given to server behaviors slightly confusing. Names like Repeat Region and Link to Detail Page certainly don't make any sense if you're not familiar with programming jargon. This makes using a server behavior for the first time quite difficult, but this section gives you a sound overview with helpful examples.

The Server Behaviors tab is used to insert server behaviors. Unlike client-side behaviors, you don't need to specify target browsers. You do, however, need to select an appropriate application server.

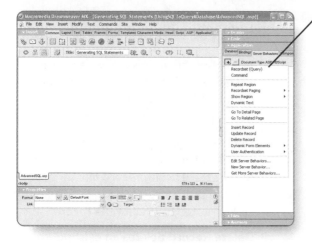

Use the following server behaviors to display search results on a Web page:

- The **Recordset (Query)** server behavior allows you to query a database and bind the returned data to a Web page.

- The **Repeat Region** server behavior allows multiple records to be displayed on a Web page. If your database contains many records, you need only display a few records at a time by splitting the results across multiple pages.

- The **Move to Record** server behavior enables you to create a navigation panel for paged search results. You can create links to move to the next and previous pages.

- The **Show Region** server behavior makes the navigation panel more intuitive to use. The previous link can be disabled on the first page, while the next link can be disabled when the last page is reached. You also can use the Show Region server behavior to display a message if the search request returned no records.

- A search results Web page usually only displays summary data from a record. You need to provide the user with an opportunity to view the entire record. The **Go To Detail Page** server behavior is used to link to a detail page, a Web page that displays all the important fields in a record. The ID of the chosen record is appended to the URL of the detail page.

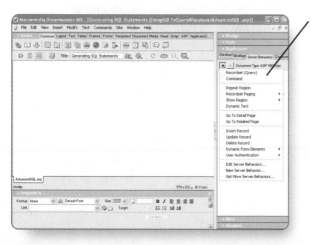

Use the following server behaviors to create a detail page:

- The **Recordset (Query)** server behavior retrieves the record that matches the ID appended to the URL of the detail page, and then binds the record to the Web page.

- The **Go To Related Page** server behavior can be used to create a link to a page that contains related information.

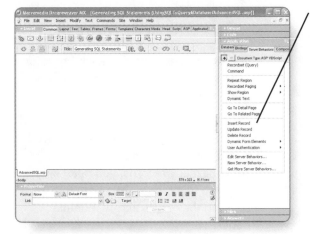

Use the following server behaviors to maintain a database from a Web interface:

- **Insert Record** inserts a new record into a database table. You need to create a form that contains all the fields to populate a record in a database.

- **Update Record** updates an existing record in a database table. You need to display the existing record in a form, so that the user can edit the data and then click a button to update the record.

- **Delete Record** deletes an existing record in a database. You need to let users preview the record so that they know what will be deleted.

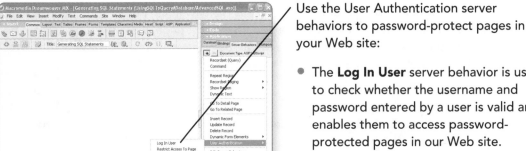

Use the User Authentication server behaviors to password-protect pages in your Web site:

- The **Log In User** server behavior is used to check whether the username and password entered by a user is valid and enables them to access password-protected pages in our Web site.

- The **Restrict Access To Page** server behavior enables you to define the pages in your site that should be password-protected.

- The **Log Out User** server behavior is used when you enable users to register before they can access restricted areas on your Web site. It checks to see if a username is already in use.

- The **Check New Username** server behavior provides a link or button that the user can click on to log out of the Web site.

7

Using HTML Forms

HTML forms are fundamental to building interactive Web sites. Forms are used to gather information from users that require processing. They contain standard graphical interface elements such as text fields, check boxes, radio buttons, and drop-down lists. Forms are extremely important in database-driven Web sites where users are required to insert, update, and search data. In this chapter, you'll learn how to do the following:

- Add form objects (text fields, password fields, check boxes, radio buttons, and drop-down lists)
- Use a table to format a form
- Use a button to submit a form
- Use a button to reset a form

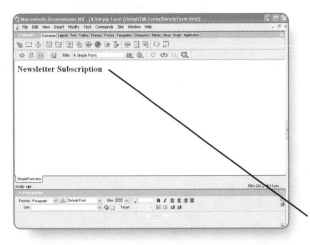

Creating HTML Forms

The Forms tab on the Insert panel enables you to insert form elements into a Web page. This is done in a visual and intuitive manner. The available form objects include text fields, check boxes, radio buttons, drop-down lists, and menus. Form object properties can be edited from the Properties Inspector.

1. Create a new Web page. A blank Web page is displayed in the Document window.

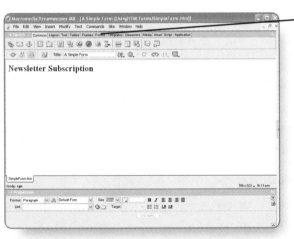

2. Click on the Forms tab. The available form objects are displayed.

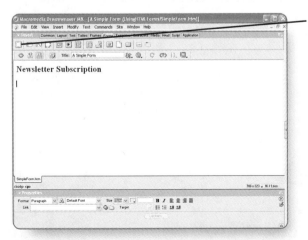

3. Click on the Insert Form button. A form is inserted.

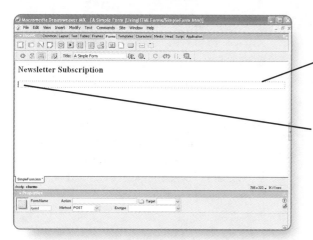

4. Click inside the form. The cursor appears where you click.

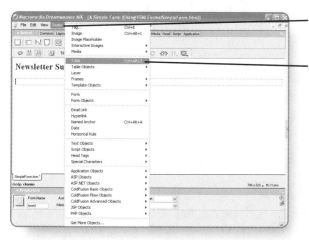

5. Click on the Insert menu. The Insert menu appears.

6. Click on Table. The Insert Table dialog box opens.

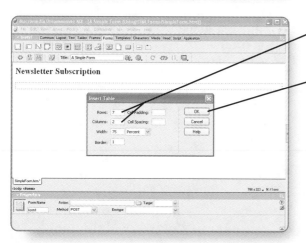

7. Enter the number of rows and columns for your table.

8. Click on OK. The table is inserted within the form on the Web page.

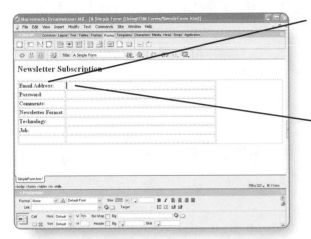

9. Type the titles for all the information you would like to collect in the left column of cells.

NOTE

In the next column, you determine the appropriate form elements to be used to collect data from your visitors. You can choose from the following element types:

- Text fields
- Password fields
- Multiline text fields
- Radio buttons
- Check boxes
- Drop-down lists

The following sections discuss each type of element in more detail.

Inserting Text Fields

Text fields enable free-form data entry. A text field is ideal for users to enter data such as names, addresses, and telephone numbers. Text fields only allow users to enter a single line of text. Use a multiline text field if you would like users to be able to enter lengthy sentences.

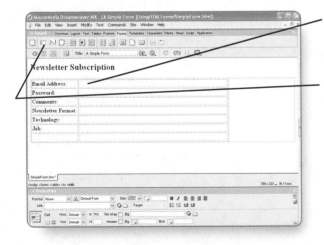

1. Click in the table cell where you want to insert the text field. The cursor appears where you click.

2. Click on the Insert Text Field button. The text field is inserted.

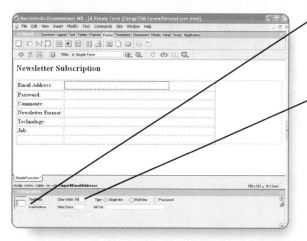

3. Type a name for the Text field. All form objects must be given a unique name. The name of a form object is required when retrieving posted form data.

4. Enter the number of characters the field should hold. This determines the length of the field when displayed in a browser. The number of characters that a text field should hold depends on the data you wish to collect.

Inserting Password Fields

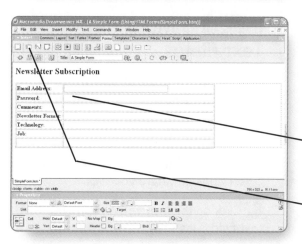

A password field is a text field that uses asterisks to mask the data being entered. Use a password field when the user has to enter sensitive data that should not be viewed by anybody else, such as a password or credit card number.

1. Click in the table cell where you would like to insert a password field. The cursor appears where you click.

2. Click on the Insert Text Field button. The text field is inserted.

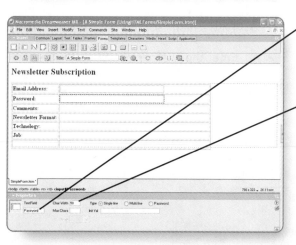

3. Type a name for the Text field. All form objects must be given a unique name. The name of a form object is required when retrieving posted form data.

4. Enter the number of characters the field should hold. This determines the length of the field when displayed in a browser. The number of characters that a text field should hold depends on the data you wish to collect.

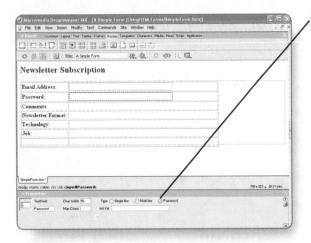

5. Click on the Password radio button. The option is selected.

Inserting Multiline Text Fields

Unlike a text field, a multiline text field can handle large amounts of information that span multiple lines.

1. Click inside the table cell where you want to insert the multiline text field. The cursor appears where you click.

2. Click on the Insert Text Field button. A text field is inserted.

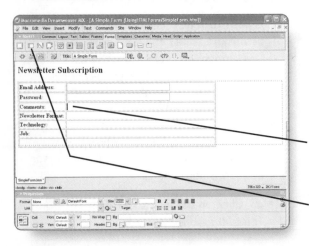

3. Type a name for the multiline text field.

4. Enter the number of characters the field should hold. This defines the width of the multiline text field when displayed in a Web browser.

5. Click on the Multi line radio button to change the text field into a multiline text field. The option is selected.

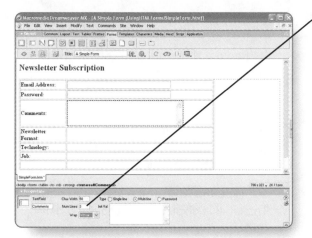

6. Type the number of lines required in the Num Lines field. This defines the number of lines that can be displayed at any one time. The number that you specify depends on the data you wish to collect.

> ### NOTE
>
> A multiline text field enables the user to enter text beyond the constraints that you set. When the user enters more data than the browser can display, scrollbars are included in the display.

7. Select Virtual from the Wrap drop-down list. This wraps text automatically as the user types. The user does not have to press Enter to go to a new line.

Inserting Radio Buttons

Radio buttons provide the user with a set of options from which only one option can be selected. Radio buttons must be grouped, and only one button in a group can be selected at a time. Selecting another option deselects the previously selected option. The minimum number of radio buttons that you can place in a group is two.

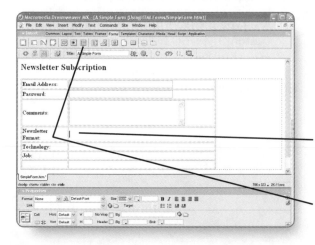

1. Click inside the table cell where you would like to insert the group of options. The cursor appears where you click.

2. Click on the Radio Group button. The Radio Group dialog box opens.

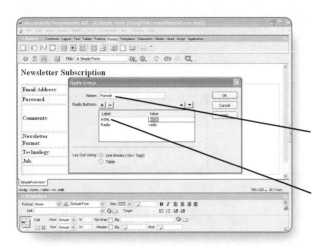

3. Type a name for the Radio Button group. The name is used to define the group of radio buttons.

4. Type the label of the first radio button. The label is displayed next to the radio button.

5. Enter a value for the first radio button. The value attribute of a radio button represents the data that is posted if the user selects this option. Each radio button in a group must have a unique value.

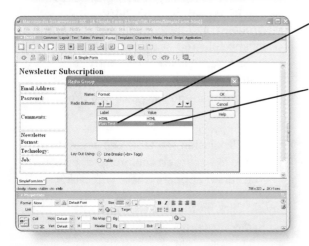

6. Type the label of the second radio button. The label is displayed next to the radio button.

7. Enter a value for the second radio button.

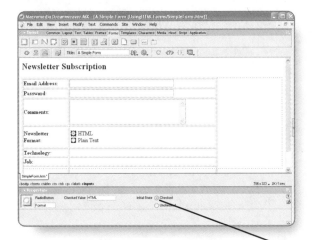

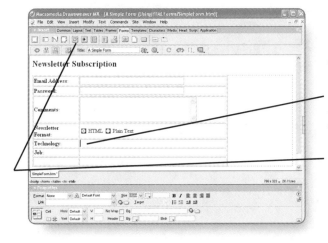

Inserting Check Boxes

Check boxes enable users to enter True/False or Yes/No answers in a form.

1. Click inside the table cell where you want to insert a group of check boxes. The cursor appears where you click.

2. Click on the Check Box button. A check box is inserted.

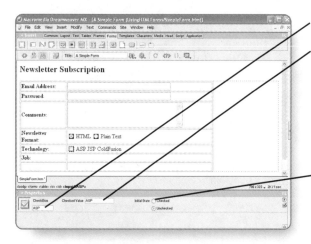

3. Type a name for the check box.

4. Type a value for the check box. The value contains the data that is posted to the server when the form is submitted if the user has checked the box.

NOTE

Click on the Checked radio button if you want a check box to be selected by default when the Web page loads.

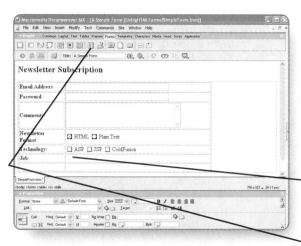

Inserting Drop-Down Lists

Drop-down lists should be used when several options are available but you only want the user to be able to select one of them. Drop-down lists preserve valuable screen space compared to radio button groups.

1. Click inside the table cell where you want to insert a drop-down list. The cursor appears where you click.

2. Click on the List/Menu button. A drop-down list is inserted.

3. Type a name for the drop-down list.

4. Click on the List Values button. The List Values dialog box opens.

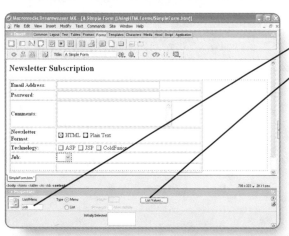

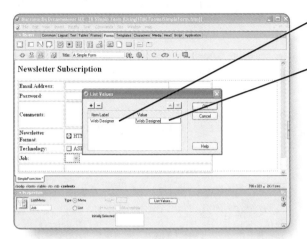

5. Type the name of the option into the Item Label column.

6. Type the value of the option into the Value column.

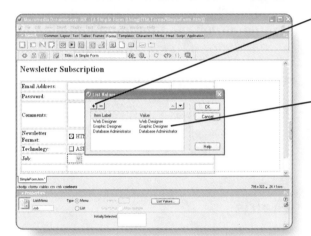

7. Click on the + button to add new options to the drop-down list. A new row is inserted for you to enter the names and values of new options.

8. Repeat this process for each option you add.

TIP

- To remove a List Value option, select it and then click on the – button.
- To change the order of options, select the option you want to re-order and click on either the up or down arrow to move it into its new position.

---

9. Click on OK. The List Values dialog box closes.

Inserting List Menus

List menus should be used when a large number of options are available to the user and more than one can be selected. Unlike drop-down lists, list menus can be scrolled and can display multiple items at a time.

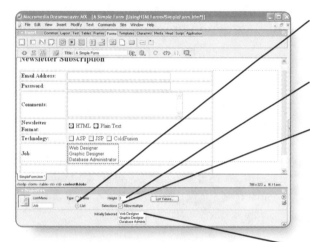

1. Click on List to change the drop-down box to a list. The Height and Selections fields are enabled.

2. Type the number of lines the list should occupy in the Height field.

3. Click on the Allow multiple check box if you want to enable the user to select multiple options. A check is placed in the check box.

TIP

Click on the List Item that you want to be selected by default when the page loads.

Inserting Hidden Form Fields

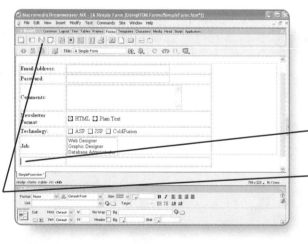

Hidden fields are used to store data within a form that can't be viewed or edited by a user. They provide a way to send additional information to the server for processing. Hidden fields are not displayed and do not affect the layout of your form.

1. Click anywhere within the form. The cursor appears where you click.

2. Click on the Hidden Field button. A Hidden Field icon is inserted in the document.

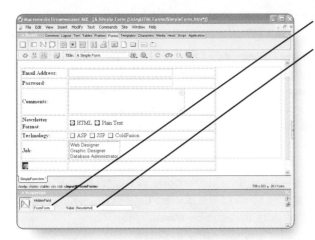

3. Type a name for the hidden field.

4. Type a value for the hidden field.

Submitting a Form

Submitting a form involves transferring all of the data entered by a user to a server where it is retrieved and processed. Before a form can be submitted, you need to set the Action and Method attributes of the form. The Method attribute defines how the data is sent, while the Action attribute tells the browser where to send the form data.

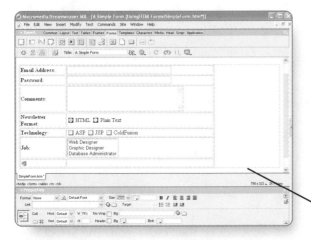

1. Click on the form border (a dashed red line). The entire contents of the form are highlighted.

2. Type a name for the form.

3. Click on the down arrow of the Method drop-down list. A list of options appears.

4a. Click on GET. The GET method is selected.

OR

4b. Click on POST. The POST method is selected.

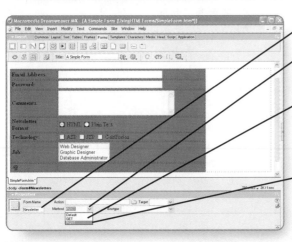

NOTE

- The **GET method** tells the browser to append all of the submitted form data to the URL. The appended data is known as the *QueryString*. The GET method is restricted by the maximum amount of characters allowed for a Web address. This varies from server to server. Your data will be truncated if it exceeds this limit. You will also be able to see the contents of the form in the address field of your browser. For example: http://www.yoursite.com/sample.asp?formfield1=value1&formfield2=value2

- The **POST method** sends all of the form data in the body of the HTTP POST command. You will not be able to read the posted data in the URL. There is no limit on the amount of data that can be transferred. This should be your preferred method for submitting form data.

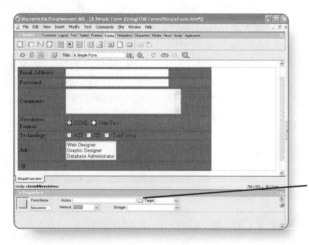

NOTE

The method you select affects the way you retrieve the posted information on the server. Both methods are covered in Chapter 8, "Validating and Retrieving Form Data."

5. Click on the Folder icon. The Select File dialog box opens.

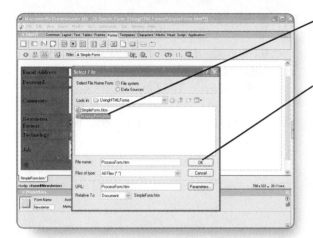

6. Click on the file that will process the form. Any simple Web page will do at the moment.

7. Click on OK. The file name is entered into the Action field.

NOTE

The Action attribute tells the browser where to send the form data. This is usually a Web page that can process the form data. You will learn to create such a file in the next chapter.

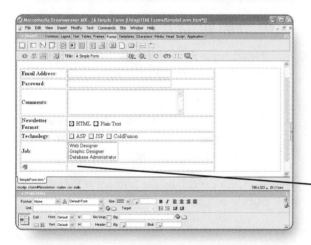

Using a Button to Submit a Form

A Submit button, once pressed, collects all of the information and sends it to the server.

1. Click inside a table cell where you would like to insert a Submit button. The cursor appears where you click.

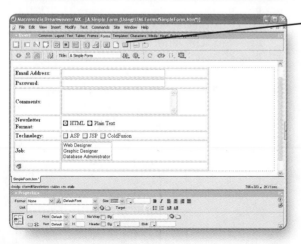

2. Click on the Insert button. A Submit button is inserted and has a default name and label.

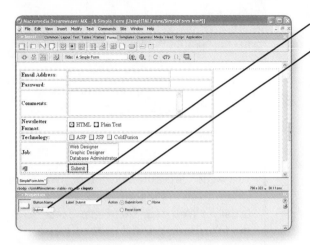

3. Type a name for the button.

4. Type a label for the button. This appears when the button is displayed in a Web browser. The label must describe the purpose of the button, which in this case is to send the information entered by the user to the server.

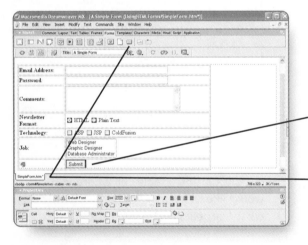

Resetting a Form

Resetting a form clears all the data that has been entered by a user and returns the form to its default settings.

1. Click inside the table cell where you want to insert a Reset button. The cursor appears where you click.

2. Click on the Insert button. A Submit button is inserted.

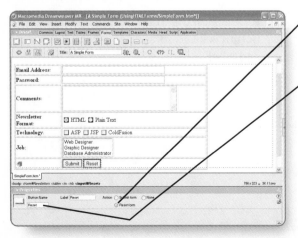

3. Click on Reset form. The option is selected. The label will be changed to Reset.

4. Type a name for the Reset button. When the user clicks on this button, any data in his or her form will be cleared from the screen.

8

Validating and Retrieving Form Data

To create a powerful Web site, you need to be able to process and respond to data sent by users. The first step in this process involves retrieving the data. It is also useful to verify that the information entered by the users is in the correct format before it gets processed. This prevents errors from occurring. In this chapter, you'll learn how to do the following:

- Validate form data
- Retrieve form data posted using the GET method
- Retrieve form data posted using the POST method
- Retrieve environment/server variables

Validating Form Data

Before you process data, you must make sure that data have been entered and are in the correct format. This process is known as *form validation* and can be performed before the information is submitted to the server. We will use a behavior to insert JavaScript code to validate the data from the form before it is submitted. JavaScript is a scripting language that runs within a Web browser on the client's machine. This is known as *client-side scripting* (as opposed to *server-side scripting*, which runs on the server). You can also perform validation on the server, but using a client-side behavior is faster and more efficient.

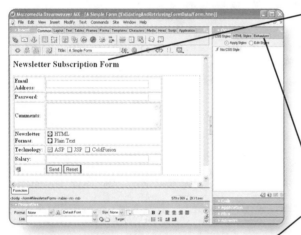

1. Open the Web page that contains a form you wish to validate. All the form fields must be named. The previous chapter covered the basics of creating a form in Dreamweaver MX. Please refer to Chapter 7, "Using HTML Forms," if you are not familiar with creating a form.

2. Click on the Behaviors tab in the Design Panel group. The Behaviors tab is displayed.

3. Click on the form border, a dashed red line. The form is highlighted.

4. Click on the + sign. A submenu containing available client-side behaviors is displayed.

5. Click on Validate Form. The Validate Form dialog box opens. A list of all named form element fields is displayed in the Named Fields list.

NOTE

The Validate Form behavior only allows you to verify the data entered into text fields.

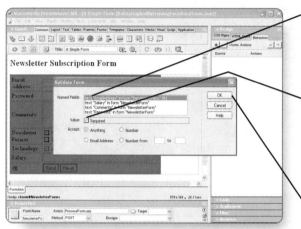

6. Click on the name of a form object you want to make mandatory. Users must enter a value in the field before the form is submitted to the server for processing.

7. Click inside the Required check box. A check is placed inside the box. (R) appears next to the form object name. This indicates that the form will not be submitted if the field is left blank.

8. Click on OK. The Validate Form dialog box closes.

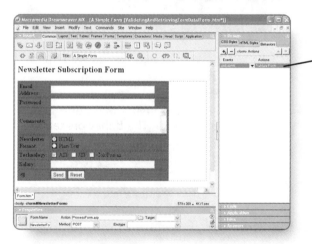

NOTE

The Validate Form action has been added to the OnSubmit form event. Dreamweaver MX does all of this automatically.

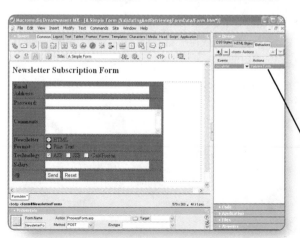

Validating Numeric Data

Sometimes you require only numeric data in a field. To prevent the user from entering other data, you need to make sure that the field can only contain numbers.

1. Double-click on the Validate Form action in the Behaviors tab. The Validate Form dialog box opens.

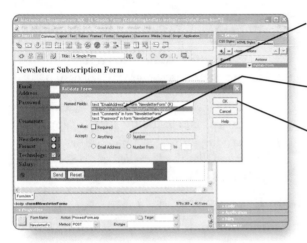

2. Click on the name of the field that must contain only numeric data. The field name is highlighted.

3. Click on the Number option button. The option is selected.

4. Click on OK. The field is set to receive only numeric data from users.

Validating E-mail Addresses

A valid e-mail address must contain the @ sign and no invalid characters (such as /:,;'). Users might accidentally include a space or colon when typing their e-mail addresses. You should validate e-mail addresses if you don't want to encounter any problems when sending messages back to the users.

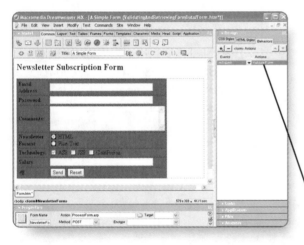

1. Double-click on the Validate Form action in the Behaviors tab. The Validate Form dialog box opens.

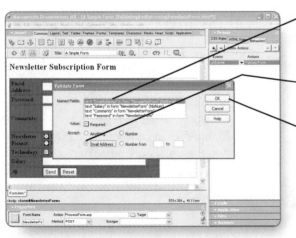

2. Click on the name of the field that must contain an e-mail address. The field name is highlighted.

3. Click on the Email Address option button. The option is selected.

4. Click on OK. The field is set to receive only an e-mail address entry from users.

Retrieving Form Data

Once data is posted to a server, it must be retrieved and processed. This is achieved by using a server-side script that is embedded within the Web page. The Web page that processes the information must be specified in the Action attribute of the form. Dreamweaver MX takes care of the scripting; all you have to do is tell it which form elements to retrieve. The process of retrieving data sent using the POST method is slightly different from retrieving data sent with the GET method. Both methods are explained in the following sections.

Retrieving Form Data Submitted with the GET Method

When a form is submitted using the GET method, the form data is appended to the URL of the file requested in the form action. A question mark (?) is inserted between the file name and the form data. The form data tagged onto the URL is known as a QueryString. The GET method appends data in name-pair values, in other words, each field is paired with the value that the user has entered. The GET method may truncate the data if it exceeds a certain limit, which varies from server to server. The GET method also encodes certain characters (&, +, and $) that are used to define a QueryString. URL encoding involves converting the character to ASCII and preceding it with a % symbol. The Request Variable behavior is used to retrieve data posted with the GET method.

1. Create a new Web page with an .asp extension. This Web page will process form data.

CAUTION

Don't use the GET method when you want your users to enter private information—it can be viewed in the address field of the Web browser.

Use the GET method when you want to enable users to bookmark the Web page. Data in the QueryString is also saved when a URL is bookmarked.

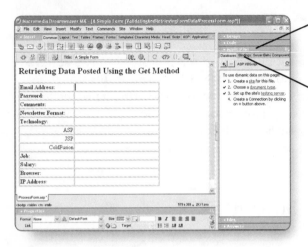

2. Expand the Application Panel Group. The Databases, Bindings, Server Behaviors, and Components tabs are displayed.

3. Click on the Bindings tab. The Bindings tab is displayed.

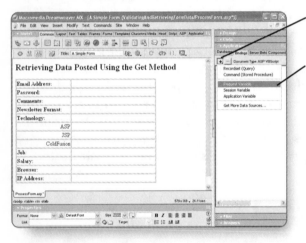

4. Click on the + sign. A submenu appears.

5. Click on Request Variable. The Request Variable dialog box appears.

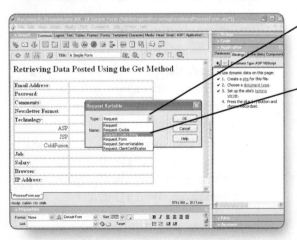

6. Click on the down arrow of the Type drop-down list. A list of request types appears.

7. Click on Request.QueryString. The option is selected.

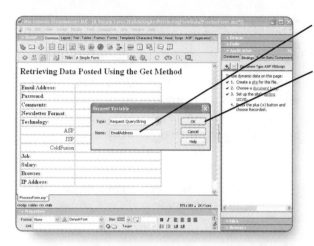

8. Type the name of the form object into the Name field.

9. Click on OK. The retrieved form element is displayed in the Bindings tab. The form element name is preceded by "QueryString."

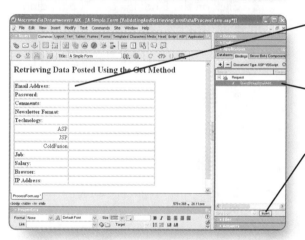

10. Click inside your document where you want to insert the retrieved form data. The cursor appears where you click.

11. Click on the form field that has the contents you want to retrieve. The form field is highlighted.

12. Click on Insert. The field placeholder is inserted as dynamic text.

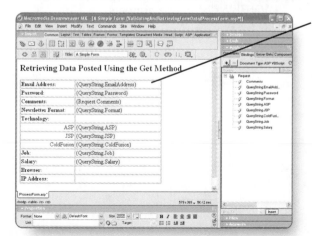

13. Repeat steps 3–12 for each field value you want to retrieve.

Retrieving Form Data Submitted with the POST Method

The POST method allows unlimited amounts of data to be transferred to the server without appending anything onto the URL. The POST method is much more secure because the posted form data is not displayed. You should also use the POST method when you don't want users bookmarking or returning directly to the processing Web page.

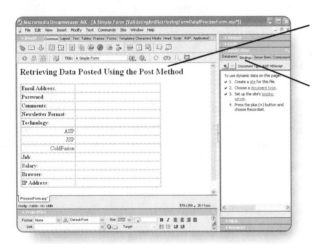

1. Create a new Web page with an .asp extension. This Web page will process form data.

2. Click on the Bindings tab. The Bindings tab is displayed.

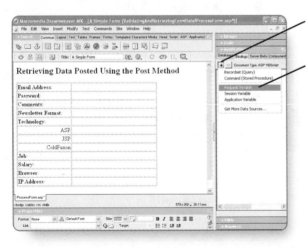

3. Click on the + sign. A submenu appears.

4. Click on Request Variable. The Request Variable dialog box appears.

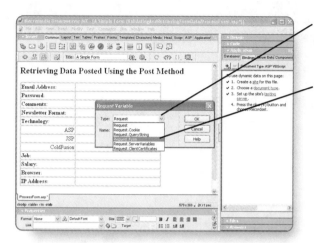

5. Click on the down arrow of the Type drop-down list. A list of request types appears.

6. Click on Request.Form. The option is selected.

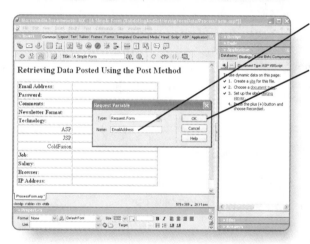

7. Type the name of the form field into the Name field.

8. Click on OK. The Retrieved form field is displayed on the Bindings tab.

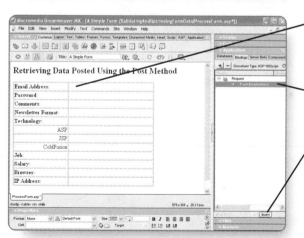

9. Click inside your document where you want to insert the retrieved form data. The cursor appears where you click.

10. Click on the form field that has the contents you want to retrieve. The form field is highlighted.

11. Click on Insert. The field placeholder is inserted as dynamic text.

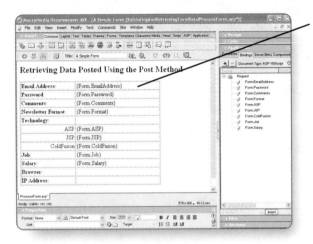

12. Repeat steps 3–11 for each field value you want to retrieve.

Retrieving Environment/Server Variables

When a form is submitted, data about the user is also sent to the Web server. This data is referred to as an *Environment/Server Variable*. Among other things, you can retrieve the user's Web browser and IP address.

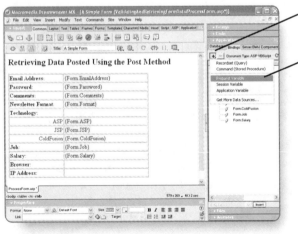

1. Click on the + sign. A submenu appears.

2. Click on Request Variable. The Request Variable dialog box opens.

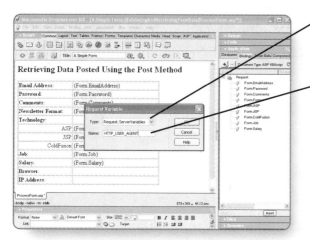

3. Select Request.ServerVariables from the Type drop-down list. The option is selected.

4. Type the name of the server variable into the Name field. Environment variables include those shown in Table 8.1.

Table 8.1 Environment Variables

Description	Variable Name
Virtual Path of Script	SCRIPT_NAME
Length of Posted Content	CONTENT_LENGTH
Browser Name	HTTP_USER_AGENT
Referring Web Page Address	HTTP_REFERER
Client's IP Address	REMOTE_ADDR
QueryString	QUERY_STRING

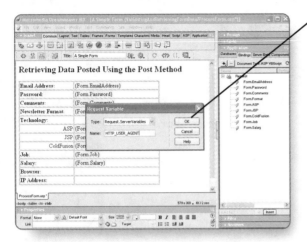

5. Click on OK. The retrieved environment variable is displayed in the Bindings tab.

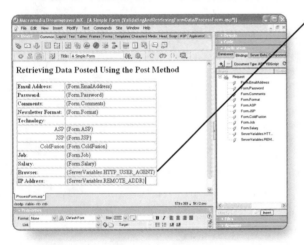

6. Bind the server variables to the page.

7. Repeat steps 1–6 for each variable you want to retrieve.

9

Designing a Database

You have probably figured out by now that you first need a database before you can create a dynamic database-driven Web site. Dreamweaver MX has revolutionized the manner in which database-enabled Web sites are built. The process is much simpler, and you don't need to write a line of code unless you require complex functionality. The irony, though, is that you still need to know how to design a relational database. Relational databases are not very complex. You only need to know some basic background theory and you'll be on your way. In this chapter, you'll learn how to do the following:

- Work with relational databases
- Create a Microsoft Access database
- Create a System DSN (Data Source Name) for your database

Understanding Relational Databases

RDMS (Relational Databases Management Systems) store data in tables. A database table is not much different from a table in Word or a spreadsheet in Excel. A table is made up of columns and rows.

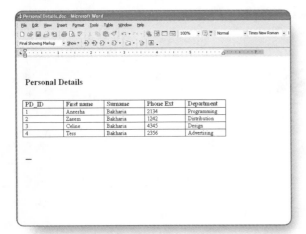

NOTE

- Each column has a heading that describes the type of data stored in a field.

- Each row represents a unique record in the table.

- Each cell is known as a field in a record.

- Each record must have a field that uniquely identifies the record. This is known as the *primary key*.

At this stage, you're probably wondering why you need a database to store data when you can already use both Word and Excel. The answer is simple: Word and Excel are not capable of handling large amounts of data in an efficient manner. A relational database, on the other hand, is designed to store and manage large amounts of information. A relational database has powerful query capabilities and the ability to extract meaningful information. Relational databases are also flexible and easy to maintain.

A relational database comprises one or more tables. Each table must contain unique data that is not duplicated in another table. This ensures that you only need to search and update data in one place. Tables are linked. The link between two tables is known as a *relationship*. A relationship is established by linking common fields from both tables.

Designing Database Tables and Relationships

Once you have determined the purpose of your database, you need to determine what tables are required. Each table should contain information about one subject, and no two tables should contain duplicate information. I can't stress this point enough. It is key to creating a database that can be maintained easily and does not contain duplicate data. There should only be one place to update data.

Each table should be normalized. Data normalization simply means that you are optimizing the storage of data in tables. Normalization will help you to eliminate duplication and store data in an efficient way. Here are some guidelines:

- A field can't contain multiple values. Each field can only contain a single value. You should also avoid repeating columns of similar data stored in a table.

- Every field that makes up a record in a table must be dependent upon the primary key. All fields that are not dependent upon the primary key should be stored in another table.

- A field that is not a primary key should not be linked to another field that is also not a primary key.

When you design required tables, you need to determine

- The type of data that each field in a table will store. A field could store numeric, text, or date information.

- Which field to use as the primary key in each table. The primary key must be unique for each record.

- How tables are related in your database. You can store another table's primary key to identify the linked record stored in another table. This is known as a *foreign key*.

Creating a Microsoft Access Database

Microsoft Access is a relational database that is very easy to learn. If you have never created a database before, this section is just for you. You'll learn to create and relate tables in Access. As you become comfortable with designing databases and relational theory, you should consider scaling up to a client/server database like Microsoft SQL Server.

1. Open Microsoft Access from the Start menu. Access is part of Microsoft Office but can also be purchased separately.

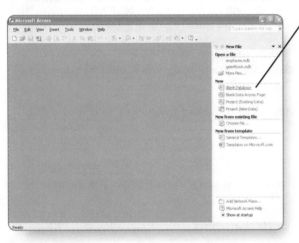

2. Click on the Blank Database link. The File New Database dialog box opens.

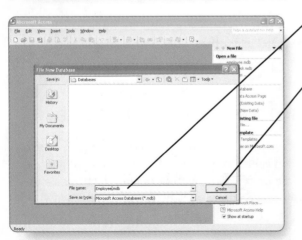

3. Enter the database name into the File name field. The file name must have an .mdb extension.

4. Click on Create. The database is created.

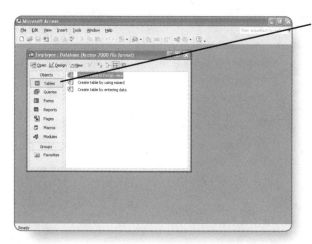

5. Click on the Tables tab, and then click on New. The New Table dialog box opens.

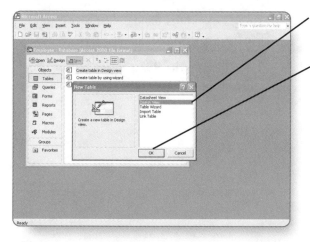

6. Click on Design View. The option is selected.

7. Click on OK. The Table Design View window opens.

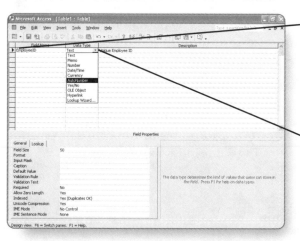

8. Type a field name in the Field Name column. The first field is usually the primary key. Don't include spaces, periods, exclamation marks, or square brackets in field names. Use an underscore to replace spaces.

9. Click on the down arrow of the Data Type column. All the types of data that Access can store are displayed.

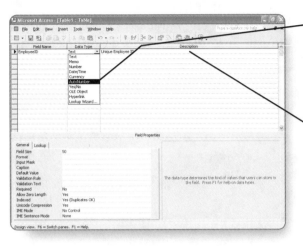

10. Click on AutoNumber. The option is selected. AutoNumber is a sequential number that is automatically inserted when a new record is added to a table. This is ideal for creating a unique primary key.

11. Type in a description for the field. This helps you when you return to modify the database.

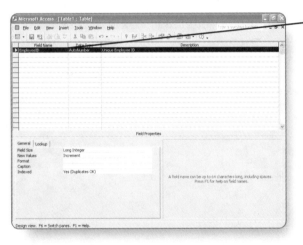

12. Click on the Field Selection button. The field is selected.

13. Click on the Primary Key button. The selected field is converted to a primary key.

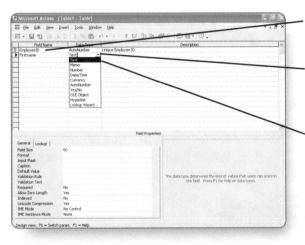

14. Type a field name in the Field Name column.

15. Click on the down arrow of the Data Type column. All the types of data that Access can store are displayed.

16. Click on the appropriate data type. The data type is selected.

> ## NOTE
> The following data types are available:
> - **Text**. A text field can hold up to 255 alphanumeric characters.
> - **Memo**. A memo field can store about 64,000 alphanumeric characters.
> - **Number**. A number field stores numeric data that can be included in calculations.
> - **Date/Time**. A date/time field stores date- and time-formatted data.
> - **Currency**. A currency field stores data with a currency sign and allows you to perform calculations.
> - **Yes/No**. A yes/no field stores logical values (true/false, yes/no, 1/0).

17. Type in a description for the field.

18. Repeat steps 15–17 for each field in the table.

19. Click on the Close icon. You are asked if you want to save the table.

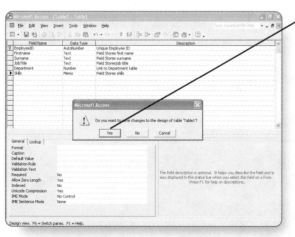

20. Click on Yes. The Save As dialog box opens.

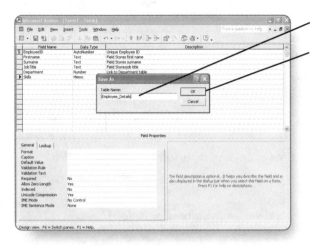

21. Type in the table name.

22. Click on OK. The table is saved.

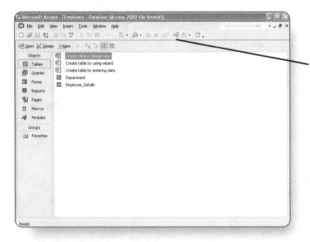

23. Repeat steps 6–22 for each table in your database.

24. Click on the Relationships button. The Show Table dialog box opens.

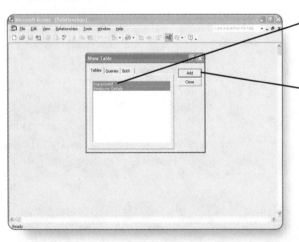

25. Ctrl+click on the tables you would like to relate to each other. The tables are selected.

26. Click on Add. The selected tables are added to the Relationships window.

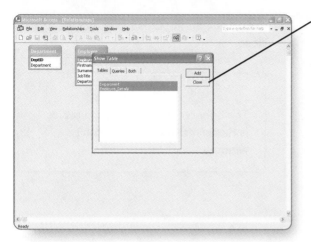

27. Click on Close. The Show Table dialog box closes.

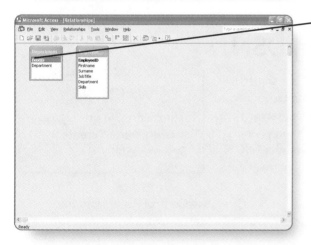

28. Click on the field that you would like to link to another table.

29. Drag the field that you want to relate from one table to the related field in the other table. The Edit Relationships dialog box will open.

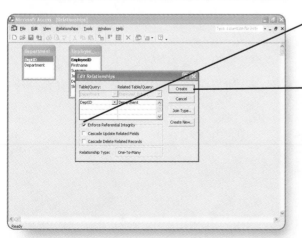

30. Click inside the Enforce Referential Integrity check box. A check is placed in the box.

31. Click on Create. A One-To-Many relationship is created. This means that each record links to many related records in the linked table. You can also use One-To-One and Many-To-Many relationships.

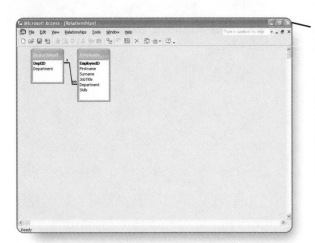

32. Click on the Close icon. Access will close.

> ### NOTE
> The connection between the tables is displayed in the Relationships window.

Creating a System DSN

A System DSN (Data Source Name) is a shortcut to your database. It contains the path to your database, the driver, username, and password required to access your database. When your database is Web-enabled in Dreamweaver MX, all you need to do is specify the DSN name.

> ### WARNING
> Administrative privileges are required to create a System DSN.

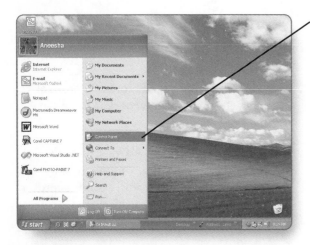

1. Open the Control Panel from the Windows Start menu.

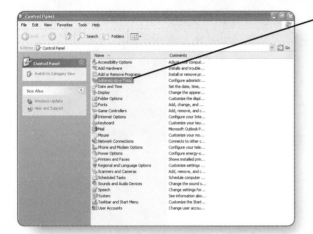

2. Double-click on the Administrative Tools icon. The contents are displayed.

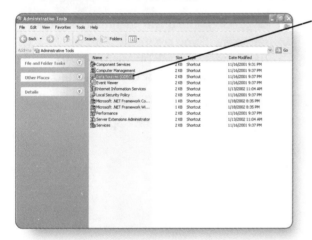

3. Double-click on Data Sources (ODBC). The ODBC Data Source Administrator dialog box opens.

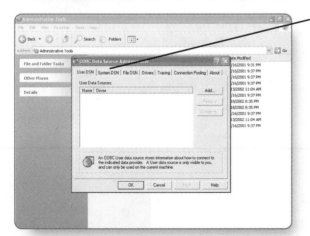

4. Click on the System DSN tab. The System DSN page comes to the front.

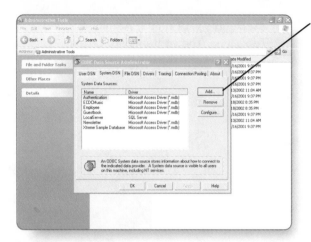

5. Click on Add. The Create New Data Source dialog box opens.

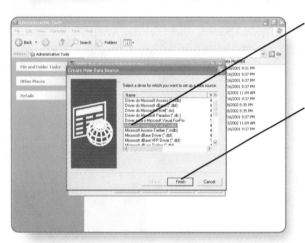

6. Click on the driver that matches your database. If you created an Access database, then click on Microsoft Access Driver (*.mdb). The option is selected.

7. Click on Finish. The ODBC Microsoft Access Setup dialog box opens.

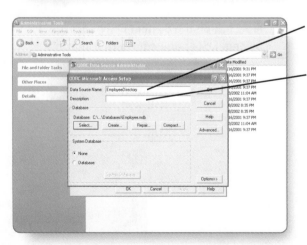

8. Type the DSN name into the Data Source Name field.

9. Type in a description for the DSN. This should be a description of what the database stores.

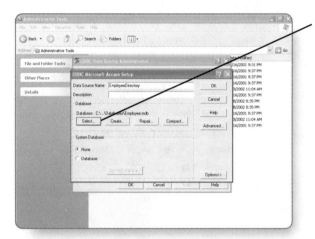

10. Click on Select. The Select Database dialog box is displayed.

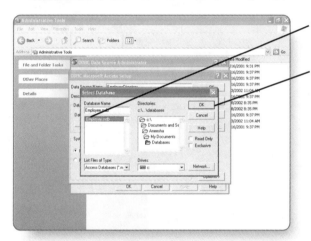

11. Click on the database file. The file name is highlighted.

12. Click on OK. The Select Database dialog box closes.

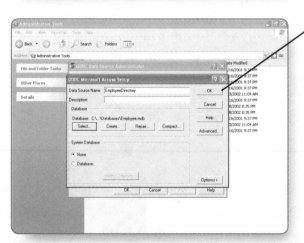

13. Click on OK. The ODBC Microsoft Access Setup dialog box closes.

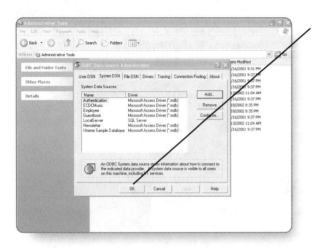

14. Click on OK. The ODBC Data Source Administrator dialog box closes.

> ## NOTE
>
> That's all that is required to create a System DSN. You need to create a System DSN for each database that will be Web-enabled.

10

Retrieving Data from a Database

You are now ready to create your first dynamic, database-driven Web site. This used to be a tedious process before Dreamweaver MX came to the rescue. You can now bind data to a Web page in a totally visual environment. In this chapter, you'll learn how to do the following:

- Define a database connection
- Create recordsets
- Bind data to a Web page
- Use the Live Data window
- Create simple database queries

Defining a Database Connection

When you create a database connection, you have to specify the DSN (Data Source Name) of the database and the type of connection required. Dreamweaver MX enables you to set up separate connections for your run-time and design-time environments. This means that you can easily publish your dynamic Web site without having to change the connection settings manually.

If you're using ASP as a server-side technology, you must create an ADO (ActiveX Data Objects) connection.

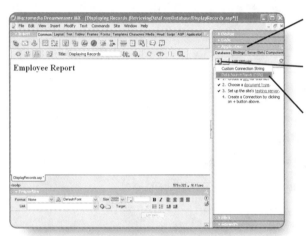

1. Expand the Application panel. The Databases tab is displayed.

2. Click on the + sign. A submenu appears.

3. Click on Data Source Name (DSN). The Data Source Name dialog box opens.

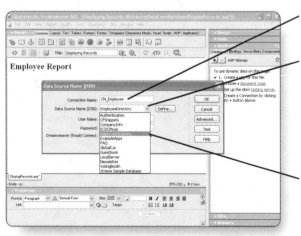

4. Type a name for the database connection into the Connection Name field.

5. Click on the down arrow of the Data Source Name drop-down list. A list of all available system DSNs on your local machine is displayed. Chapter 9, "Designing a Database," covers creating a DSN for a database.

6. Click on a DSN. The option is selected.

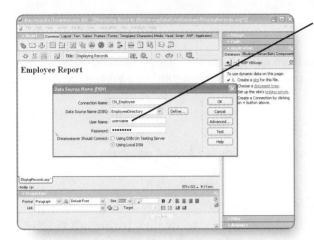

7. Enter the username and password if the database is password-protected.

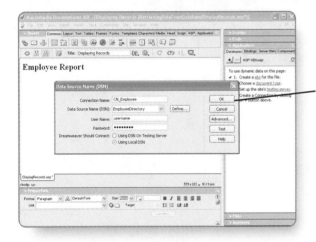

8. Click on OK. The database connection is created.

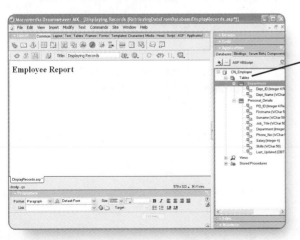

Data Binding

Data binding means retrieving data from a database and displaying it on a Web page. A recordset must be created before data can be bound to a Web page.

Creating Recordsets

A recordset contains records that have been retrieved from a database because they match specific criteria.

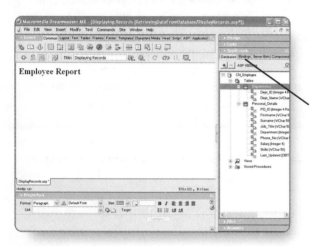

1. Create a new Web page with an .asp file extension. The Web page must have an .asp extension for data binding to be successful.

2. Click on the Bindings tab. The Bindings tab is displayed.

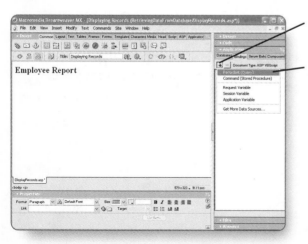

3. Click on the + sign. A submenu appears.

4. Click on Recordset (Query). The Recordset dialog box opens.

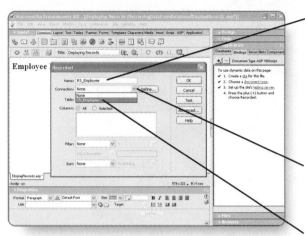

5. Type a name for the recordset.

> ### TIP
>
> It is handy to name all recordsets with an RS prefix. This enables you to identify recordsets easily.

6. Click on the down arrow of the Connection drop-down list. A list of available database connections appears.

7. Click on a connection. The connection is selected. All the tables in the database are loaded.

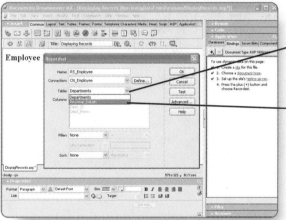

8. Click on the down arrow of the Table drop-down list. A list of tables in your database is displayed.

9. Click on the name of the table you want to include in the query. The table is selected.

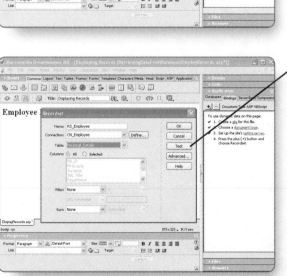

10. Click on Test. The Test SQL Statement dialog box opens.

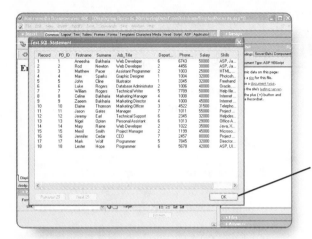

11. Click on OK. The Test SQL Statement dialog box closes.

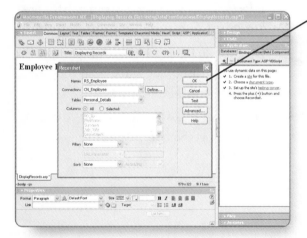

12. Click on OK. The Recordset dialog box closes. A Recordset node is added to the Bindings palette.

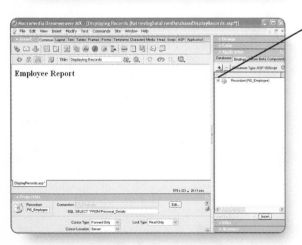

13. Click on the + sign to open the Recordset node. A list of all retrieved fields is displayed.

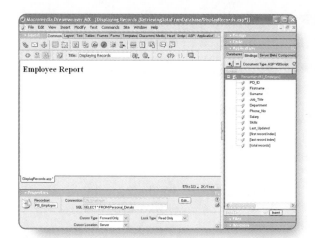

NOTE

In the next section you will learn to bind these fields to a Web page.

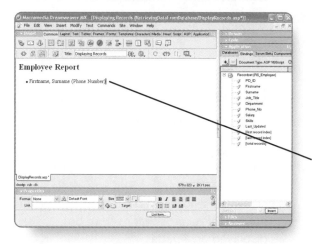

Binding Data to a Web Page

A recordset field can be bound to a Web page to produce dynamic text. You can drag fields from the Bindings tab and drop them anywhere on your page.

1. Insert placeholder text for the database fields.

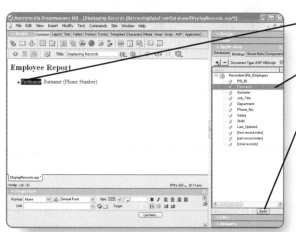

2. Select the placeholder field. The selected text is highlighted.

3. Click on the field you want to display. The field is highlighted.

4. Click on Insert. The placeholder text is replaced by dynamic text.

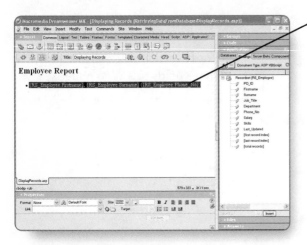

5. Repeat steps 2–4 for each field you want to bind to the Web page.

6. Press F12 to preview the Web page in a browser. The browser opens and loads the Web page.

NOTE

Only the first record in the recordset is displayed. Use the Repeat Region server behavior to display multiple records.

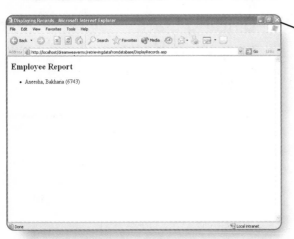

7. Click on Close. The Web browser closes.

Using the Repeat Region Server Behavior

When data is bound to a Web page, only the first record that was returned by the recordset is displayed. The Repeat Region server behavior must be used to specify the number of records that need to be displayed on a page.

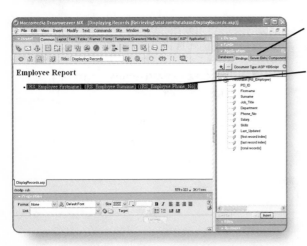

1. Click on the Server Behaviors tab. The Server Behaviors tab is displayed.

2. Select the region you want to repeat. The selection is highlighted.

DATA BINDING 145

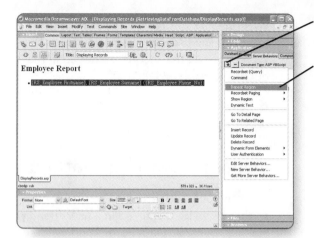

3. Click on the + sign. A submenu appears.

4. Click on Repeat Region. The Repeat Region dialog box opens.

NOTE

The recordset that is bound to the region is automatically selected in the Recordset drop-down list.

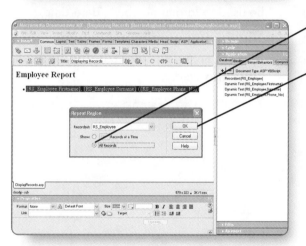

5. Click on the All Records option button. The option is selected.

6. Click on OK. The Repeat Region behavior is inserted.

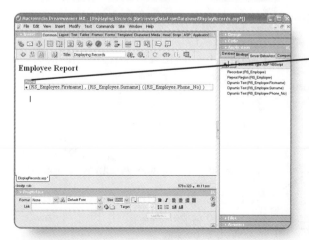

NOTE

The Repeat Region code is enclosed in a tabbed gray outline.

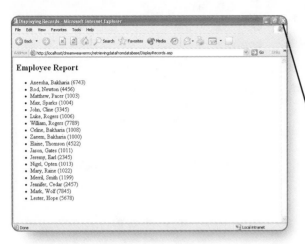

7. Press F12 to preview the Web page in a browser. The browser opens and loads the Web page. All the records retrieved in the query are displayed.

8. Click on the Close icon. The Web browser closes.

Dynamic Data Formatting

You can apply formatting to retrieved data so that it can be displayed in a user-friendly manner. Dynamic Data Formatting can also be used to format numbers, date/time, text, and percentages.

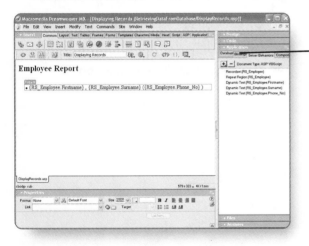

1. Click on the Bindings tab. The Bindings tab is displayed.

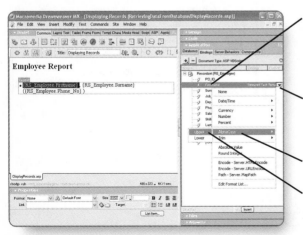

2. Click on a dynamic text element. A dynamic text element is a database field that has been bound to a Web page. The field name is selected in the Bindings tab.

3. Click on the down arrow in the Format column. A list of all available formatting options is displayed.

4. Click on AlphaCase. A submenu appears.

5. Click on Upper. This option converts the text to uppercase when it is previewed in a Web browser.

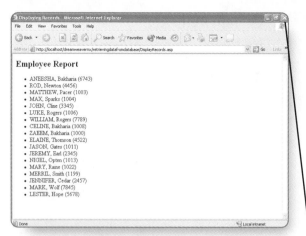

6. Press F12 to preview the Web page in a browser. The Web browser opens and loads the Web page.

7. Click on the Close icon. The Web browser closes.

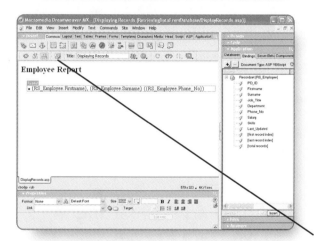

Live Data Preview

There is no need to preview your Web page in a browser each time you need to test your dynamic Web page. You can preview and format data within the Dreamweaver MX interface.

Enabling the Live Data Window

1. Click on Live Data View. Live Data View is enabled.

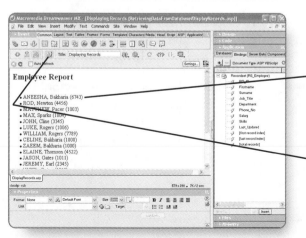

2. Click on Live Data View. Design View is enabled.

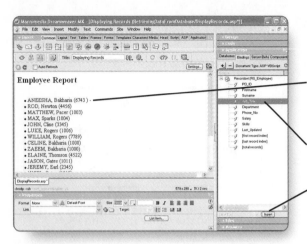

Binding Data in Live Data Window

1. Click on the field you would like to insert in the Bindings tab. The selection is highlighted.

2. Click where you would like the field to be inserted. The cursor appears.

3. Click on Insert. The field is inserted.

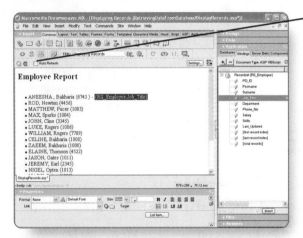

4. Click inside the Auto Refresh check box. The contents of the fields will automatically be refreshed.

Applying Formatting in Live Data Preview

1. Select the text you would like to format. The text is highlighted.

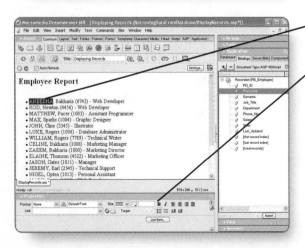

2. Apply formatting by setting the properties found in the Properties Inspector. There is no difference between applying formatting in the Document or Live Data windows. Chapter 2, "Dreamweaver MX Basics," covers formatting in detail.

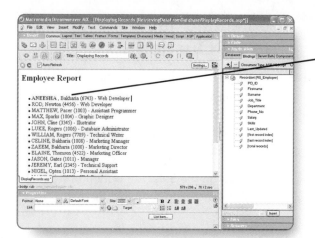

NOTE

The formatting of the selected text will change.

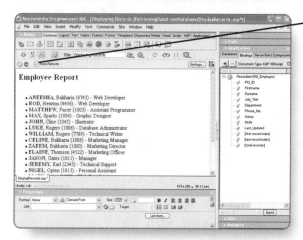

3. Click on Auto Refresh. All fields are updated.

Creating Simple Queries

Queries retrieve the records you require from a database. The Recordset dialog box enables you to create simple queries intuitively, without writing a single line of code.

Editing a Recordset

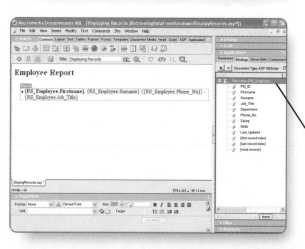

The Recordset dialog box is opened by creating a new Recordset (Query) in the Bindings tab. You can edit a recordset at any time.

1. Double-click on the Recordset node in the Bindings tab. The Recordset dialog box opens.

2. Follow the steps in the next sections depending on the type of selection you want to make.

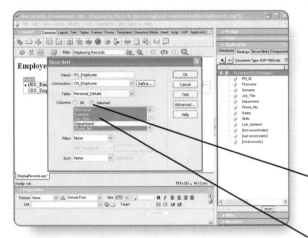

Selecting Table Fields to Be Queried

It is wise to include only tables containing data that will be inserted in a Web page when creating a query. This will improve the speed at which your pages are generated.

1. Click on the Selected option button. The list containing the table fields is enabled.

2. Click on a field to select it. (Use Ctrl+click to select multiple fields.) The selection is highlighted.

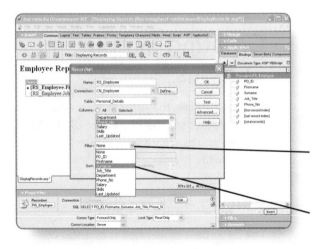

Filtering Data

A filter enables you to search for specific field values and can be placed on any field in your database. You can enter the value that the filter must match manually or retrieve it from a form.

1. Click on the down arrow of the Filter drop-down list. A list of all fields in the table is displayed.

2. Click on the field you want to filter. The field is highlighted.

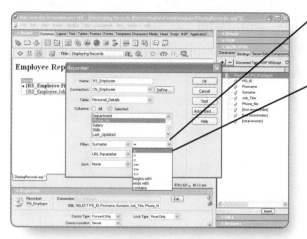

3. Click on the down arrow of the comparison operators. All the comparison operators are displayed.

4. Click on a comparison operator sign. The option is selected.

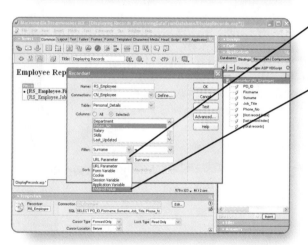

5. Click on the down arrow of the URL Parameter drop-down list. All the filter options are displayed.

6. Click on Entered Value. The option is selected. The Entered Value filter option enables you to enter the filter criteria manually. In Chapter 12, "Using SQL to Query a Database," you will learn to create dynamic queries.

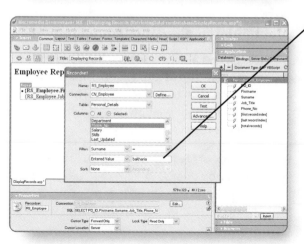

7. Type the value that the field must match. Records that match the filter are returned in the recordset.

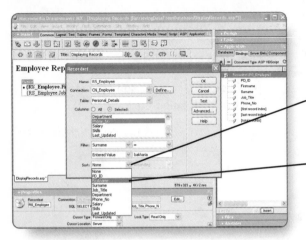

Sorting Data

The records returned in a recordset can be sorted in ascending or descending order.

1. Click on the down arrow of the Sort drop-down list. A list of all table fields is displayed.

2. Click on the field in which you would like to sort records. The field is highlighted.

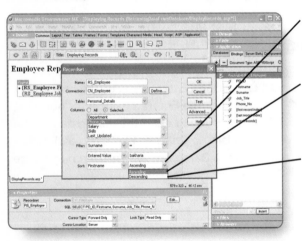

3. Click on the down arrow of the Sort drop-down list. Records can be sorted in ascending or descending order.

4a. Click on Ascending. The option is selected.

OR

4b. Click on Descending. The option is selected.

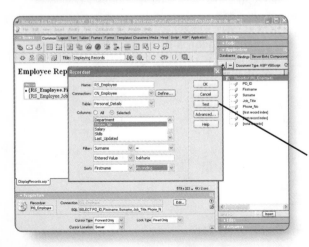

Testing a Query

It is always a good idea to check whether a query can be executed successfully before you bind data to a Web page. The Test SQL Statement window enables you to view the results of a query.

1. Click on Test. The Test SQL Statement dialog box opens.

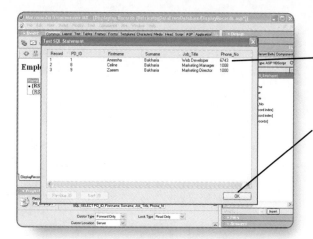

2. Click on OK. The Test SQL Statement dialog box closes.

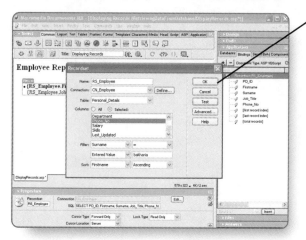

3. Click on OK. The Recordset dialog box closes.

11

Using Application Objects

Application objects encompass features present in most database-driven Web applications. These include displaying search results, linking to more specific information, inserting new records, and updating existing records in a database. Server behaviors can certainly be used to incorporate this functionality, but Application objects can automate the whole process. You can now spend more time developing complex solutions. In this chapter, you'll learn how to do the following:

- ◉ Insert Recordset statistics
- ◉ Insert a Recordset Navigation panel
- ◉ Create a Master-Detail Page set
- ◉ Insert new records into a database
- ◉ Update existing records in a database

Application Objects—An Overview

Application objects are wizards that automatically insert server behaviors to perform common database functionality. You still have control over page layout and the ability to modify the server behaviors. You can insert Recordset navigation bars, Recordset statistics and Master-Detail Page sets. Forms that insert and update data in a database can also be created.

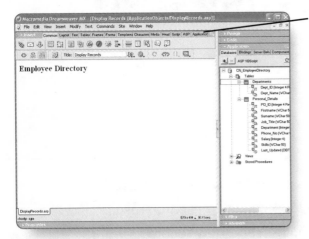

1. Click on the Application tab. The Application tab is displayed.

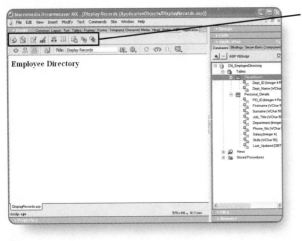

2. The Following Live Data objects are available:

- Recordset
- Repeated Region
- Dynamic Table
- Dynamic Text
- Insert Recordset Navigation bar
- Insert Recordset Navigation Status
- Insert Master-Detail Page set
- Insert Record Insertion form
- Insert Record Update form

Inserting a Record Counter

The Insert Recordset Navigation Status object is used to display the number of records returned in a search and the location of the records currently being viewed.

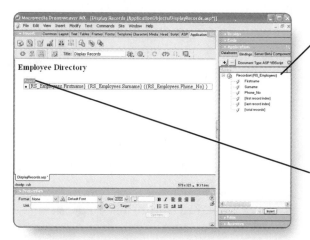

1. Create a search results page.

● Use the Recordset (Query) data source from the Bindings tab to create a recordset. The retrieved recordset must be bound to the search results page. The steps involved in creating a recordset are covered in Chapter 10, "Retrieving Data from a Database."

● Use the Repeat Region server behavior to display multiple records.

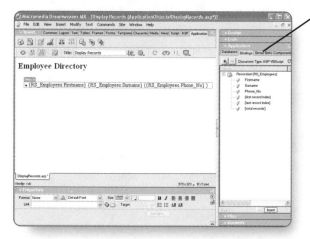

2. Click on the Server Behaviors tab. The Server Behaviors tab is displayed.

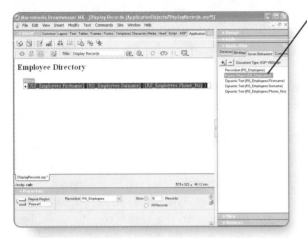

3. Double-click on Repeat Region in the list of utilized server behaviors. The Repeat Region dialog box opens.

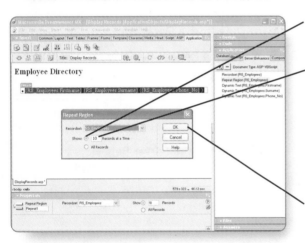

4. Click on Show a specified number of Records at a Time. The option is selected.

5. Type the number of records to display on a page. You have to make a decision about the amount of records that should be displayed at any one time. The value you select depends upon the layout of your search result Web page. You should generally try to prevent too much scrolling.

6. Click on OK. The Repeat Region dialog box closes.

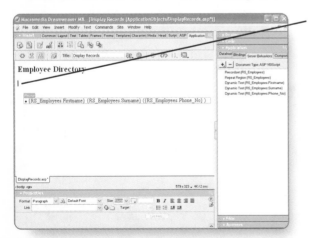

7. Click inside the Document window where you would like to insert the Recordset Navigation Status Bar.

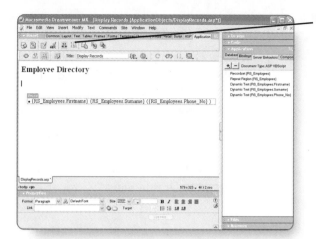

8. Click on the Insert Recordset Navigation Status object. The Recordset Navigation Status dialog box opens.

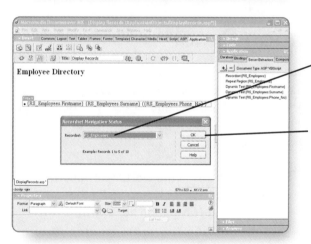

9. Click on OK. The Recordset Navigation Status dialog box closes.

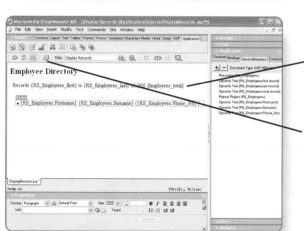

10. Click on the Live Data View icon. Live Data View is enabled.

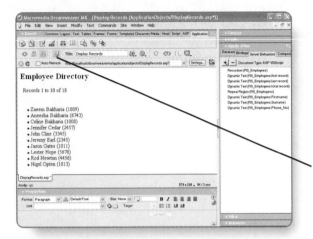

11. Click on the Live Data View icon. You are returned to Design View.

Inserting a Navigation Panel

Databases can contain millions of records. When you display the results of a database search, you should always split the results across multiple pages to enable users to easily navigate between pages. This technique is employed by most popular Internet search engines. The Insert Navigation Panel object creates a set of text or image links to the first, last, next, and previous pages.

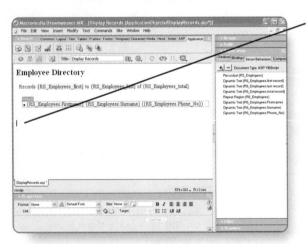

1. Click inside the Document window where you would like to insert the Recordset Navigation bar.

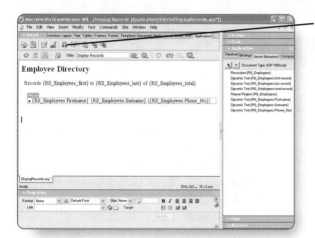

2. Click on the Insert Recordset Navigation Bar object. The Recordset Navigation Bar dialog box opens.

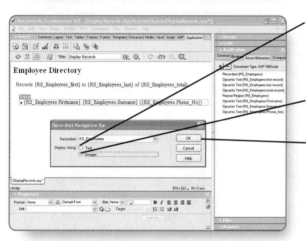

3a. Click on the Text option button. The option is selected.

OR

3b. Click on the Images option button. The option is selected.

4. Click on OK. The Recordset Navigation Bar dialog box closes.

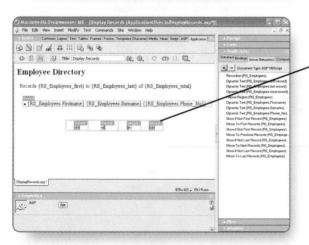

NOTE

The Recordset Navigation Bar is inserted.

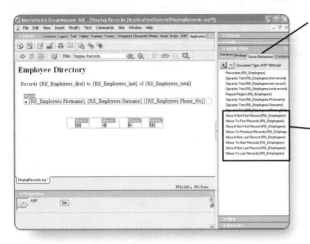

5. Click on the Server Behaviors tab, if it is not already selected. The Server Behaviors tab is displayed.

NOTE

You can see that the Show and Move To server behaviors have been used to create the navigation panel. In Chapter 13, "Searching a Database," you learn to use these server behaviors and create a custom navigation panel.

Testing the Recordset Navigation Bar

1. Press F12 to preview the current Web page in a browser. The browser opens and displays the Web page.

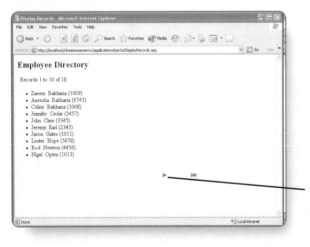

NOTE

The first page of records does not contain a link to the First page and Previous page. The last page also does not contain a link to the Last page and the Next page.

2. Click on the Next button. The Next page containing results is displayed.

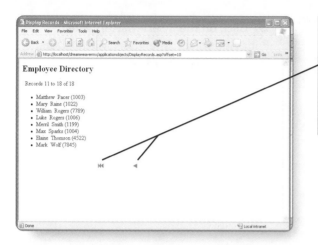

Creating a Master-Detail Page Set

A Master page only displays summary data for each record returned in a search. A Master page also contains a link, which the user must click on to view the record in detail. This enables users to view multiple records on a single page and then decide which record they would like to display in full.

The Master page displays the results in a table. You decide on the amount of records that can be displayed on a single page. The object automatically inserts a navigation panel and recordset status information if the search results span multiple pages. The resulting Master and Detail pages are both fully editable.

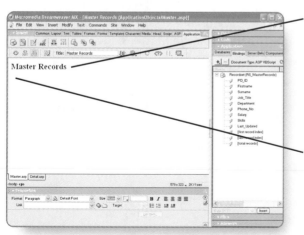

1. Create a new Web page to display master records. Use the Recordset (Query) data source from the Bindings tab to create a recordset. The steps involved in creating a recordset are covered in Chapter 10, "Retrieving Data from a Database."

2. Click inside the Document window where you would like to insert the Master Records table.

3. Click on the Insert Master-Detail Page Set object. The Insert Master-Detail Page Set dialog box opens.

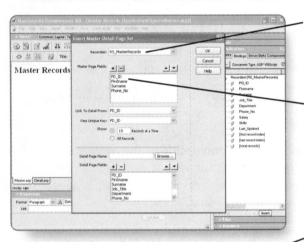

4. Select the recordset that will be used to create the Master-Detail Page set. The fields retrieved are included in the Master and Detail pages.

5. Include only essential fields on the Master page. Select the table column/field name.

You can

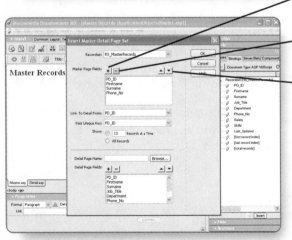

- Click on the + sign to include additional fields on the Master page.

- Click on the – sign to remove the field from the Master page.

- Use the up and down arrows to change the order in which the fields are displayed.

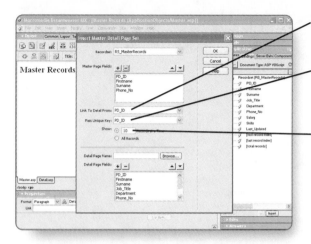

6. Select the field that must link to the Detail page.

7. The unique record ID/primary key is automatically selected. It will be passed to the Detail page via the QueryString.

8. Type in the number of records that can be displayed on the Master page at one time.

NOTE

If you limit the number of records displayed per page of search results, a Recordset Navigation Bar will be inserted.

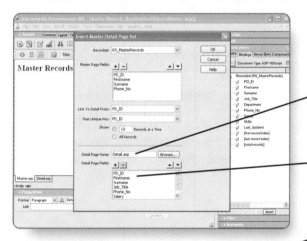

9. Type in the name of the Detail page. The Detail page must have an .asp extension.

10. Select the fields that must be included in the Detail page.

You can

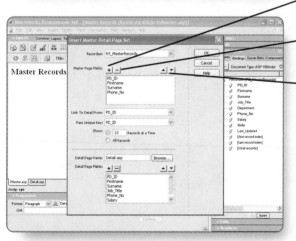

- Click on the + sign to include additional fields on the Detail page.

- Click on the – sign to remove the field from the Detail page.

- Use the up and down arrows to change the order in which the fields are displayed.

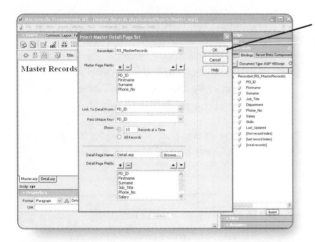

11. Click on OK. Both the Master and the Detail pages are created.

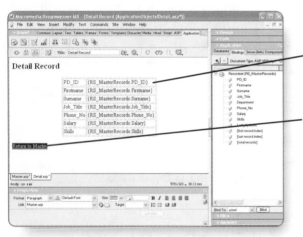

NOTE

The Detail record is displayed in a table.

12. Create a link back to the Master page so that the user can view Detail pages for other records as well.

Testing the Master-Detail Page Set

You can only test a Master-Detail Page set from a browser because Live Data View does not support links.

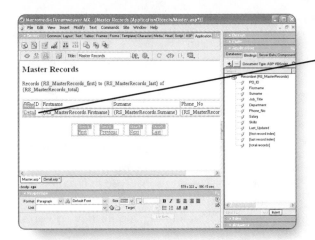

NOTE

The Master page displays summary records in a table and links to a Detail page for each record. A Recordset Navigation and Status bar will both be included if all records are not displayed on a single page.

1. Press F12 to preview the Master page in a Web browser. The Master page is displayed in a Web browser.

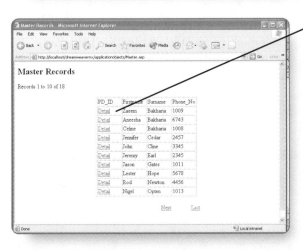

2. Click on the Link for a record that you wish to view in detail. The Detail page that contains the full record is displayed.

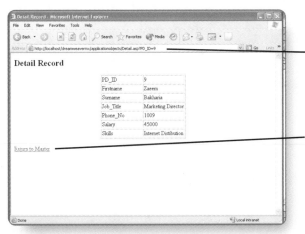

NOTE

You can see the records unique ID number passed to the Detail page in the QueryString.

3. Click on the link to return to the Master page, from which you can choose to view more records in detail.

Inserting a New Record in a Database

The Insert Record object creates a form in the current Web page that enables users to insert new records in a database. You need to select the appropriate form objects and the database columns where the data will be inserted. Common form objects like text fields, drop-down lists, radio buttons, and check boxes can all be used.

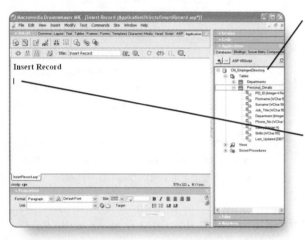

1. Create a database connection. Records are inserted into a table within this database. The steps involved in creating a database connection are covered in Chapter 8, "Validating and Retrieving Form Data."

2. Click inside the Document window where you would like to insert the form generated by the Insert Record object.

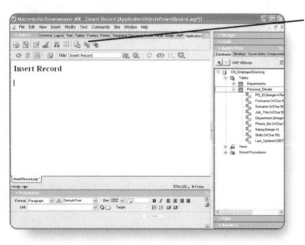

3. Click on the Insert Record Insertion object. The Record Insertion Form dialog box opens.

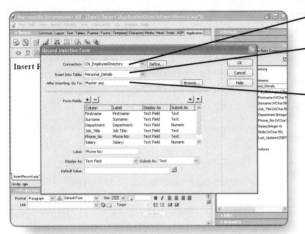

4. Select the database connection.

5. Select the table where the new record will be inserted.

6. Type in the name of the Web page that must be displayed after the record is successfully inserted.

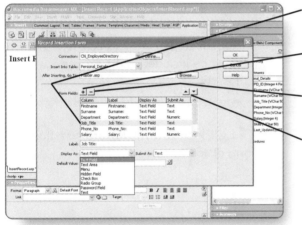

7. Click on a database table column name. You can

- Click on the + sign to add a field to the Insertion form.

- Click on the – sign to remove the field from the Insertion form.

- Use the up and down arrows to change the order in which the fields are displayed in the Insertion form.

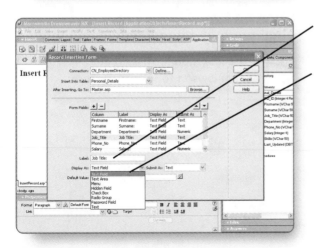

8. Type in a label for the field. The table column name is used by default.

9. Select the form object that the user will use to enter the data. You could select a text field, text area, menu, check box, or a radio button group.

TIP

You could even specify a default value for each field, which will be displayed when the page loads. This could aid data entry.

10. Select the format of the data that will be inserted into the table column.

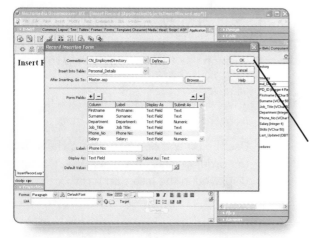

NOTE

Repeat steps 7–10 for each field that must be included in the Record Insertion form.

11. Click on OK. The Record Insertion Form dialog box closes.

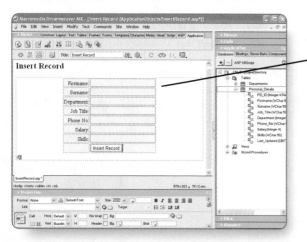

NOTE

The Insertion form is created. A table is used to format the form.

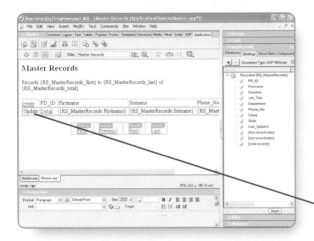

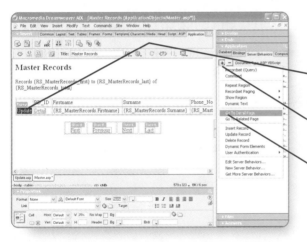

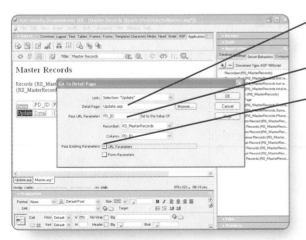

Updating an Existing Record

The Update Record object creates a form that enables users to edit the existing data and then update the record stored in the database. You will need to select the appropriate form object for each field that needs to be updated in the database table.

1. Open the Master page that you created earlier in this chapter. You can insert an Update link for each record. This enables a user to select the record they would like to update. A new column needs to be added to the table.

2. Select the Update link. The text is highlighted.

3. Click on the + sign. A submenu appears.

4. Click on Go To Detail Page. The Go To Detail Page dialog box opens.

5. Type in the name of the Web page that will contain the Update form.

6. Type in the primary key/unique ID field.

7. Click inside the URL Parameters check box. A check is placed inside the box. The unique identifier of the current record will be passed to the Update form as a URL Parameter. This means that it will be appended to the URL as a QueryString.

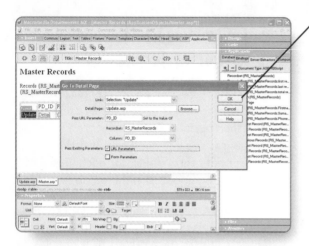

8. Click on OK. The Go To Detail dialog box closes and the Update link is created.

Inserting an Update Form

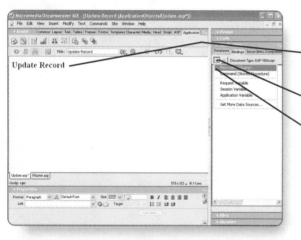

1. Create the Web page that will contain the Update form.

2. Click on the + sign. A submenu appears.

3. Click on Recordset (Query). The Recordset dialog box opens.

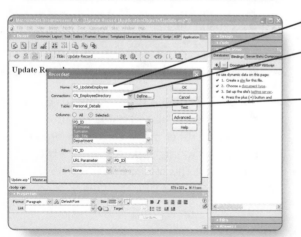

4. Type a name for the recordset.

5. Select a database connection. The option is selected.

6. Select the table that contains the record you need to retrieve. The option is selected.

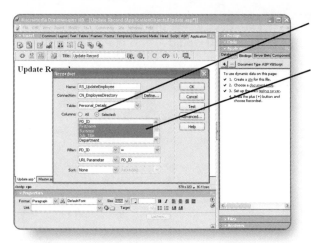

7. Click on the Selected option button. The option is selected.

8. Select the fields that must be included in the Update form. To select more than one field, hold down the Ctrl key, and then click on the fields you want to include. Only select the fields that the user will be allowed to update. These fields will be bound to the form objects on the update form.

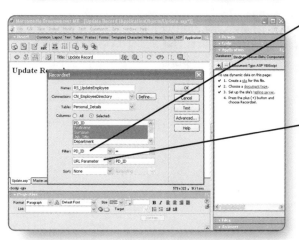

9. Select the field that corresponds to the value that is being passed to the Update form via the QueryString. In this case it must be the unique ID field also known as the primary key. The field is highlighted.

10. Select URL Parameter because the ID number must be retrieved from the QueryString. The option is selected.

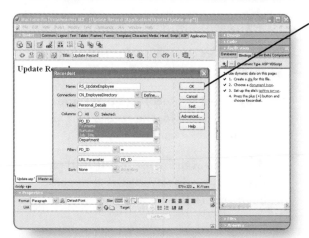

11. Click on OK. The Recordset dialog box closes.

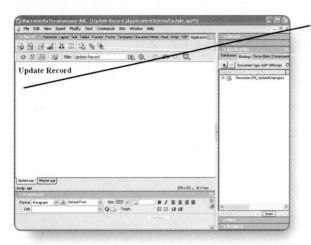

12. Click inside the Document window where you would like to place the Update form.

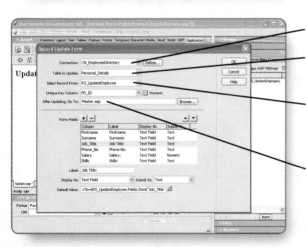

13. Click on the Insert Record Update Form object. The Record Update Form dialog box opens.

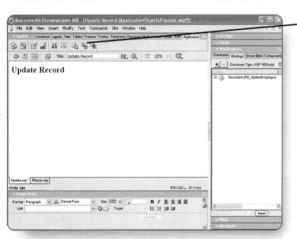

14. Select the database connection.

15. Select the table that contains the records that will be updated.

16. Select the recordset that retrieves the unique ID value for the record that must be updated.

17. Type in the name of the Web page that must be displayed after the record has been updated.

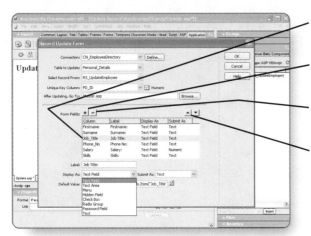

18. Click on a database table column name. You can

- Click on the + sign to add a field to the Update form.

- Click on the – sign to remove the field from the Update form.

- Use the up and down arrows to change the order in which the fields are displayed in the Update form.

NOTE

The table column name, by default, is used as the field label. You can change the label.

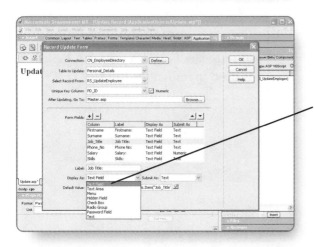

19. Select the form object that the user will use to enter the data. You could select a text field, text area, menu, check box, or a radio button group.

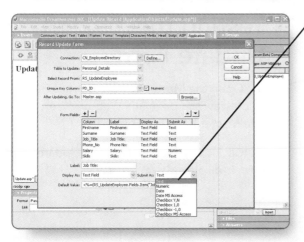

20. Select the format of the data that will be inserted into the table column.

NOTE

Repeat steps 18–20 for each field that must be included in the Insertion form.

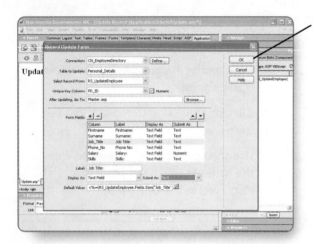

21. Click on OK. The Record Update Form dialog box closes.

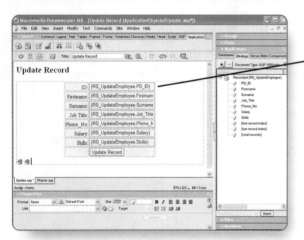

NOTE
The Update Form is created. A table is used to format the form.

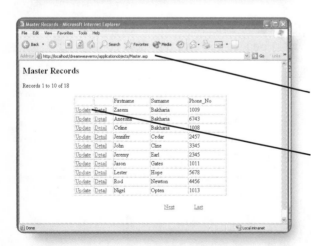

Testing the Update Form

1. Open the Master page and press F12 to preview the page in a Web browser. The Master page is displayed.

2. Click on an Update link. The Update form is displayed.

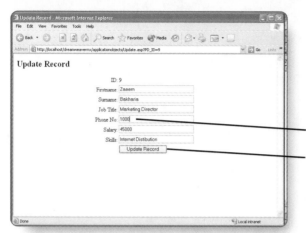

3. Edit the data as needed.

4. Click on Update Record. After the record is updated, you are returned to the Master page.

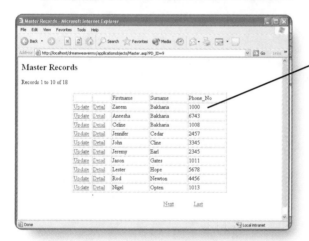

12

Using SQL to Query a Database

In the previous chapter, you learned to create simple queries that returned all the available records in a table. However, to create truly powerful database-enabled Web applications, you need to learn to select and retrieve only specific data from a database. In simple terms, you need to build customized queries in SQL (Structured Query Language). Dreamweaver MX will help you generate the SQL commands for manipulating data, but you will still have to customize the statements it generates. In this chapter, you'll learn how to do the following:

- ○ Create SQL queries
- ○ Define search criteria
- ○ Use Boolean operators
- ○ Retrieve distinct records
- ○ Use wildcards to search strings
- ○ Retrieve summary data from a table
- ○ Work with related tables

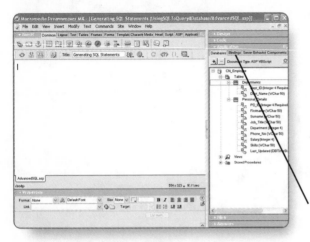

Generating SQL Statements

SQL is used to build database queries. It is a simple yet powerful language that allows databases to be queried based upon specific criteria. The Advanced Recordset dialog box allows you to generate and test SQL queries intuitively.

1. Click on the Bindings tab. The tab is displayed.

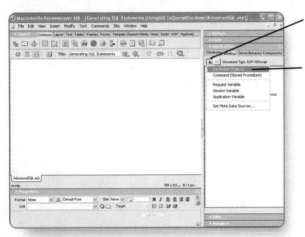

2. Click on the + sign. A submenu appears.

3. Click on Recordset (Query). The Recordset dialog box opens.

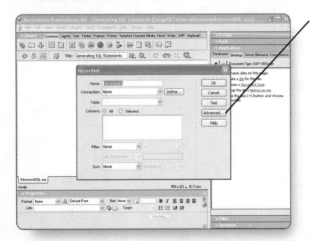

4. Click on Advanced. The dialog box expands.

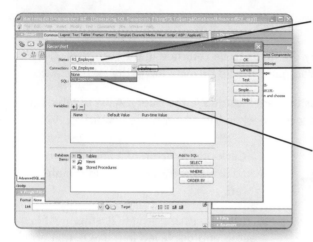

5. Type the name of the recordset in the Name field.

6. Click on the down arrow of the Connection drop-down list. The DSNs available on your local computer are displayed.

7. Click on a DSN title. The connection is selected.

NOTE

If you would like to follow the example in this chapter, create a System DSN for the Employee Directory Microsoft Access database (employee_directory.mdb). The employee_directory.mdb file is included in the source code for Chapter 12 that can be downloaded from http://www.premierpress books/downloads.asp.

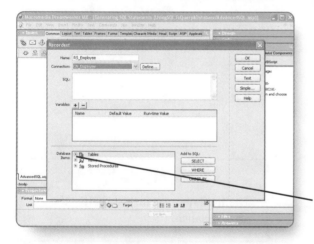

8. Click on the + sign to expand the Tables tree. A list of tables are displayed.

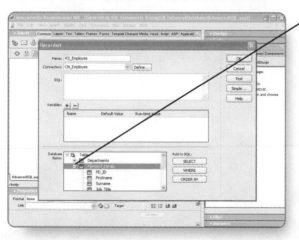

9. Click on the + sign next to the name of a table. All of the fields in the table are displayed.

Selecting Fields and Tables

The SELECT clause is used to specify the fields to be returned in the recordset. Only the fields that are required on a Web page should be included in the SELECT clause.

The FROM clause specifies the tables that are included in the query. A list of tables is automatically inserted after the FROM clause when the SELECT button is clicked.

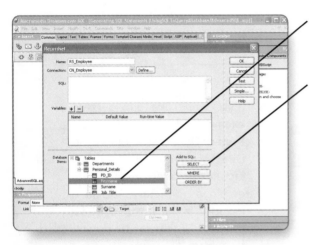

1. Click on the name of a field that you would like to retrieve. The field is highlighted.

2. Click on SELECT. The SQL statement is created and displayed in the SQL text area.

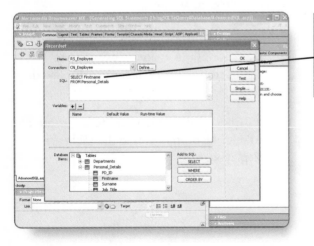

NOTE

The field name is inserted after the SELECT clause.

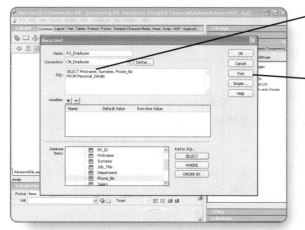

3. Repeat steps 1 and 2 to include more fields in the query. A comma separates fields returned in the recordset.

4. Click on Test. The Test SQL Statement dialog box opens.

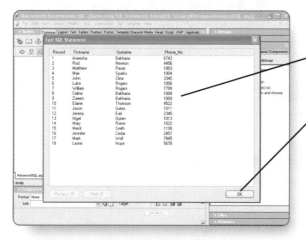

TIP

Only the fields included in the SELECT clause are returned in the query.

5. Click on OK. The Test SQL Statement dialog box closes.

Defining Search Criteria

The number of records returned can be limited by filtering the data. The WHERE clause is used to set search criteria.

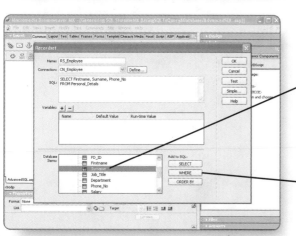

1. Click on the field you want to use as a filter. You will need to expand the branches of the Tables tree until you find the required table and field. The field is highlighted.

2. Click on WHERE. The WHERE clause is inserted into the SQL text area.

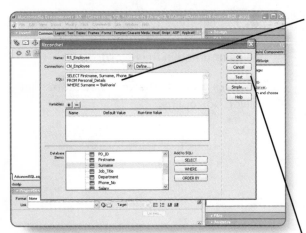

3. Type the search criteria into the SQL text area.

NOTE

Search criteria are made up of a comparison operator and the value with which the field should be compared. The value must be surrounded by apostrophes. Table 12.1 contains a list of comparison operators.

---

4. Click on Test. The Test SQL Statement dialog box opens.

Table 12.1 Comparison Operators

Operator	Description
=	Equal to (case sensitive)
LIKE	Equal to (not case sensitive)
<>	Not equal to (case sensitive)
NOT LIKE	Not equal to (not case sensitive)
<	Less than
>	Greater than
<=	Less than or equal to
>=	Greater than or equal to

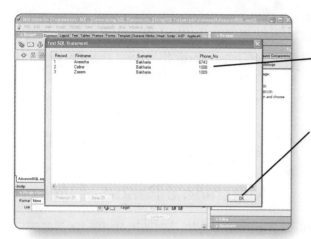

5. Click on OK. The Test SQL Statement dialog box closes.

Using Boolean Operators

Boolean operators provide a way to specify multiple criteria in a query. The AND operator is used when each criteria must be met before a record will be returned. The OR operator will return records if any of the specified criteria are matched.

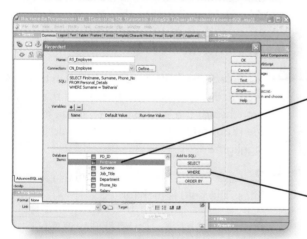

1. Click on another field that you want to use as a filter. You will need to expand the branches of the Tables tree until you find the required table and field. The field is highlighted.

2. Click on WHERE. The field is added to the WHERE clause. The AND Boolean operator is automatically inserted between the fields. Records will only be returned if the criteria for all fields are met. If you want records to be returned if any of the set criteria are met, replace AND with OR.

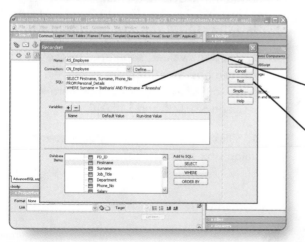

3. Type the value for the field's search criteria.

4. Click on Test. The Test SQL Statement dialog box opens.

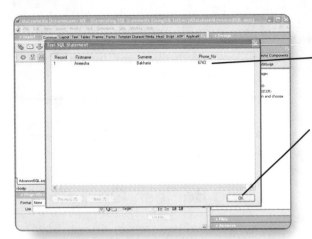

NOTE

Only records that meet the specified criteria are returned.

5. Click on OK. The Test SQL Statement dialog box closes.

Matching a Range of Values

Sometimes it's handy to search for records that contain values within a specified range. You could use comparison operators (<, >, <>, <=, and >=), but using the BETWEEN keyword is much easier.

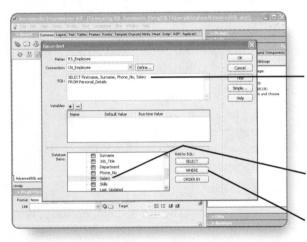

1. Select the fields to be included in the recordset. You will need to expand the branches of the Tables tree until you find the required table and field. The field is highlighted.

2. Click on the field you want to use as a filter. The field is highlighted.

3. Click on WHERE. The WHERE clause is added in the SQL text area.

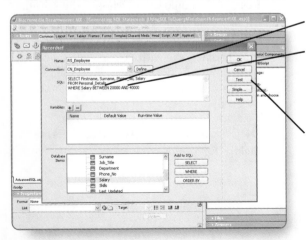

4. Type BETWEEN after the field name.

5. Type the values, separated by the AND Boolean operator. In this example, we are trying to find all employees that earn between $20,000 and $40,000.

6. Click on Test. The Test SQL Statement dialog box opens.

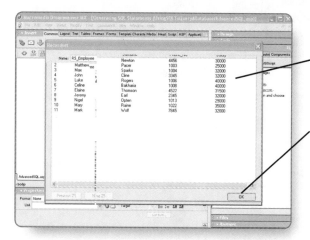

7. Click on OK. The Test SQL Statement dialog box closes.

Ordering Results

SQL allows for returned records to be sorted in either ascending or descending order. You'll use the ORDER BY clause to specify which fields to sort.

1. Click on the field on which you want to order the returned records. The field is highlighted.

2. Click on ORDER BY. The ORDER BY clause is inserted in the SQL text area.

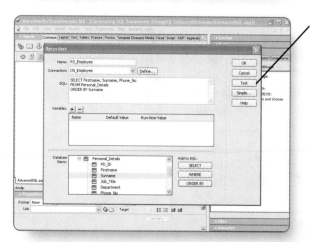

3. Click on Test. The Test SQL Statement dialog box opens.

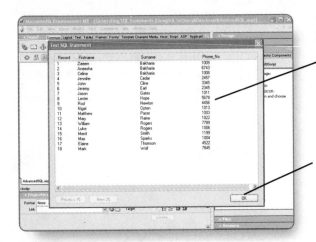

NOTE

The records will be returned in ascending order based upon the field that was specified in the ORDER BY clause.

4. Click on OK. The Test SQL Statement dialog box closes.

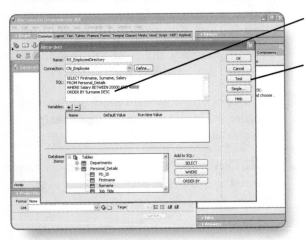

5. Type DESC after the field name. This will return records in descending order.

6. Click on Test. The Test SQL Statement dialog box opens.

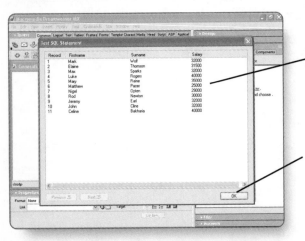

NOTE

The records will be returned in descending order based upon the field that was specified in the ORDER BY clause.

7. Click on OK. The Test SQL Statement dialog box closes.

Retrieving Distinct Records

Sometimes a table column contains duplicate values. The DISTINCT keyword is used to retrieve all unique values in a column.

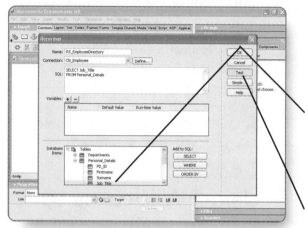

1. Select the field from which you want to retrieve distinct values. You will need to expand the branches of the Tables tree until you find the required table and field. The field is highlighted.

2. Click on Test. The Test SQL Statement dialog box opens.

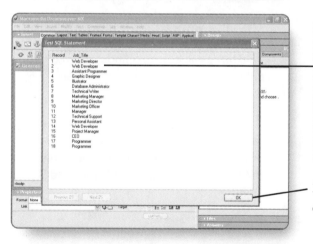

NOTE

Duplicate records are returned. In this example, I want to list all of the available Job Titles. Duplicate records are returned because multiple people can have the same job title.

3. Click on OK. The Test SQL Statement dialog box closes.

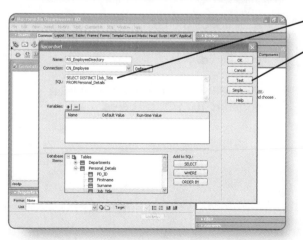

4. Type DISTINCT after the SELECT clause.

5. Click on Test. The Test SQL Statement dialog box will open.

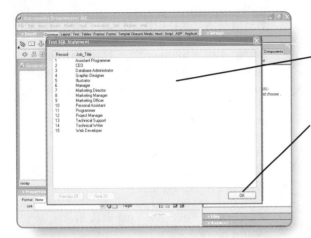

6. Click on OK. The Test SQL Statement dialog box will close.

Using Wildcards to Search Strings

Wildcards can be used as placeholders for other characters when querying fields. Wildcards will help you find data when you only know part of a value or are searching for a specific pattern.

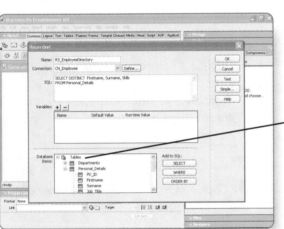

1. Select the fields to be returned in the recordset. You will need to expand the branches of the Tables tree until you find the required table and field. The field is highlighted.

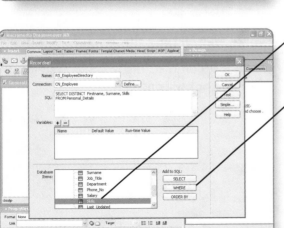

2. Click on the field you want to use as a filter. The field cannot be numeric. The field is selected.

3. Click on WHERE. The WHERE clause is added to the SQL text area.

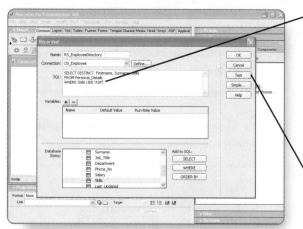

4. Type search criteria into the SQL text area. In this example, we are searching for employees that have ASP skills. The skill field contains a list of skills, separated by commas. ASP could be anywhere within the string. The LIKE (equal to) operator will return all employees who can create ASP applications.

5. Click on Test. The Test SQL Statement dialog box opens.

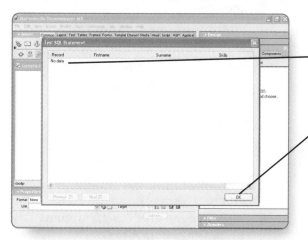

NOTE

Only records that match the search criteria exactly will be returned. In this case, no records are returned.

6. Click on OK. The Test SQL Statement dialog box closes.

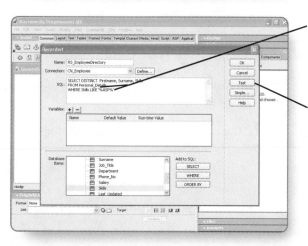

7. Type % before and after the value to be searched. The % wildcard allows any number of characters to occur before and after the search value.

8. Click on Test. The Test SQL Statement dialog box opens.

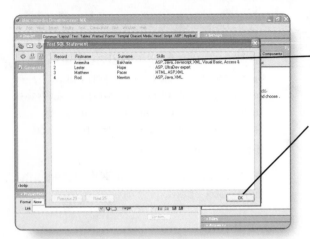

9. Click on OK. The Test SQL Statement dialog box closes.

Retrieving Summary Data from a Table

The SQL Aggregate function can be used to return summary data such as the number of records in a table, the average value of a column, the sum of column values, or the maximum/minimum values in a column.

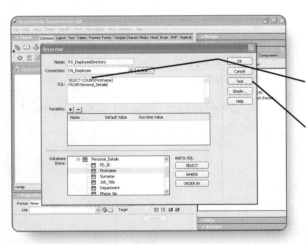

Counting Records

1. Type COUNT(*field name*) into the SQL text area.

2. Click on Test. The Test SQL Statement dialog box opens.

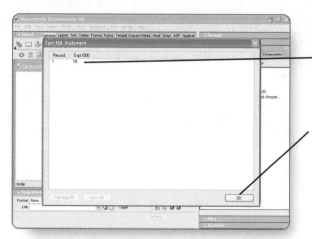

NOTE

The total number of records in the table is returned.

3. Click on OK. The Test SQL Statement dialog box closes.

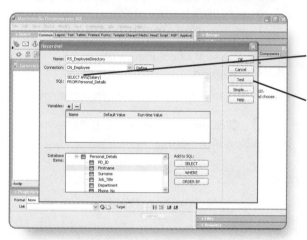

Average Column Value

1. Type AVG(*field name*) into the SQL text area.

2. Click on Test. The Test SQL Statement dialog box opens.

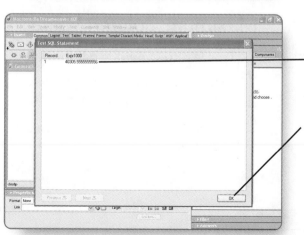

NOTE

The average column value is returned.

3. Click on OK. The Test SQL Statement dialog box closes.

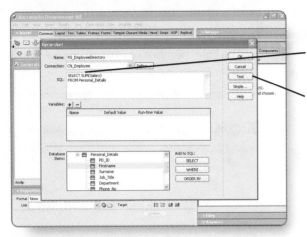

Sum of Column Values

1. Type SUM(*field name*) into the SQL text area.

2. Click on Test. The Test SQL Statement dialog box opens.

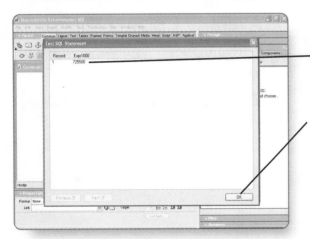

NOTE
The sum of column values is returned.

3. Click on OK. The Test SQL Statement dialog box closes.

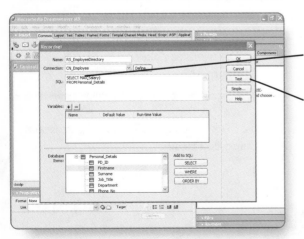

Maximum Column Value

1. Type MAX(*field name*) into the SQL text area.

2. Click on Test. The Test SQL Statement dialog box opens.

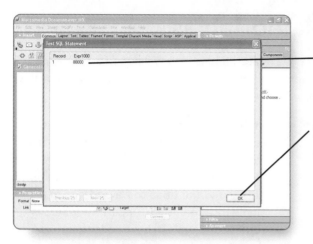

NOTE

The maximum column value is returned.

3. Click on OK. The Test SQL Statement dialog box closes.

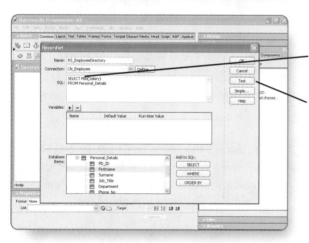

Minimum Column Value

1. Type MIN(*field name*) into the SQL text area.

2. Click on Test. The Test SQL Statement dialog box opens.

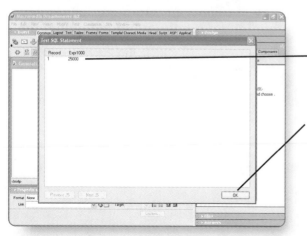

NOTE

The minimum column value is returned.

3. Click on OK. The Test SQL Statement dialog box closes.

Working with Related Tables

When working with a database that has related tables, you will need to define the table connection in the SQL statement. This is achieved by establishing a relationship between columns from each table.

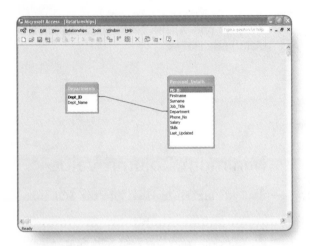

In this Microsoft Access example, there is a relationship between the Department field from the Personal_Details table and the Dept_ID field from the Department table. This allows the titles to be updated in a single location. If the Department field is retrieved, users will have to look up department titles manually in the Departments table. You can avoid this by writing an SQL statement that joins the Department and Dept_ID fields and retrieves the Dept_Name field.

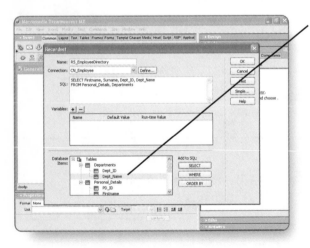

1. Select the fields to be retrieved. You will need to expand the branches of the Tables tree until you find the required table and field. The field is highlighted.

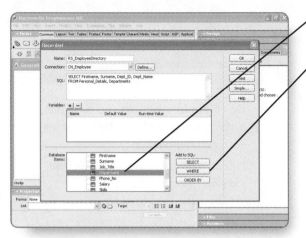

2. Select the related field. The field is highlighted.

3. Click on WHERE. A WHERE clause is inserted.

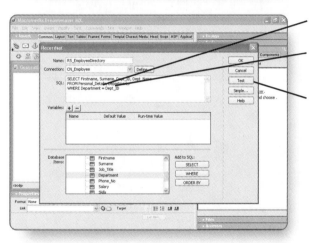

4. Type a comparison operator.

5. Type the name of the field from the related table.

6. Click on Test. The Test SQL Statement dialog box opens.

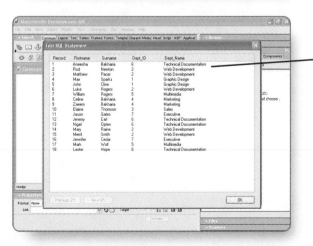

NOTE

The contents of the related field are displayed.

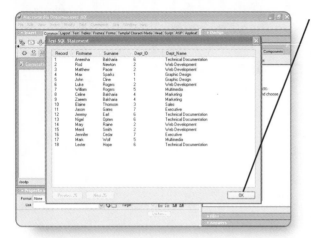

7. Click on OK. The SQL Statement dialog box closes.

> ### NOTE
>
> Dot Notation can be used to avoid ambiguity by prefixing table names with column names:
>
> SELECT Personal_Details.Firstname, Personal_Details.Surname, Departments.Dept_Name_
>
> FROM Personal_Details, Departments
>
> WHERE Personal_Details.Department = Departments.Dept_ID_

13

Searching a Database

It's time you stopped hard-coding search criteria and developed a forms-based interface to collect and process search requests. This technique provides a much more efficient way for users to find exactly what they need. It is also essential that you display search results in a visually appealing and user-friendly manner. In this chapter, you'll learn how to do the following:

- Create a simple search form
- Process a search form
- Search multiple database fields
- Display search results in a table
- Create paged search results
- Create Master-Detail page sets

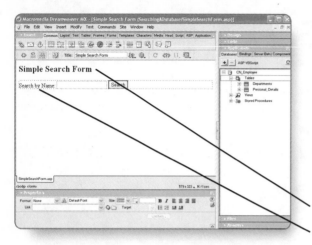

Creating a Simple Search Form

In the following steps, you will create a form that enables the user to enter a search request in a text box. It is useful to indicate which field will be searched. The search request is sent to the server for processing when the Search button is clicked.

1. Create a search form.

2. Type a name that describes the type of search being performed.

3. Insert a Text field for the user to enter their search request.

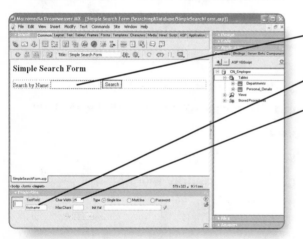

4. Type a name for the Text field.

5. Type in the character width of the text field. You should use the type of data stored in the field that the user can search as a guide when defining the width. Be sure to give users ample room to enter their search request.

6. Insert a Submit button. The user will click on this button to send their search request to the server for processing.

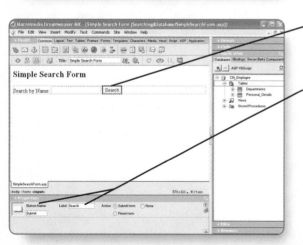

7. Type in a name for the button in the Button Name field. The label should clearly describe the purpose of the button, which in this case is to search the database.

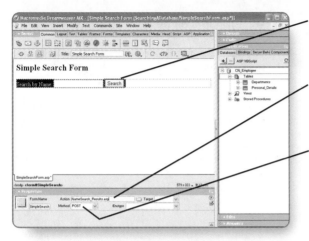

8. Click on the dashed red line that surrounds the form. The contents of the form are highlighted.

9. Type the name of the page that will process the search request into the Action field.

10. Select POST, from the Method drop-down list. The POST option is selected.

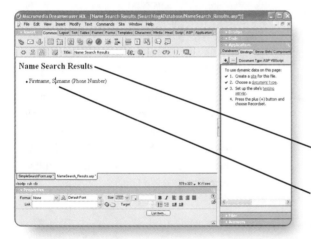

Processing a Search Form

To process a search request, you will need to include the retrieved form data in the database query.

1. Create a new Web page with an .asp extension.

2. Type in placeholder text for the fields. Each record is displayed in a bulleted list. Later in this chapter you'll learn to display search results in a table.

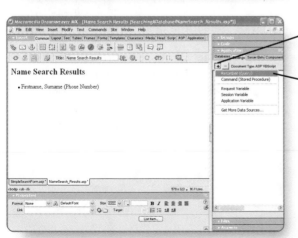

3. Click on the + sign. A submenu appears.

4. Click on Recordset (Query). The Recordset dialog box opens.

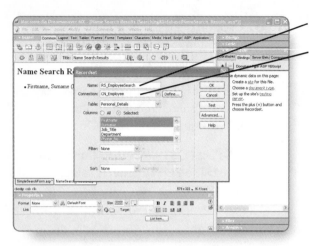

5. Type in a name for the recordset.

6. Select a database connection. All the tables in the database are loaded.

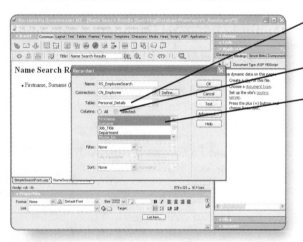

7. Select the table that contains the field that must be searched.

8. Click on the Selected option button.

9. Select the fields that must be returned by the query. To select more than one field, hold down the Ctrl key, and then click on the fields you want to include. Only select fields that are bound to the search results Web page.

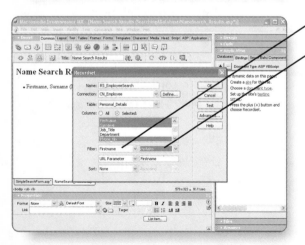

10. Select the field that will be searched.

11. Select Contains as the comparison operator. This allows the search criteria to be matched to any portion of the field.

NOTE

You could also select

- **Begins with** to return a match if the search criteria are found at the start of the text stored in the field.
- **Ends with** to return a match if the search criteria are found at the end of the text stored in the field.

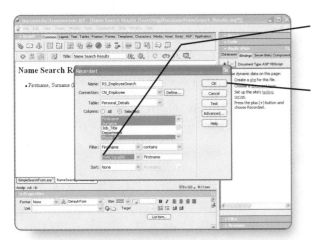

12. Select Form Variable from the Filter drop-down list. This option retrieves the search request from the form.

13. Click on OK. The Recordset dialog box closes.

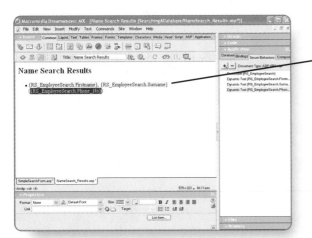

NOTE

You now have to bind the fields returned in the recordset to the Web page and use the Repeat server behavior to display multiple records. Chapter 10, "Retrieving Data from a Database," covers this topic in depth.

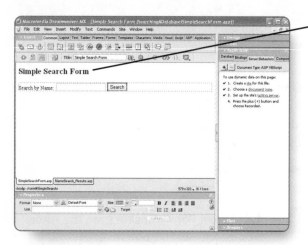

14. Open the Search form that you created in the previous section.

15. Press F12 to preview the Web page in a browser. The Web browser opens and loads the search form.

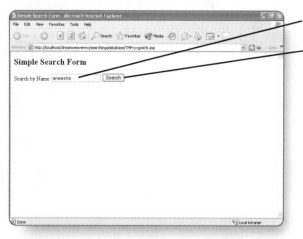

16. Type in your search request.

17. Click on Search. The search results page loads.

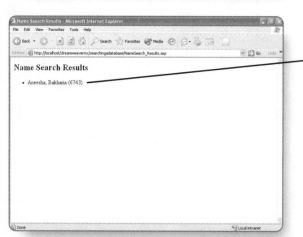

NOTE

Records that match the search criteria are displayed.

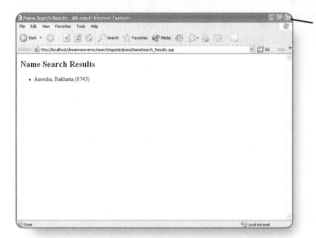

18. Click on the Close icon. The Web browser closes.

Searching Multiple Database Fields

Because a table is usually made up of several search fields, it might be useful to perform a search across multiple fields. Data entered into a text field can be compared with numerous fields in a database. You will need to retrieve the form data, store it in a variable, and then include it in the SQL query.

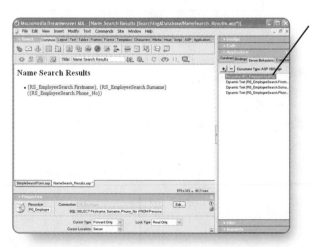

1. Double-click on Recordset.

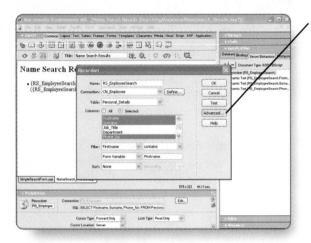

2. Click on Advanced. The Recordset dialog box is expanded.

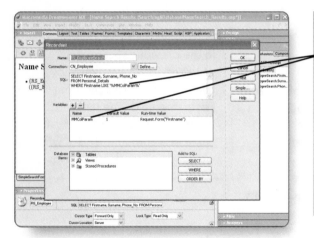

NOTE

The Query contains a variable called `MMColParam`. This variable is created by Dreamweaver MX when you use a form field to filter a recordset. The variable `MMColParam` will be replaced by the data entered in the form element called `Firstname`. The `Request.Form` object is used to retrieve the posted form data.

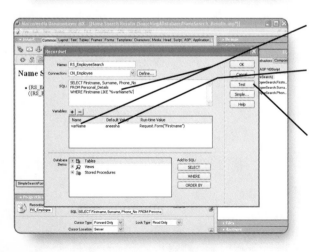

3. Change the variable name to something more descriptive.

4. Enter a default value for the variable. The value is used when a test on a query is performed in Dreamweaver MX.

5. Click on Test. The Test SQL Statement dialog box opens.

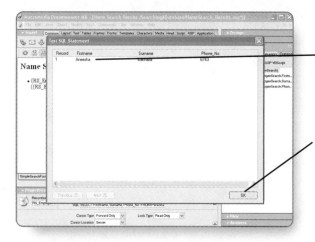

NOTE

The records that match the default value entered for the variable are returned.

6. Click on OK. The Test SQL Statement dialog box closes.

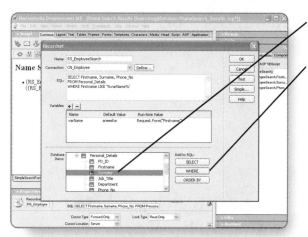

7. Click on the field that the user will be able to search. The field is highlighted.

8. Click on WHERE. The WHERE clause is added to the SQL statement.

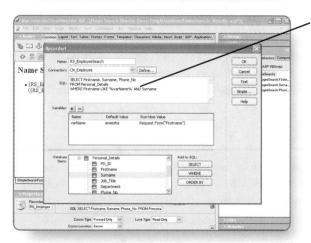

9. Change AND to OR. The query needs to return records where either the Firstname or Surname fields match the data entered into the form element.

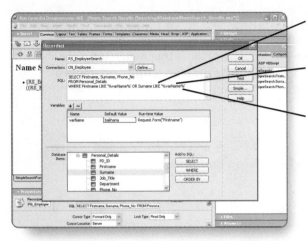

10. Type `LIKE` after the field name in the `WHERE` clause.

11. Type in a variable name enclosed by apostrophes.

12. Type the % wildcard before and after the variable name. This allows the search criteria to be matched to any portion of the field.

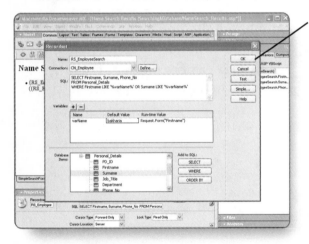

13. Click on OK. The Recordset dialog box closes.

Displaying a User-Friendly Search

Databases can hold thousands of records. When enabling users to search a database, you never know how many records will be returned. You can easily achieve this goal by displaying a reasonable amount of records on a page and letting users page through the returned results at their own pace. Search engines take a similar approach by splitting results across multiple pages.

Displaying Search Results in a Table

Tables provide a handy way to display multiple records from a database because they have a grid-like structure. Each column within the table can represent a field in the database. In Chapter 2, "Dreamweaver MX Basics," you learned to use Dreamweaver MX as a visual tool to create and modify tables. You will now learn how to bind data to a table cell.

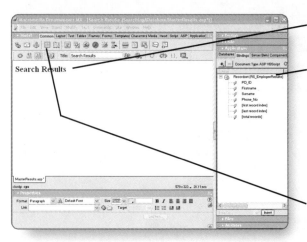

1. Create a new Web page with an .asp extension.

2. Use the Recordset (Query) Data Source from the Bindings tab to create a recordset. The retrieved recordset will be bound to the table cells. The steps involved are fully explained in Chapter 10, "Retrieving Data from a Database," and Chapter 11, "Using Application Objects."

3. Click on the Insert Table icon on the Common tab. The Insert Table dialog box opens.

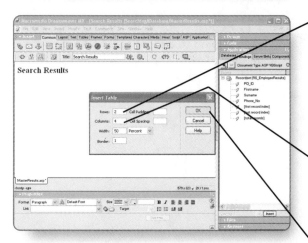

4. Type in the number of rows required. You only need to include a row that will be used to display the column headings and another that will be bound to the database. The Repeat server behavior will be used to create a new row for each record retrieved from the database.

5. Type in the number of columns required. This value depends upon the number of fields you have retrieved in your recordset and wish to display.

6. Click on OK. The table is inserted.

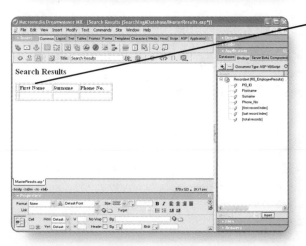

7. Label the table columns. The column headings should reflect the data that will be displayed. Refer to Chapter 2, "Dreamweaver MX Basics," for information on adding text to a table cell.

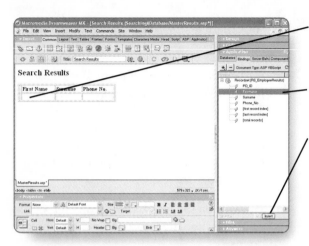

8. Click inside the table cell where the field should be bound. The cursor appears where you click.

9. Click on a field in the Bindings tab. The field is selected.

10. Click on Insert. The field placeholder is inserted as dynamic text in the table cell.

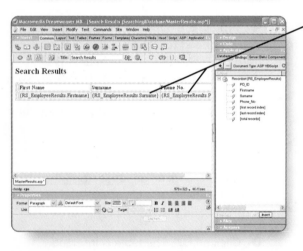

11. Repeat steps 9–10 for each field you want to bind to a table cell. Make sure the cells are all within the same table row.

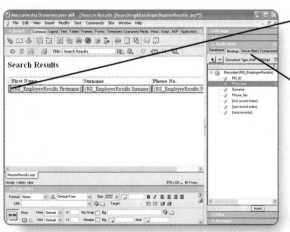

12. Select the row that contains the dynamic text elements. The row is highlighted.

13. Click on the Server Behaviors tab. The Server Behaviors tab is displayed.

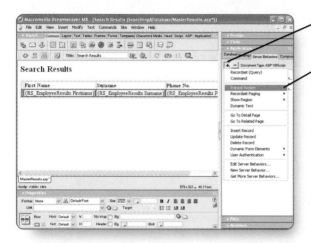

14. Click on the + sign. A submenu appears.

15. Click on Repeat Region. The Repeat Region dialog box opens.

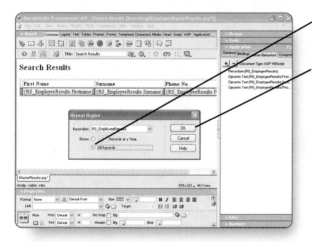

16. Click on the All Records option button. The option is selected.

17. Click on OK. The Repeat Region dialog box closes. A tabbed gray outline appears around the table row. This signifies a Repeat Region.

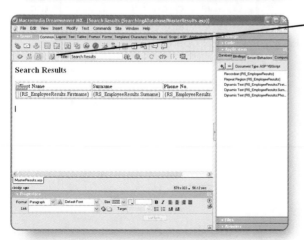

18. Click on the Live Data View icon. Live Data View is enabled.

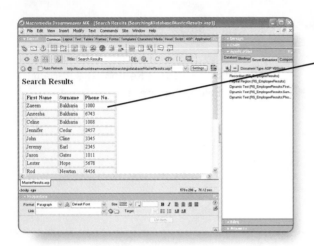

A table row is inserted for each record retrieved from the database. All records are displayed on a single page.

Displaying Paged Search Results

You will now learn how to display results in smaller groups and enable users to step through the results at their own pace. This is essential when a search can return hundreds of records.

Limiting the Number of Records

Reducing the number of records displayed on a page saves server resources and decreases the time it takes a page to load. The Repeat Region server behavior is used to specify the number of records that can be displayed on a page.

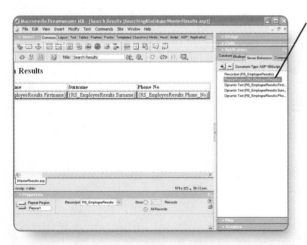

1. Double-click on Repeat Region in the list of server behaviors. The Repeat Region dialog box opens.

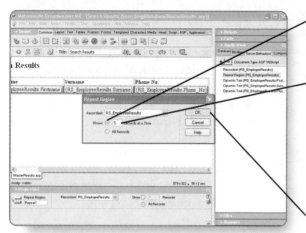

2. Click on the Show option button to show a specified amount of records. The option is selected.

3. Type the number of records to display on a page. You have to make a decision about the number of records that should be displayed at any one time. The value you select depends upon the layout of your search results Web page. You should generally try to prevent too much scrolling.

4. Click on OK. The Repeat Region dialog box closes.

5. Click on the Live Data View icon. Live Data View is enabled.

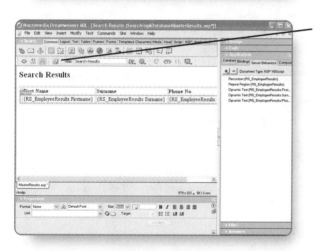

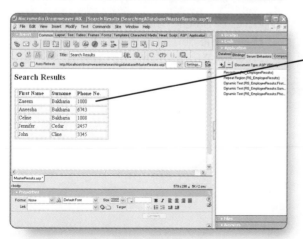

NOTE

Only the specified number of records are displayed on the page. But what if more results are returned in the search? In the next section, you will create a navigation panel so that users can page through returned results.

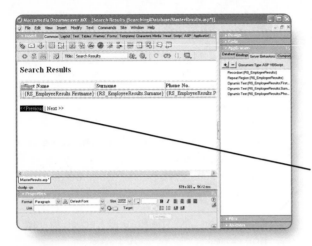

Creating a Navigation Panel

A navigation panel enables users to navigate quickly through paged search results. The navigation panel must contain a link/button to move forward to the next page and a link/button to return to the previous page.

1. Insert text for the recordset navigation panel. Ideally, you will have placeholder text for Previous and Next links.

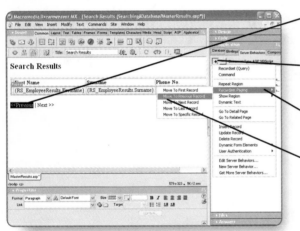

2. Select the Previous link. The text is highlighted.

3. Click on the + sign. A submenu appears.

4. Point the mouse to Recordset Paging. A submenu appears.

5. Click on Move To Previous Record. The Move To Previous Record dialog box opens.

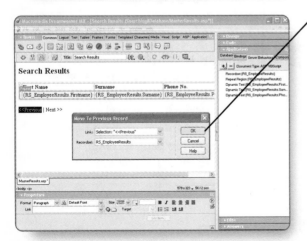

6. Click on OK. There is usually no need to change the default settings. The Move To Previous Record dialog box closes.

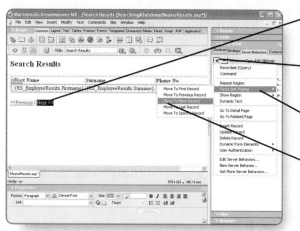

7. Select the Next link. The text is highlighted.

8. Click on the + sign. A submenu is displayed.

9. Move the mouse pointer to Recordset Paging. A submenu appears.

10. Click on Move To Next Record. The Move To Next Record dialog box opens.

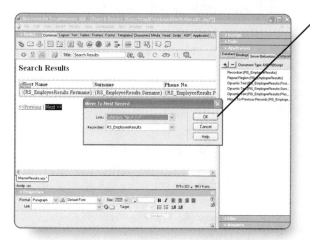

11. Click on OK. There is usually no need to change the default settings. The Move To Next Record dialog box closes.

NOTE

You can't follow links while in Live Data Mode. The functionality of the navigation panel must be tested in a browser.

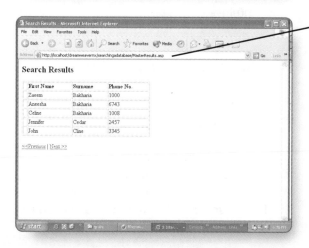

12. Press F12 to preview the current Web page in a browser. The browser opens and displays the Web page.

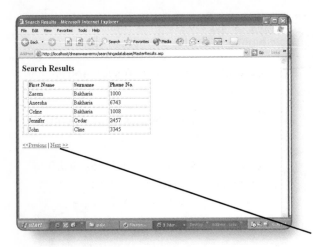

13. Click on the Next link. The Next page of search results is displayed.

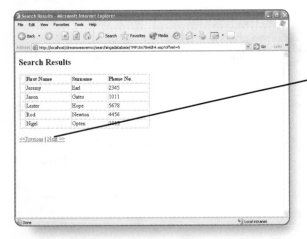

14. Click on the Close icon. The browser closes.

Disabling Navigation Links

We will use the Show Region server behavior to disable the links when there are no more records to display. The Show Region server behavior must be applied to both the Next and Previous links.

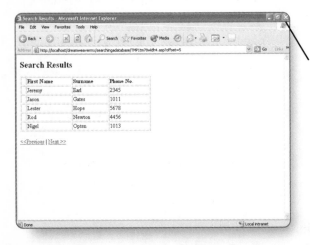

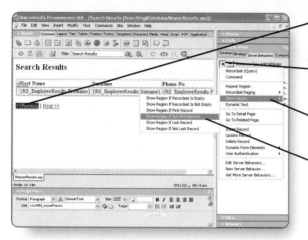

1. Select the Previous link. The text is highlighted.

2. Click on the + sign. A submenu appears.

3. Click on Show Region. A submenu appears.

4. Click on Show Region If Not First Record. The Show Region If Not First Record dialog box opens.

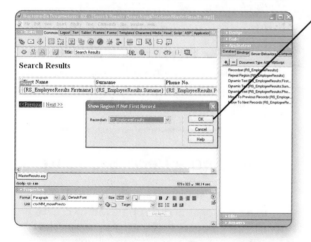

5. Click on OK. The Show Region If Not First Record dialog box closes.

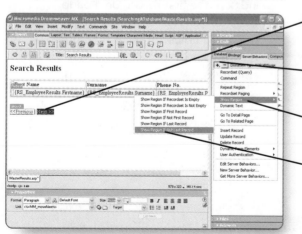

6. Select the Next link. The text is highlighted.

7. Click on the + sign. A submenu appears.

8. Click on Show Region. A submenu appears.

9. Click on Show Region If Not Last Record. The Show Region If Not Last Record dialog box opens.

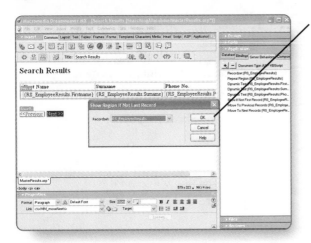

10. Click on OK. The Show Region If Not Last Record dialog box closes.

11. Press F12 to preview the current Web page in a browser. The browser opens and loads the Web page.

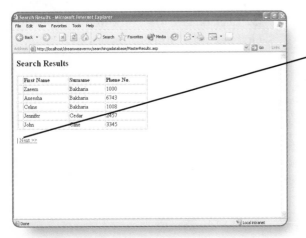

NOTE

The first page of records does not contain a Previous link. When the last page is reached, the Next link will not be displayed.

Creating a Record Counter

Recordset statistics are always returned in a recordset and can be used to create a record counter. Every query returns the index of the first record on a page, the index of the last record on a page, and the total number of records returned. A record count informs users about the amount of search results returned.

1. Click on the Bindings tab. The Bindings tab is displayed.

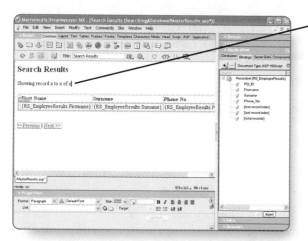

2. Insert placeholder text for the record counter. Ideally, you will have placeholder text to display the first record, the last record, and the total number of records.

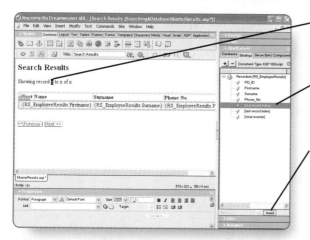

3. Select the text that should be replaced by the index of the first record on a page. The text is highlighted.

4. Click on [first record index] in the Bindings tab. The [first record index] option is highlighted.

5. Click on Insert. The [first record index] placeholder is inserted as dynamic text.

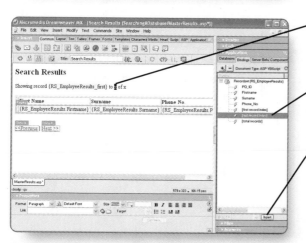

6. Select the text that should be replaced by the index of the last record on a page. The text is highlighted.

7. Click on [last record index] in the Bindings tab. The [last record index] option is highlighted.

8. Click on Insert. The [last record index] placeholder is inserted as dynamic text.

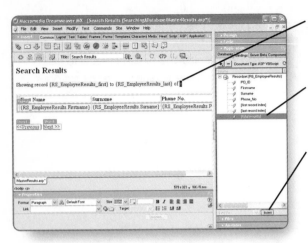

9. Select the text that should be replaced by the total number of records returned. The text is highlighted.

10. Click on [total records] in the Bindings tab. The [total records] option is highlighted.

11. Click on Insert. The [total records] placeholder is inserted as dynamic text.

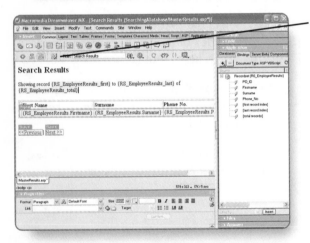

12. Click on the Live Data View icon. Live Data View is enabled.

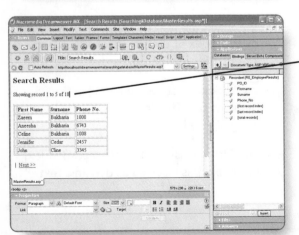

NOTE

The record counter will be displayed. The record counter indicates the user's position in the paged recordset.

Linking to a Detail Page

The search results pages should ideally display only summary data from each record and provide a link, which the user can click on to view detailed information. This enables the user to evaluate the search results and then decide which result they want to view in full.

Creating a Detail Link

A detail link must pass the unique ID number of the record to the detail page. The best way to achieve this is to append the ID number to the detail page URL, in other words, the QueryString. Move To Specific Record takes care of all the hard work.

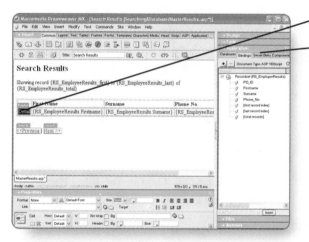

1. Select the Detail link.

2. Click on the Server Behaviors tab, if not already selected. The Server Behaviors tab is displayed.

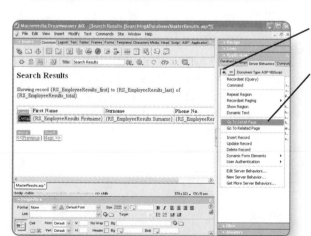

3. Click on the + sign. A submenu appears.

4. Click on Go To Detail Page. The Go To Detail Page dialog box opens.

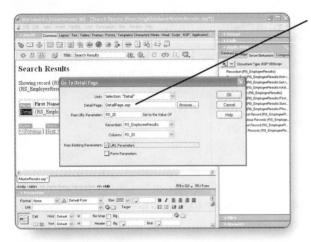

5. Type the name of the file that will display the full record. This is known as the *Detail Page*. The file name is inserted into the name field.

> ## NOTE
>
> The primary key/unique ID of the record is detected by Dreamweaver MX.

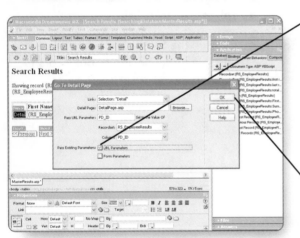

6. Click inside the URL Parameters check box. A check mark is placed in the box. This means that the record ID will be passed to the Detail Page as a QueryString, in other words, it will be appended to the URL. Refer to Chapter 7, "Using HTML Forms," for more information about the QueryString.

7. Click on OK. The Go To Detail Page dialog box closes.

Creating a Detail Page

A detail page must retrieve the record that matches the unique ID passed to it in the QueryString. In this section, you will set up a query that retrieves the ID number from the QueryString and then searches the database for the record that matches the ID number. Obviously, a detail page must display comprehensive information about a record. Users will be expecting the full record to be displayed.

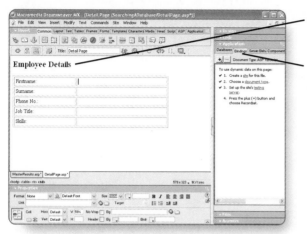

1. Create a new file with an .asp extension.

2. Click on the Bindings tab, if not already selected. The Bindings tab is displayed.

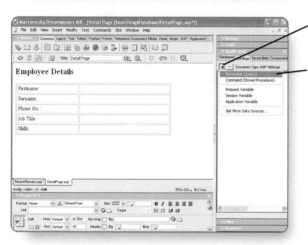

3. Click on the + sign. A submenu appears.

4. Click on Recordset (Query). The Recordset dialog box opens.

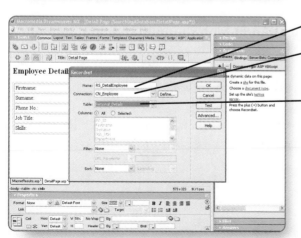

5. Type a name for the recordset.

6. Select a database connection. The option is selected.

7. Select the table that contains the record that you need to retrieve. The option is selected.

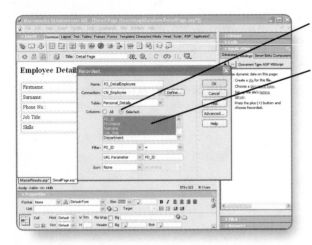

8. Click on the Selected option button. The option is selected.

9. Select the fields that must be returned by the query. To select more than one field, hold down the Ctrl key, then click the fields you want to include.

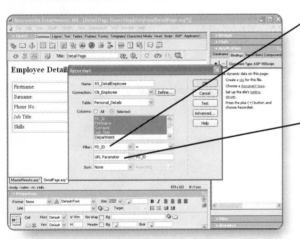

10. Select the field that corresponds to the value that is being passed to the detail page via the QueryString. It must be the unique ID field, also known as the primary key.

11. Select URL Parameter because the ID number must be retrieved from the QueryString. The option will is selected.

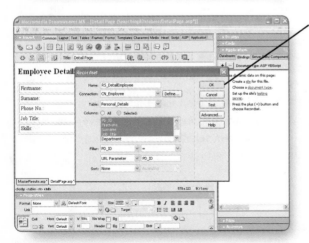

12. Click on OK. The Recordset dialog box closes.

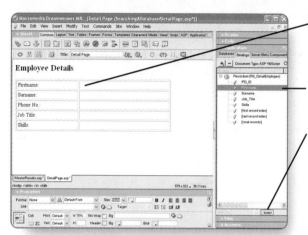

13. Click in the Document window where the field should be bound. The cursor appears where you click.

14. Click on a field in the Bindings tab. The field is selected.

15. Click on Insert. The field placeholder is inserted as dynamic text.

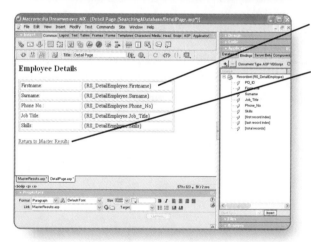

16. Repeat steps 13–15 for each field to be inserted.

17. Insert a link back to the Master Results page.

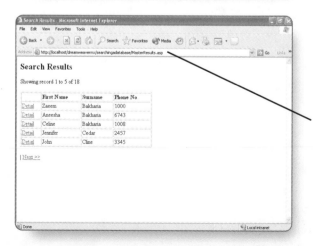

Testing the Detail Link

A detail link can't be tested with Live Data View. You will have to preview the Web page in a browser to test the detail links.

1. Press F12 to preview the current page in a browser. The browser opens and displays the Web page.

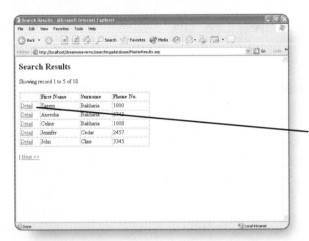

NOTE

The search page contains a Detail link for each record.

2. Click on the Detail link. The Detail page will be loaded.

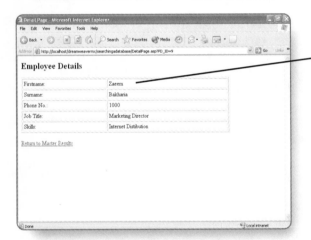

NOTE

The Detail page displays the full record.

14

Creating Dynamic Form Objects

Forms play an important role in database maintenance. Form objects (text fields, check boxes, radio buttons, and drop-down lists and menus) must be populated with the contents of a record so that the user can view and edit the data before sending it back to the server for processing. In this chapter, you'll learn to make dynamic

- Text fields
- Radio buttons
- Check boxes
- List/Menu boxes

Making Text Fields Dynamic

Text fields should only be bound to data that can be displayed in a single line. Text fields ideally are used to update fields that store data such as a name, phone number, or e-mail address. Use a multiline text field if the stored data spans multiple lines.

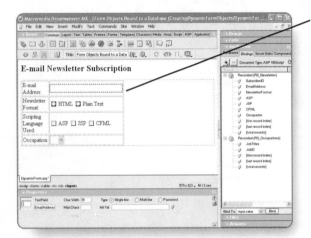

1. Create an HTML form. Use form objects (text fields, radio buttons, check boxes, and drop-down lists) that best suit your data entry needs. You will need to be familiar with creating forms in Dreamweaver MX; this was covered in Chapter 7, "Using HTML Forms," and Chapter 8, "Validating and Retrieving Form Data."

NOTE

All form objects must be named. The names given to form objects should match the table columns to which they will be bound.

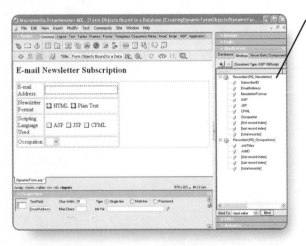

2. Create a recordset called RS_Newsletter from the Bindings tab. The retrieved recordset will be bound to form objects. You can only display one record at a time in a form. You must therefore create a query that only retrieves a single record from a database. The steps involved to create a recordset that retrieves a specific record are covered in Chapter 8, "Validating and Retrieving Form Data," and Chapter 12, "Using SQL to Query a Database."

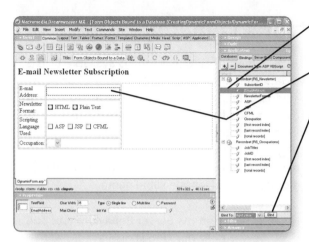

3. Click on the field that will be bound to a text field. The field name is highlighted.

4. Click on the text field. The field is selected.

5. Click on the Bind button. The field is bound to the text field.

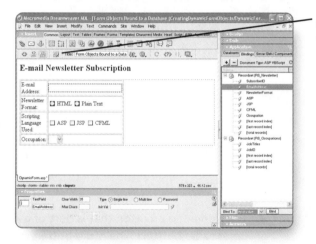

6. Click on the Live Data View icon. Live Data View is enabled.

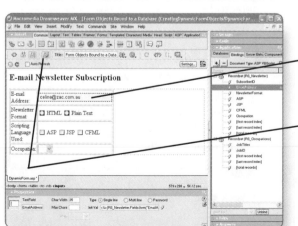

NOTE

The text field displays the data retrieved from the database.

7. Click on the Live Data View icon. Design View is enabled.

Making Radio Buttons Dynamic

Radio buttons can only be used correctly if more than one option is available to the user. You should use them to update data where the user has a number of options available but must select only one. A good example of this is a field that stores whether a person is under or over 18 years old. If the button group is dynamic, it only appears when triggered by information stored in the database. For example, if the form is related to legally binding agreements, you may want the user to be prompted to state that he or she is over 18 years of age. Radio buttons must be grouped, and grouped radio buttons must all be given the same name.

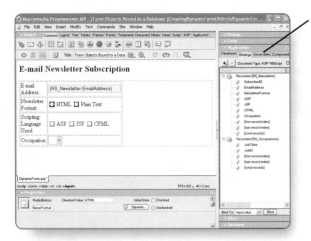

1. Click on the Server Behaviors tab. The Server Behaviors tab is displayed.

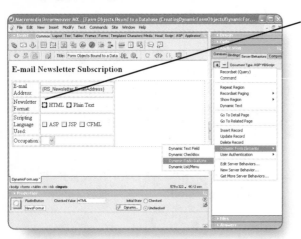

2. Click on a radio button that is part of a group of radio buttons. The radio button is selected.

TIP

Make sure that all radio buttons in a group have the same name, but different values. Refer to Chapter 7, "Using HTML Forms," to refresh your knowledge.

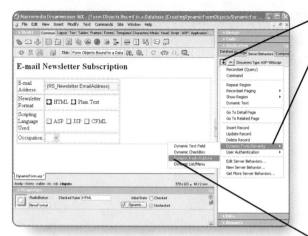

3. Click on the + sign. A submenu appears.

4. Click on Dynamic Form Elements. A submenu appears.

NOTE

The Dynamic Form Elements server behavior will help you bind data to all the different types of form objects.

5. Click on Dynamic Radio buttons. The Dynamic Radio buttons dialog box opens.

6. Click on the Lightning Bolt icon. The Dynamic Data dialog box opens.

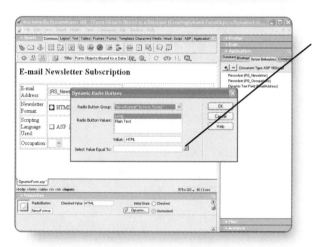

NOTE

Dreamweaver MX detects the group to which the selected radio button belongs. All the radio button values are also inserted in the Radio Button Values list.

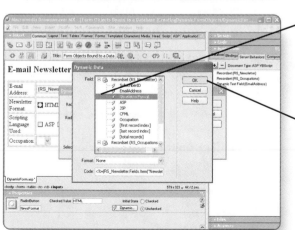

7. Click on the field that will be bound to the radio button. The Code field is generated. The radio button that matches the data stored in the field will be selected when the page loads.

8. Click on OK. The Dynamic Data dialog box closes.

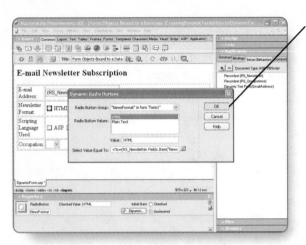

9. Click on OK. The Dynamic Radio Buttons dialog box closes. The group of radio buttons are bound to the selected database field.

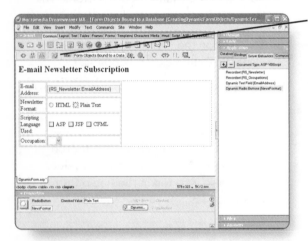

10. Click on the Live Data View icon. Live Data View is enabled.

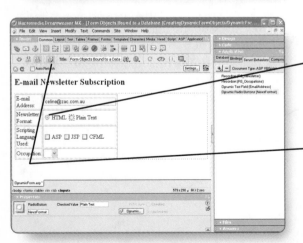

NOTE

The radio button that matches the value stored in the database is selected.

11. Click on the Live Data View icon. Design View is enabled.

Making Check Boxes Dynamic

Use check boxes for a list of fields that can be selected or deselected. The user is allowed to select any combination of fields. Typically, the field must contain data that can be represented in Boolean form, such as Yes/No or True/False. Boolean means that the form object is only capable of storing two values.

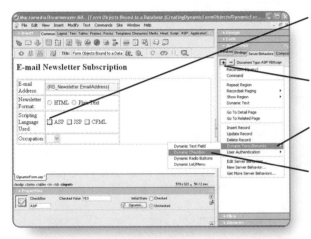

1. Click on the check box that you would like to bind to a database field. The check box is selected.

2. Click on the + sign. A submenu appears.

3. Click on Dynamic Form Elements. A submenu appears.

4. Click on Dynamic CheckBox. The Dynamic CheckBox dialog box opens.

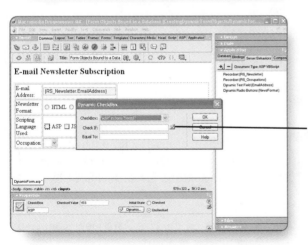

NOTE

The name and value of the check box are detected.

5. Click on the Lightning Bolt icon. The Dynamic Data dialog box opens.

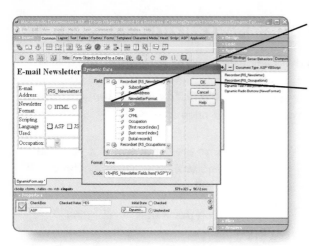

6. Click on the database field you want to bind to the check box. The Code field is generated.

7. Click on OK. The Dynamic Data dialog box closes.

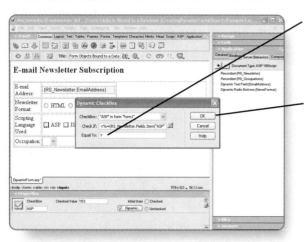

8. Type the value that must be stored in the database field for the check box to be selected by default when the Web page loads. This is usually a Boolean value.

9. Click on OK. The Dynamic CheckBox dialog box closes.

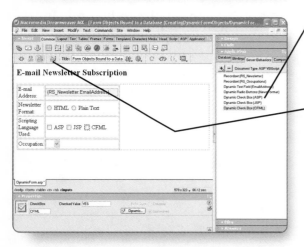

10. Repeat steps 1–9 for each check box on your form. A Dynamic Check Box server behavior is added for each check box that you add.

11. Click on the Live Data View icon. Live Data View is enabled.

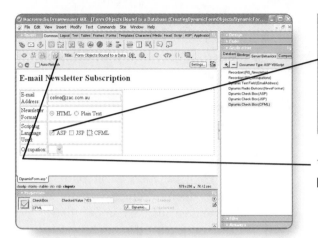

NOTE

Check boxes are selected if the data retrieved matches the value you entered into the Equal To field in the Dynamic CheckBox dialog box.

12. Click on the Live Data View icon. Design View is enabled.

Making a List or Menu Dynamic

Dreamweaver menus are also commonly known as drop-down lists. They allow the user to make a selection from a long list of options without wasting valuable screen space. They are ideal if you want to restrict the values that can be stored in a database field to a predefined list. You can enter the options manually or dynamically populate the list with the results of a database query.

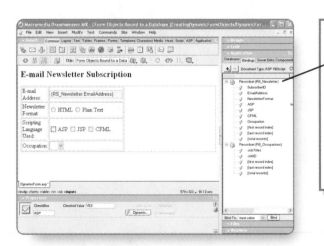

NOTE

You will need two recordsets to create a dynamic drop-down list.

The first recordset will be bound to the drop-down list. This means the option that matches the data stored in the database will be selected when the Web page loads.

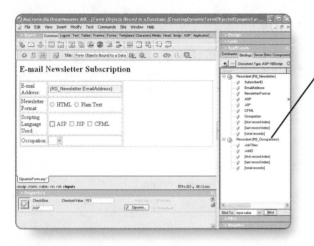

NOTE

The second recordset will populate the drop-down list with options. This recordset must return distinct records so that the drop-down list does not contain duplicate options. Creating a query that returns distinct records was covered in Chapter 12, "Using SQL to Query a Database." You may need to return both option labels and values. Remember that labels are displayed in the browser, while the value of the selected option is sent to the server when the form is submitted. Depending on your data, you may find that some-times the labels and values are equal.

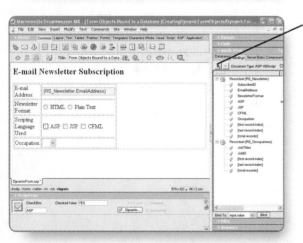

1. Click on the drop-down list. The drop-down list is selected.

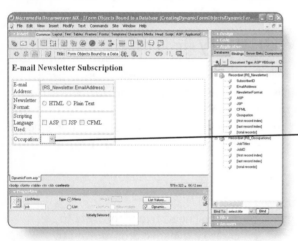

2. Click on the Server Behaviors tab. The Server Behaviors tab is displayed.

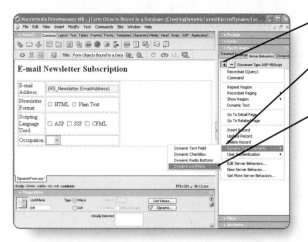

3. Click on the + sign. A submenu appears.

4. Click on Dynamic Form Elements. A submenu appears.

5. Click on Dynamic List/Menu. The Dynamic List/Menu dialog box opens.

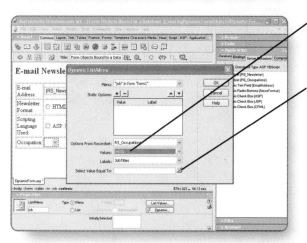

6. Select the field that will be used to set the values of the drop-down list options. The field is selected.

7. Click on the Lightning Bolt icon. The Dynamic Data dialog box opens.

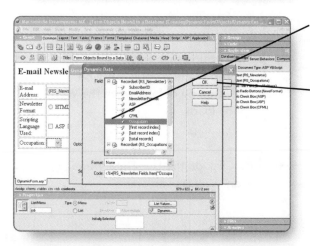

8. Click on the field that will be bound to the drop-down list. The Code field is generated.

9. Click on OK. The Dynamic Data dialog box closes.

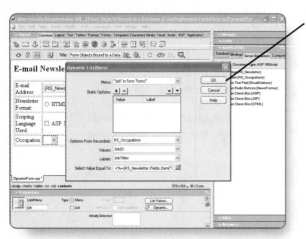

10. Click on OK. The Dynamic List/Menu dialog box closes.

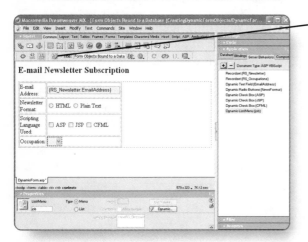

11. Click on the Live Data View icon. Live Data View is enabled.

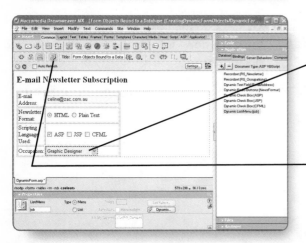

NOTE

The option that matches the value stored in the database will be selected by default when the Web page loads.

12. Click on the Live Data View icon. Design View is enabled.

15

Inserting, Updating, and Deleting Records

It is rare for the data stored in a database to remain static over a long period of time. A Web-enabled database, in particular, has the potential to be accessed by millions of people and must be maintained to prevent invalid data from being displayed. You can easily insert, update, and delete records. Dreamweaver MX comes with a set of server behaviors that will enable you to incorporate all of this functionality in your Web site. In this chapter, you'll learn how to do the following:

- Insert records
- Update existing records
- Delete records

Inserting Records

You need to provide a means for users to populate a database in the first place, as well as to add to the database at a later stage. Adding a new record to a database is not as difficult as you might think. The Insert Record server behavior takes care of all the hard work.

Creating the Insert Form

A form must be created to gather the data to be inserted as a new record in the database table. The form should contain all the fields required to create a new record.

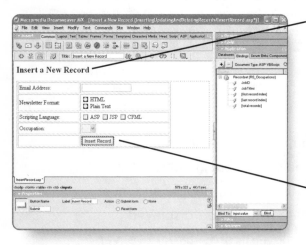

1. Create an HTML form. Use form elements (text fields, radio buttons, check boxes, and drop-down lists) that best suit your data entry needs. Consult Chapter 7, "Using HTML Forms," and Chapter 8, "Validating and Retrieving Form Data," if you do not feel comfortable with creating forms in Dreamweaver MX.

NOTE

The form must have a Submit button that indicates the purpose of the form, which in this case is to insert a new record in the database. This will be covered in the next section.

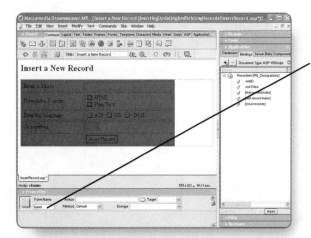

2. Type a name for the form, which indicates the purpose of the form.

NOTE

All form elements must be named. The names given to form elements must match the table columns where data will be inserted. Having named form elements makes using the Insert Record server behavior a breeze.

Using the Insert Record Server Behavior

The Insert Record server behavior generates all of the code required to insert a new record. All you need to do is specify the database connection and the table where the record must be inserted, then match the form elements to the table columns.

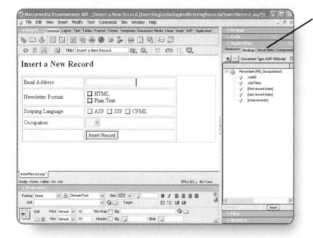

1. Click on the Server Behaviors tab. The Server Behaviors tab is displayed.

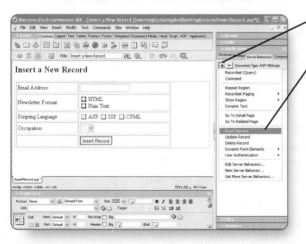

2. Click on the + sign in the Server Behaviors tab. A submenu appears.

3. Click on Insert Record. The Insert Record dialog box opens.

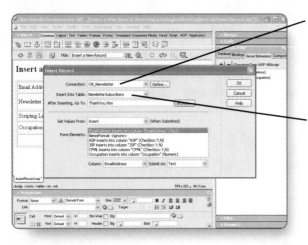

4. Select the connection for the database that needs a Web-based interface to insert data. Creating a connection is covered in Chapter 8, "Validating and Retrieving Form Data."

5. Select the table where the record will be inserted. The table name is selected.

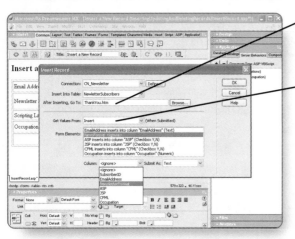

6. Type a file name in the After Inserting, Go To field. This file will be displayed after the record has been inserted.

7. Select the form that will be used to insert data if the form that Dreamweaver MX has selected is incorrect. This will only happen if there is more than one form on your Web page.

NOTE

Dreamweaver MX automatically matches form elements to the database table columns where the data will be inserted, provided the form element and the database columns have the same names. This is why you should always label your form elements correctly. If Dreamweaver MX fails to match a form element to any column in the database table, <ignore> will be placed beside the field name. In this case, you will have to match the form elements to table columns manually.

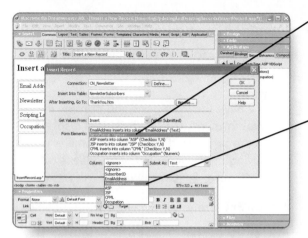

8. Select the column name where the data in the currently selected form element must be inserted. (You are really just matching the form elements to database columns or fields.)

9. Click on the name of the form element that must be matched to a table column. The form object is selected.

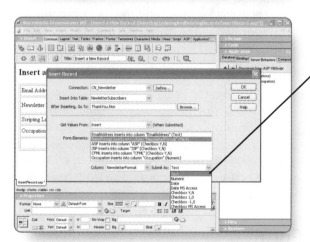

NOTE

Once a table column has been selected, the type of data that the column stores is detected. This column could hold text, numeric data, Yes/No data (usually bound to a check box), or a date.

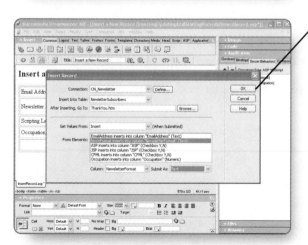

10. Click on OK. The Insert Record dialog box closes.

Testing the Insert Record Server Behavior

You can only test the Insert Record server behavior from a Web browser. The Live Data window does not currently support this function.

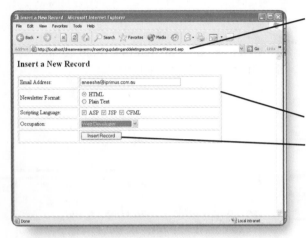

1. Save the Web page and preview it in a Web browser. The Web page is displayed in the browser. If you are not familiar with saving or previewing a page, please refer to Chapter 2, "Dreamweaver MX Basics."

2. Enter relevant data into the form fields.

3. Click on the Insert Record button. The record is inserted, and the page that you specified in the After Inserting, Go To field in the Insert Record dialog box is displayed.

Updating Records

Databases are very flexible in the way they allow records to be modified. In addition to adding new records, users often need to edit existing records. The Update Record server behavior incorporates this functionality into Dreamweaver MX.

Linking to an Update Form

Before a record can be updated, the user must first select it. You will therefore need to display a summary of records and create a Detail link to the update form. The Detail link passes the unique ID number of the record to the update form.

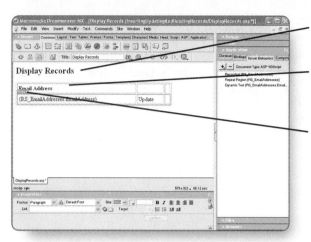

1. Create a search results page that will display summary data from each record.

- Use a table to lay out the results. Chapter 13, "Searching a Database," covered the topic in detail.

- Use the Repeat Region server behavior to display multiple records in the result table.

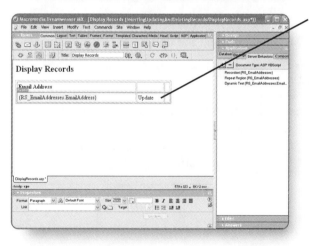

- Each record must have an Update link, which the user can click on to open the appropriate form. The link needs to be within the Repeat Region, so that an Update link is inserted for each record that is displayed.

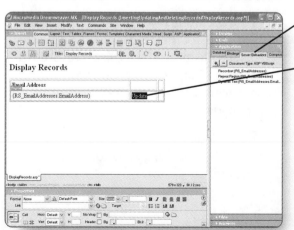

2. Click on the Server Behaviors tab. The Server Behaviors tab is displayed.

3. Select the Update link. The text is highlighted.

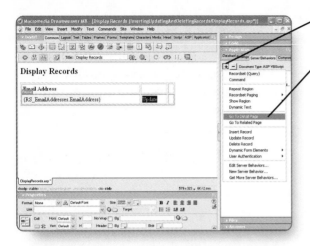

4. Click on the + sign of the Server Behaviors tab. A submenu appears.

5. Click on Go To Detail Page. The Go To Detail Page dialog box opens.

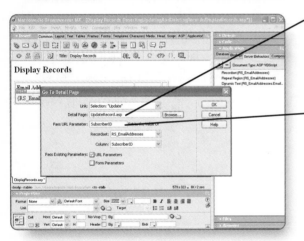

6. Type in the name of the Web page that will contain the update form.

NOTE

The primary key of the table will be detected. This value will be passed to the Web page that contains the update form.

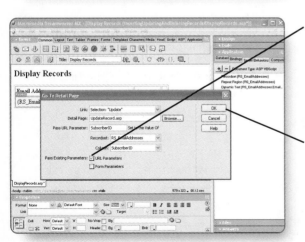

7. Click inside the URL Parameters check box. A check is placed inside the box. The unique identifier of the current record will be passed to the update form as a URL parameter. This means that it will be appended to the URL as a QueryString.

8. Click on OK. The Go To Detail Page dialog box closes, and the Update link is created.

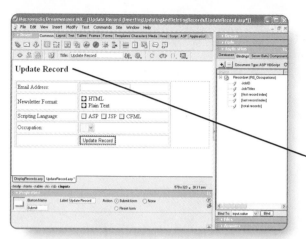

Creating an Update Form

The form objects that comprise the update form need to display the contents of the retrieved record. The update form should contain all of the fields that the user is allowed to update.

1. Create an HTML form. The update form must contain form objects (text fields, radio buttons, check boxes, and drop-down lists) that best suit your data entry requirements. Refer to Chapter 7, "Using HTML Forms," and Chapter 8, "Validating and Retrieving Form Data," if you do not feel comfortable with creating forms in Dreamweaver MX.

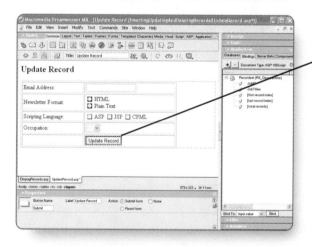

2. Create a Submit button. The form must have a Submit button that indicates the purpose of the form, which in this case is to update a record in the database.

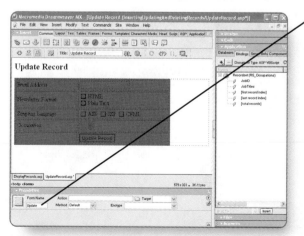

3. Type a name for the form, which indicates the purpose of the form.

NOTE

All form objects must be named. The names given to form objects must match the table columns to which they will be bound. This makes using the Update Record server behavior a breeze.

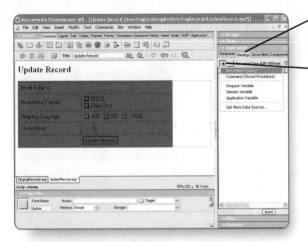

4. Click on the Bindings tab. The Bindings tab is displayed.

5. Click on the + sign. A submenu appears.

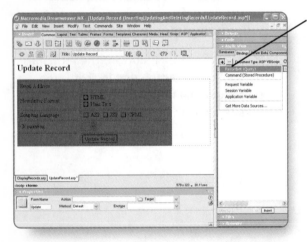

6. Click on Recordset (Query). The Recordset dialog box opens.

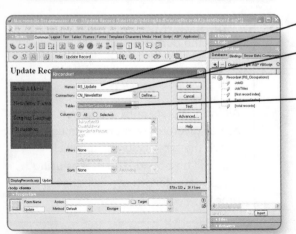

7. Type a name for the recordset.

8. Select a database connection. The option is selected.

9. Select the table that contains the record you need to retrieve. The option is selected.

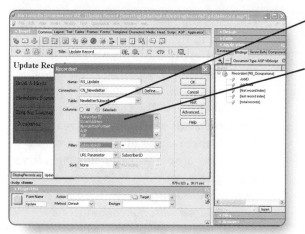

10. Click on the Selected option button. The option is selected.

11. Select the fields that must be returned by the query. To select more than one field, hold down the Ctrl key, and then click on the fields you want to include. Only select the fields that the user will be allowed to update. These fields are bound to the form objects on the update form.

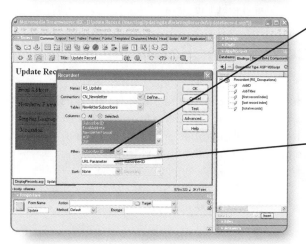

12. Select the field that corresponds to the value that is being passed to the update form via the QueryString. In this case it must be the unique ID field, also known as the primary key. The field is highlighted.

13. Select URL Parameter because the ID number must be retrieved from the QueryString. The option is selected.

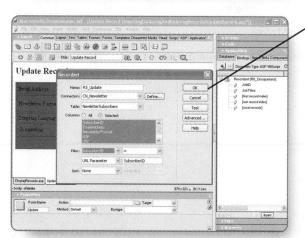

14. Click on OK. The Recordset dialog box closes.

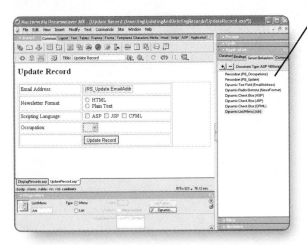

15. Bind the fields retrieved from the database to their matching form objects. You need to use the Dynamic Elements server behavior. Chapter 12, "Using SQL to Query a Database," covers this topic comprehensively. The Dynamic Elements server behavior can be used to create dynamic text fields, radio buttons, check boxes, and drop-down lists. Binding a form element to a database field means that when the Web page loads, the form objects are populated with the contents of a record. This will enable the user to view and edit the data.

Using the Update Record Server Behavior

Using the Update Record server behavior is slightly more involved than using the Insert Record server behavior. In addition to specifying the database connection and the table where the record should be updated and matching form objects to table columns, you also need to specify the unique ID number of the record to be updated. This value is passed to the update form in the QueryString.

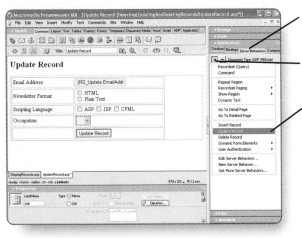

1. Click on the Server Behaviors tab. The Server Behaviors tab is displayed.

2. Click on the + sign. A submenu appears.

3. Click on Update Record. The Update Record dialog box opens.

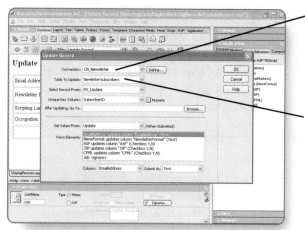

4. Select the database connection for the database that needs a Web-based interface to update data. Creating a connection is covered in Chapter 10, "Retrieving Data from a Database."

5. Select the table that contains the record to be updated. The table name is selected.

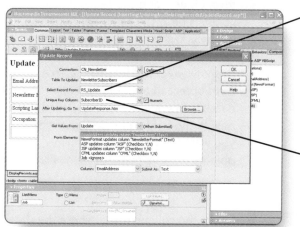

6. Select the recordset that is bound to the update form if the recordset that Dreamweaver MX has selected is incorrect. This only happens if there is more than one recordset bound to the Web page.

NOTE

The unique record identifier/primary key is automatically selected in the Unique Key Column drop-down list.

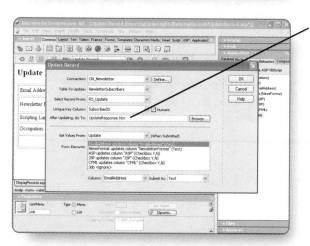

7. Type a file name into the After Updating, Go To field. This file will be displayed after the record has been updated. Ideally, you will want to acknowledge that the record has been updated.

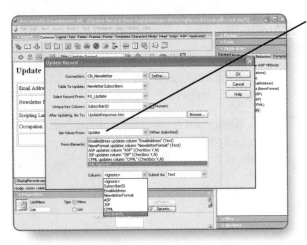

8. Select the form that will be used to update data if the form that Dreamweaver MX has selected is incorrect. This will only happen if there is more than one form on your Web page. The selection is highlighted.

NOTE

Dreamweaver MX automatically matches form objects to the database table columns where the record will be updated, provided the form objects and the database columns have the same names. This is why you should always label your form objects accordingly. If Dreamweaver MX fails to match a form object to any column in the database table, <ignore> is placed beside the field name. In this event, you will have to match the form objects to table columns manually.

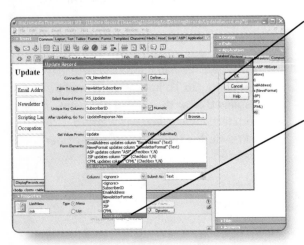

9. Select the column name where the data in the currently selected form object will update. The selection is highlighted. You are really just matching the form objects to database columns or fields.

10. Click on the name of the form elements that must be matched to a table column. The form object is selected.

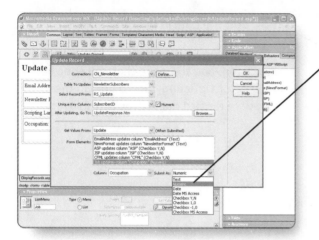

NOTE

NOTE

After a table column has been selected, the type of data that the column stores is detected. This column could hold text, numeric data, Yes/No data (usually bound to a check box,) or a date.

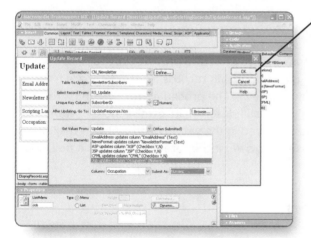

11. Click on OK. The Update Record dialog box closes.

Testing the Update Record Server Behavior

You can only test the Update Record server behavior from a Web browser. The Live Data window does not currently support this function.

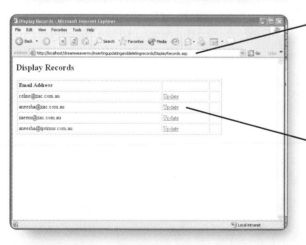

1. Preview search results in the Web page that contains the update link in a Web browser. The Web page is displayed in the Web browser. If you are not familiar with saving or previewing a page, please refer to Chapter 1, "Introducing Dreamweaver MX."

2. Click on the Update link that corresponds to a record that you wish to update. The Web page that contains the update form is displayed. The form objects display the data that has been retrieved from the database.

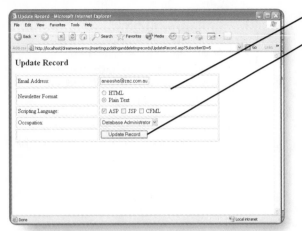

3. Edit the data in the form objects.

4. Click on Update Record. The record is updated, and the page that you specified in the After Updating, Go To field in the Update Record dialog box is displayed.

Deleting Records

The last database maintenance feature that you need to provide for your users is the ability to delete outdated or invalid data. Removing records from a database frees up valuable space and speeds up data retrieval. The procedure for deleting a record is not much different from updating, but it still deserves its own section. Beware that this capability can be very dangerous if placed in the wrong hands. Always make sure that you only allow access to users who know what they are doing because no Undo command is available.

Linking to a Delete Form

Before a record can be deleted, the user must first select the record to be deleted. You will need to display a summary of records and create a Detail link to the delete form. The Detail link passes the unique ID number of the record to the delete form.

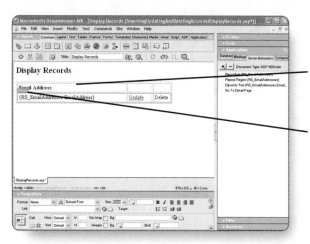

1. Create a search results page that will display summary data from each record.

- Use a table to lay out the results. Chapter 13, "Searching a Database," covers this topic in detail.

- Use the Repeat Region server behavior to display multiple records in the results table.

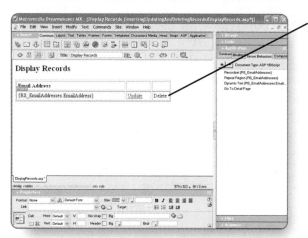

- Each record must have a Delete link, which the user can click on to open the form that will allow the record to be deleted. The link needs to be within the Repeat Region so that a Delete link is inserted for each record displayed. If you would like to allow your users to update records as well, also include an Update link. The steps involved in creating an Update link are covered in the previous section, "Updating Records."

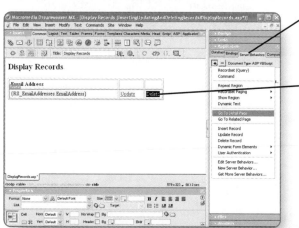

2. Click on the Server Behaviors tab, if it is not already selected. The Server Behaviors tab is displayed.

3. Select the Delete link. The text is highlighted.

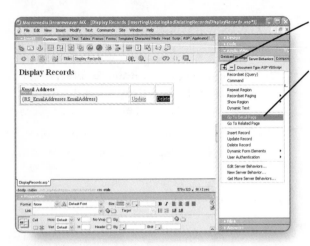

4. Click on the + sign of the Server Behaviors tab. A submenu appears.

5. Click on Go To Detail Page. The Go To Detail Page dialog box opens.

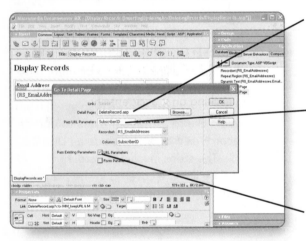

6. Type in the name of the Web page that will contain the delete form.

NOTE

The primary key of the table is detected. This value will be passed to the Web page containing the delete form.

7. Click inside the URL Parameters check box. A check is placed inside the box. The unique identifier of the current record will be passed to the delete form as a URL parameter. That means it will be appended to the URL as a QueryString.

8. Click on OK. The Go To Detail Page dialog box closes, and the Delete link is created.

Creating a Delete Form

You don't need to display the contents of a record that is going to be deleted within form objects. There is no need for users to edit fields when the record is going to be deleted. You should, however, display the entire record that will be deleted. This will give users the opportunity to preview the record before deleting it. Remember, once a record has been deleted, there is no way to restore it.

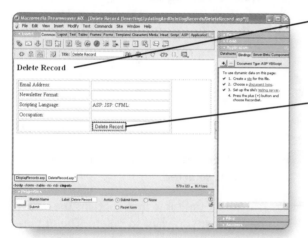

1. Create an HTML Form. The delete form should not contain form objects. You only need to display the entire record that will be deleted.

2. Create a Submit button. The form must have a submit button that indicates the purpose of the form, which in this case is to delete a record in the database. It is very important that the Delete button be appropriately labeled. This prevents users from clicking on it accidentally.

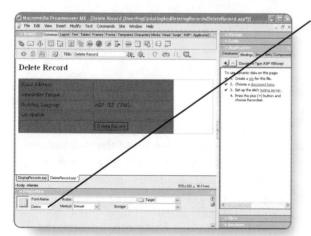

3. Type a name for the form that indicates its purpose.

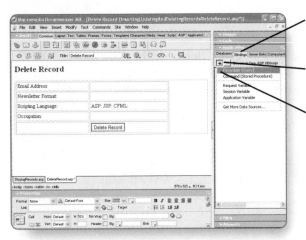

4. Click on the Bindings tab. The Bindings tab is displayed.

5. Click on the + sign. A submenu appears.

6. Click on Recordset (Query). The Recordset dialog box opens.

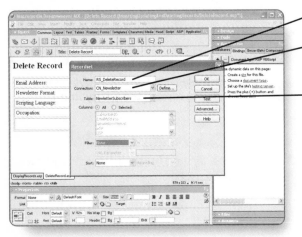

7. Type in a name for the recordset.

8. Select a database connection. The option is selected.

9. Select the table that contains the record that you want to delete. The option is selected.

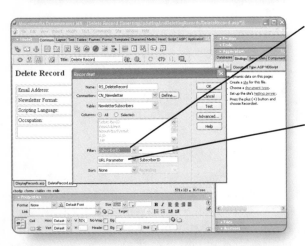

10. Select the field that corresponds to the value being passed to the delete form via the QueryString. In this case, it must be the unique ID field also known as the primary key. The field is highlighted.

11. Select URL Parameter because the ID number must be retrieved from the QueryString. The option is selected.

12. Click on OK. The Recordset dialog box closes.

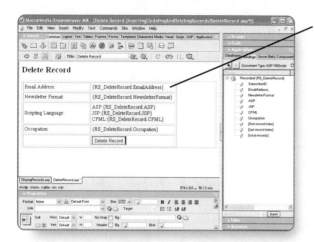

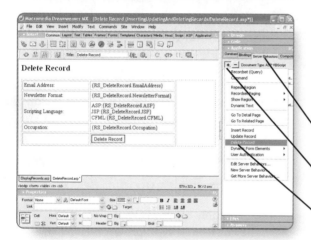

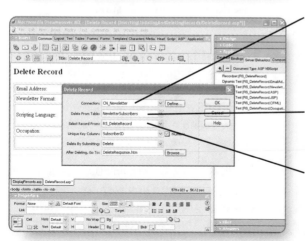

13. Bind the fields retrieved from the database to the Web page. Chapter 8, "Validating and Retrieving Form Data," covers this topic comprehensively. This enables the user to view the record before deciding to delete it.

Using the Delete Record Server Behavior

Using the Delete Record server behavior is slightly more involved than using the Insert Record server behavior. In addition to specifying the database connection and the table where the record should be deleted and matching form objects to table columns, you also need to specify the unique ID number of the record to be deleted. This value is passed to the delete form in the QueryString.

1. Click on the Server Behaviors tab. The Server Behaviors tab is displayed.

2. Click on the + sign. A submenu appears.

3. Click on Delete Record. The Delete Record dialog box opens.

4. Select the connection for the database that needs a Web-based interface to delete data. Creating a connection is covered in Chapter 8, "Validating and Retrieving Form Data."

5. Select the table that will contain the record to be deleted. The table name is selected.

6. Select the recordset that is bound to the delete form if the recordset that Dreamweaver MX has selected is incorrect. This only happens if there is more than one recordset bound to the Web page.

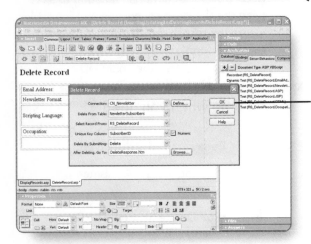

NOTE

The unique record identifier/primary key is automatically selected in the Unique Key Column drop-down list.

7. Select the form that will delete the record when submitted, if the form that Dreamweaver MX has selected is incorrect. This only happens if there is more than one form on your Web page.

8. Type a file name into the After Deleting, Go To field. This file will be displayed after the record has been deleted. Ideally you want to acknowledge that the record has been deleted.

9. Click on OK. The Delete Record dialog box closes.

Testing the Delete Record Server Behavior

You can only test the Delete Record server behavior from a Web browser. Live Data View does not currently support this function.

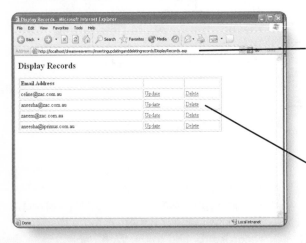

1. Press F12 to preview the search results in the Web page that contains the Delete link. The Web page is displayed in the Web browser. If you are not familiar with saving or previewing a page, please refer to Chapter 2, "Dreamweaver MX Basics."

2. Click on the Delete link that corresponds to a record you wish to delete. The Web page that contains the delete form is displayed. The contents of the record that is about to be deleted is displayed.

16

Writing Your Own ASP Code

Server behaviors are extremely powerful, but you can't use them for every situation. There will come a time when you need to customize the code generated by Dreamweaver MX. This is where a basic knowledge of a server-side scripting language, such as ASP (Active Server Pages), comes in handy. In this chapter, you'll learn how to do the following:

- Insert ASP code in a Web page
- Comment your code
- Use operators, variables, and functions
- Use loops and conditional statements
- Use the Response, Request, and Session objects

Inserting ASP Code into a Web Page

The biggest advantage of using ASP is that server-side scripts are embedded in HTML. This template-based approach is much easier than using CGI (Common Gateway Interface) languages such as Perl, in which the entire HTML file has to be printed line by line to the Web browser. ASP is embedded in a Web page using the <% and %> script delimiters. Anything within these delimiters is processed as server-side script.

Thus far you have only used Dreamweaver MX as a visual tool to create dynamic database-driven Web sites, but Dreamweaver MX is also equipped with a capable script editor. Unlike other visual Web page creation tools, Dreamweaver MX does not interfere with the code you write.

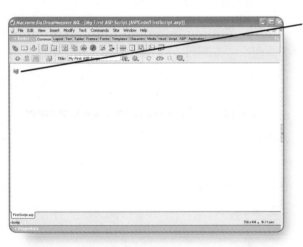

1. Create a new Web page with an .asp extension. The ASP code placed in a file with an .htm extension will be displayed as text in a Web browser. The ASP engine only interprets files that contain the .asp extension.

2. Click on the Show Code View icon. The source code of the Web page is displayed.

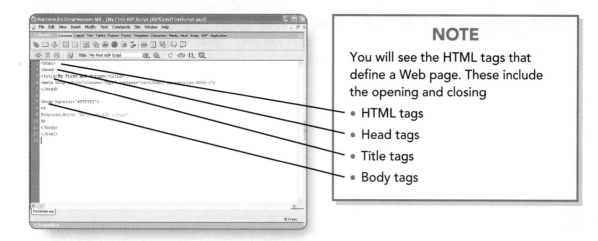

NOTE

You will see the HTML tags that define a Web page. These include the opening and closing

- HTML tags
- Head tags
- Title tags
- Body tags

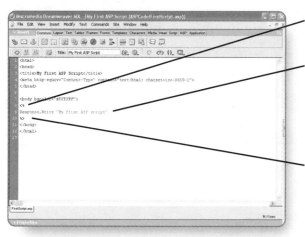

3. Type <%, the opening script delimiter, after the <body> tag.

4. Type your ASP code. If you have never written code before, just follow the example in the illustration. As the chapter progresses, you will learn to write your own code.

5. Type %>, the closing script delimiter.

6. Click on the Show Design View icon. The Web page is displayed.

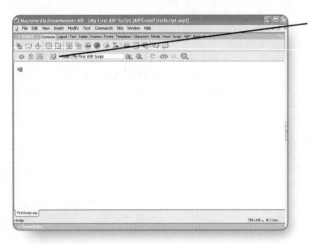

7. Click on the Live Data View icon. The result of the ASP script is displayed.

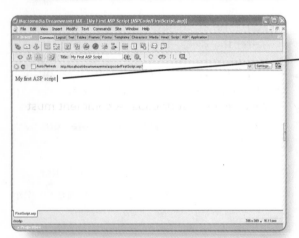

NOTE

You can preview the results of your scripts in Live Data View. This saves you from having to launch a Web browser each time you need to test your code.

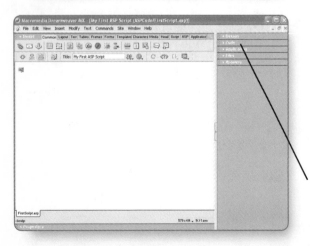

Displaying the ASP Reference

Dreamweaver MX comes with references for CSS (Cascading Style Sheets), HTML, and JavaScript. The ASP reference is very comprehensive and will help you with ASP syntax.

1. Expand the Code panel.

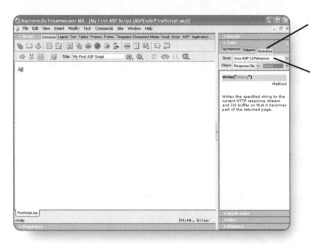

2. Click on the Reference tab. The Reference tab is displayed.

3. Select the reference you would like to view. The tag drop-down list is populated accordingly.

Commenting Your Code

Comments are used as a form of communication between yourself and other programmers who will maintain your code at a later time. As a general rule, comments should explain what may not be obvious in your code. A comment must be placed within the script delimiters and preceded by an apostrophe ('). An apostrophe can only be used to create a single comment line.

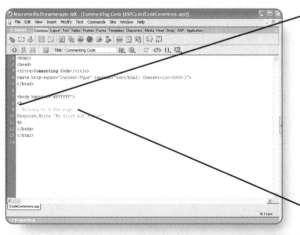

1. Type an apostrophe within the <% and %> script delimiters. The text you enter after the apostrophe will be a comment.

CAUTION

Text included outside the script delimiters is displayed when the Web page is viewed.

2. Type in the comment after the apostrophe.

Declaring Variables

Variables are used to store data so that it can be processed and updated at a later stage. You should always give your variables meaningful names. The variable name should define the type of information that is being stored. This makes your code more readable.

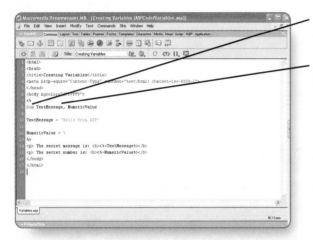

1. Use the `Dim` keyword to declare variables.

2. Type in the variable name after the `Dim` keyword.

NOTE

A string must be enclosed in quotation marks. This is not necessary for numeric values.

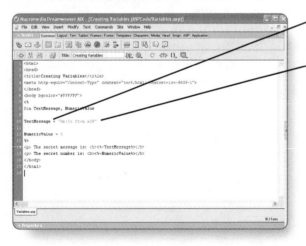

3. Use the = sign to set the value of a variable.

4. Type the value of the variable after the = sign.

NOTE

You can declare more than one variable at a time by separating the variable names with a comma.

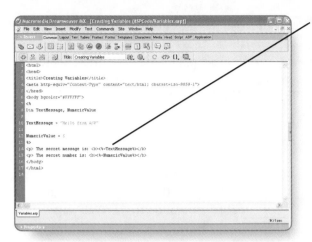

5. Type the name of a variable within the <%= and %> delimiters. The value stored in the variable will be printed to the Web page when the script is executed.

NOTE

The <%= and %> script delimiters are used to print the contents of a variable.

Using Mathematical Operators

Mathematical operators enable you to perform addition, subtraction, multiplication, and division (see Table 16.1).

Table 16.1 Mathematical Operators

Operator	Description
+	Adds two numbers
-	Subtracts one number from another
*	Multiplies two numbers together
/	Divides one number by another
mod	Returns the remainder after dividing two numbers

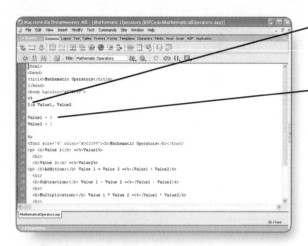

1. Use the Dim keyword to declare variables. These variables are used to perform simple mathematic operations.

2. Use the = sign to assign values to the variables.

NOTE

The <%= and %> script delimiters are used to print the result of the mathematical operation to the Web page.

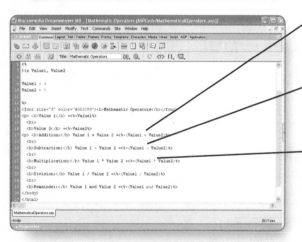

3. Type + between the variables that you want to add. The result is displayed when the Web page is previewed.

4. Type - between the variables that you want to subtract. The result is displayed when the Web page is previewed.

5. Type * between the variables that you want to multiply. The result is displayed when the Web page is previewed.

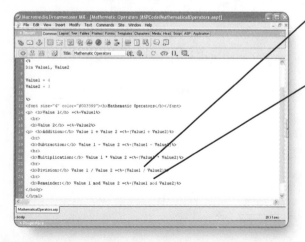

6. Type / between the variables that you want to divide. The result is displayed when the Web page is previewed.

7. Type mod between the variables that you want to divide and only return the remainder. The result is displayed when the Web page is previewed.

Using Comparison Operators

A comparison operator compares the value in one element with the value of another (see Table 16.2). Comparison operators can be used to compare both strings and numeric data. You can test whether values are equal, not equal, greater, or less than each other.

Table 16.2 Comparison Operators

Operator	Name	Description
=	equal	Returns TRUE if the variables are equal.
<>	not equal	Returns TRUE if the variables are not equal.
>	greater than	Returns TRUE if the variable on the left is greater.
>=	greater than or equal to	Returns TRUE if the variable on the left is greater than or equal to the value on the right.
<	less than	Returns TRUE if the variable on the left is less than the value on the right.
<=	less than or equal to	Returns TRUE if the variable on the left is less than or equal to the value on the right.

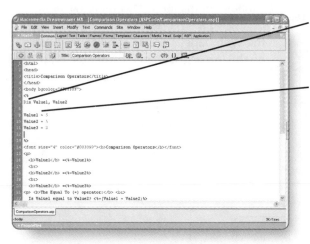

1. Use the Dim keyword to declare variables. These variables are used to illustrate the use of comparison operators.

2. Use the = sign to assign values to the variables.

NOTE

The <%= and %> script delimiters will be used to print the result returned from the comparison expression to the Web page.

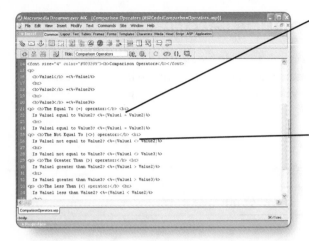

3. Type = between the variables that you want to compare. This will test whether the variables contain numeric data that is equal. The result will be displayed when the Web page is previewed. If both variables are equal, the expression returns TRUE.

4. Type <> between the variables that you want to compare. This tests whether the variables contain numeric data that is not equal. The results are displayed when the Web page is previewed. If the variables are not equal to each other, the expression returns TRUE.

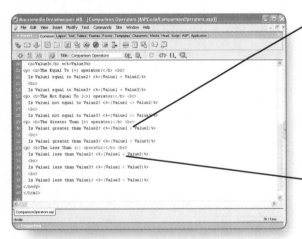

5. Type > between the variables that you want to compare. This tests whether the variable on the left is greater than the variable on the right. The result is displayed when the Web page is previewed. If the variable on the left is greater than the variable on the right, the expression returns TRUE.

6. Type < between the variables that you want to compare. This tests whether the variable on the left is less than the variable on the right. The result is displayed when the Web page is previewed. If the variable on the left is less than the variable on the right, the expression returns TRUE.

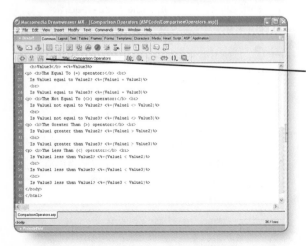

7. Click on the Show Design View icon. The Web page is displayed.

Using Logical Operators

Logical operators are useful when working with expressions that need to return logical values (see Table 16.3). These expressions mainly use comparison operators.

Table 16.3 Logical Operators

Operator	Description
AND	Returns TRUE when both expressions are true
OR	Returns TRUE if either expression is true

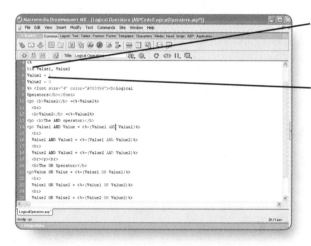

1. Use the Dim keyword to declare variables. These variables are used to illustrate the use of logical operators.

2. Use the = sign to assign values to the variables. Logical operators can only be performed on Boolean data such as 1/0 and true/false.

NOTE

The <%= and %> script delimiters are used to print the result returned from the comparison expression to the Web page.

3. Type AND between the variables. If both variables contain a true value (i.e., a value equal to 1), the expression returns TRUE. If either variable contains a false value (a value equal to 0), the expression returns FALSE. The result is displayed when the Web page is previewed.

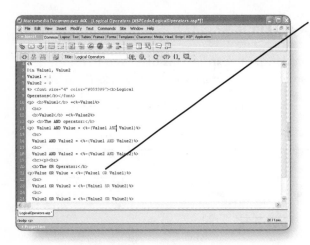

4. Type OR between the variables. As long as one variable contains a true value (a value equal to 1), the expression returns FALSE. The result is displayed when the Web page is previewed.

Using Conditional Statements

Conditional statements are used to execute code that should only be run if certain conditions are met. They enable you to make decisions.

Using the If...Then...Else Statement

The code within the If...Then block is executed only if the logical expression returns a True value. Include an Else clause if you want to execute code when a logical expression returns a False value.

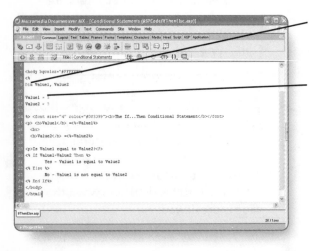

1. Use the Dim keyword to declare variables. These variables are compared within an expression.

2. Use the = sign to assign values to the variables.

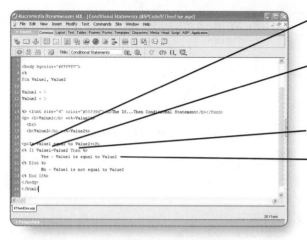

3. Type `If` within the `<%` and `%>` script delimiters.

4. Type the expression that must return a `TRUE` value for the content within the `If` statement to be displayed.

5. Type `Then` after the expression.

6. Type the content you want to display if the expression returns a `TRUE` value.

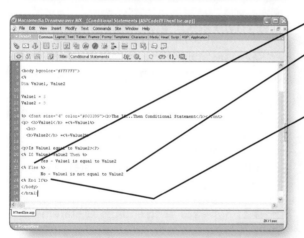

7. Type `Else` after the content.

8. Type the content you would like to display if the expression returns a `FALSE` value.

9. Type `End If` to end the `If` statement.

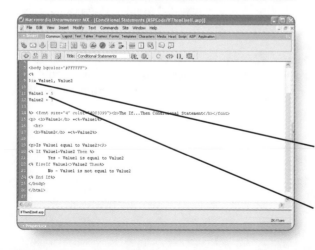

Using the `If...Then... ElseIf` Statement

The `ElseIf` statement enables you to test multiple expressions and execute the appropriate code for each condition.

1. Use the `Dim` keyword to declare variables. These variables are compared within an expression.

2. Use the `=` sign to assign values to the variables.

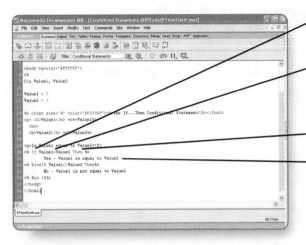

3. Type `If` within the <% and %> script delimiters.

4. Type the expression that must return a `TRUE` value for the content within the `If` statement to be displayed.

5. Type `Then` after the expression.

6. Type the content you want to display if the expression returns a `TRUE` value.

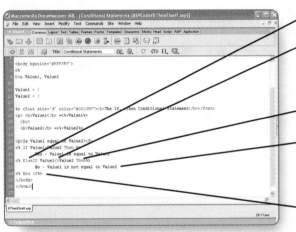

7. Type `ElseIf` after the content.

8. Type the expression that must return a `TRUE` value for the content within the `ElseIf` statement to be displayed.

9. Type `Then` after the expression.

10. Type the content you want to display if the expression in the `ElseIf` statement returns a `TRUE` value.

11. Type `End If` to end the `If` statement.

Using Loops

Each line of code that you write will only be executed once. Loops come in handy when you need to repeat a few lines of code until a condition is met. The `For` loop is very flexible and simple to use.

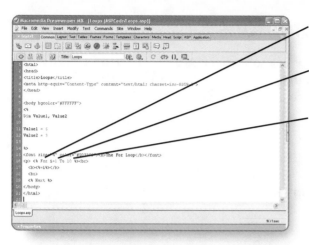

1. Type **For** within the <% and %> script delimiters.

2. Set the initial value of the counter variable.

3. Type **To** after setting the counter variable.

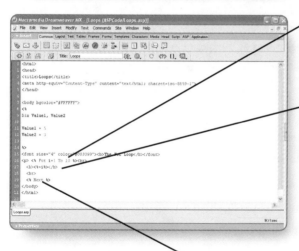

4. Type the amount of times you would like to repeat the loop. This sets the value the counter can reach before the loop finishes.

5. Type the HTML or ASP code that must be executed.

NOTE

While you're learning to use a loop, print the counter variable to the Web page. Each time the code within the loop is executed the counter will be incremented.

6. Type **Next** after the code that needs to be repeated. Any code after **Next** will not be included in the loop.

Using `String` Functions

`String` functions provide a means for you to manipulate data retrieved from a form or database. You can concatenate, search, replace, and compare strings. The following table contains a brief summary of the available `String` functions.

Table 16.4 `String` Functions

Function	Description
Concatenation	
&	Joins strings together
Removing Leading and Trailing Spaces	
LTrim(string)	Removes spaces at the beginning of the string
RTrim(string)	Removes spaces at the end of the string
Trim(string)	Removes both leading and trailing spaces
Changing the String Case	
UCase(string)	Converts the string to uppercase
LCase(string)	Converts the string to lowercase
Search Strings	
InStr(stringA,stringB)	Searches for stringB within stringA
Replace Text in a String	
Replace(stringA, stringB,stringC)	If stringB is found in stringA, replace it with stringC.

Using Built-In ASP Objects

ASP includes a number of objects that aid Web development. These objects include the Response, Request, and Session objects. In simple terms, an object is made up of numerous methods and properties. A method defines a specific function that the object can perform. Object properties can either be set or read from a script.

Using the **Response** Object

The Response object is used to send output to a Web browser. The Response object is used to write text, HTML code, and variables to a Web page.

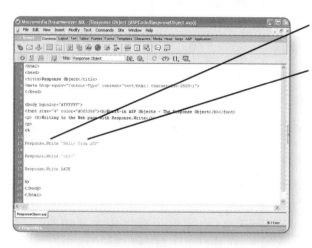

1. Type Response.Write within the <% and %> script delimiters.

2. Pass the string that needs to be printed to the Response.Write method. A string needs to be enclosed in quotation marks. The string is printed to the Web page when it is previewed.

NOTE

You can also use the Response.Write method to print

- HTML code that can be rendered by a Web browser.
- The result of a function or subroutine.

Using the **Request** Object

The Request object is used to retrieve all the data that the browser has sent to the Web server. This includes information sent using either the GET or POST method of a form. The Request object is also used to retrieve Server/Environmental variables. In Chapter 8, " Validating and Retrieving Form Data," you learned how to use the Request Variable Data Source from the Bindings tab. The Request Variable Data Source enabled you to retrieve this information and bind it to a Web page. This section shows you how to use the ASP code.

1. Type `Request.Form()` within the `<%=` and `%>` script delimiters. This prints the value retrieved from the form to the Web page. The `Request.Form()` method is used to retrieve data sent using the POST method.

NOTE

You can also assign the value retrieved from the `Request.Form` method to a variable, which you then could process. For example, you could store the contents of a form to a text file, send it as an e-mail message, or insert it into a database.

---

2. Pass the name of the form object to the `Request.Form` method. The name of the form object must be placed in quotation marks.

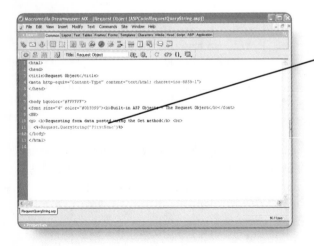

NOTE

You can retrieve data sent using the GET method by passing the form object name to the `Request.QueryString` method.

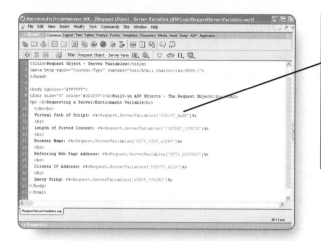

NOTE

You can retrieve Server/Environment variables using the `Request.ServerVariables` method. For a list of `Server` variables, please refer to Chapter 8, "Validating and Retrieving Form Data."

Using the `Session` Object

The `Session` object allows data to be stored in variables that can be accessed by other pages in your Web site. These variables are only stored while a user is visiting your Web site and will expire when they leave. Sessions provide an easy solution to maintaining state across your Web site.

You need to identify users and track their activities when creating complex Web applications. Unfortunately HTTP (HyperText Transfer Protocol) does not store any information between page requests because it is a stateless protocol. This certainly presents a challenge because without a permanent connection between the server and browser you won't be able to create shopping carts, authenticate users, and personalize content. Sessions provide a practical solution for sharing the information entered by a user across multiple pages in your Web site.

A session starts when a user enters your Web site and ends when a user leaves. Sessions can only be used to store information while a user is visiting your Web site. Sessions are much simpler to implement because you don't need to specify an expiration date. They rely on cookies, but this is taken care of in the background. When a session begins, a unique session ID is generated and stored as a cookie. All `Session` variables are actually stored on the Web server. This is very secure because no information is stored as a cookie. `Session` variables are specific to a particular user and can't be shared with other users.

Creating `Session` Variables

The `Session` object is used to create a new `Session` variables and assign an initial value. Each `Session` variable that you store must be given a unique name. When a user leaves the Web site or has not requested a page from the Web server in 20 minutes the session expires. When a session expires, all the `Session` variables associated with the inactive user are deleted.

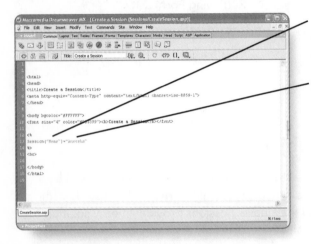

1. Pass the name of the `Session` variable to the `Session` object. This creates a `Session` variable with the specified name.

2. Set the value of the `Session` variable.

Reading `Session` Variables

The `Session` object is used to retrieve the value stored in a `Session` variable. You must know the name of the `Session` variable. You also can retrieve the unique session ID that is stored for each user. Sessions provide a simple way for variables to be shared across multiple Web pages.

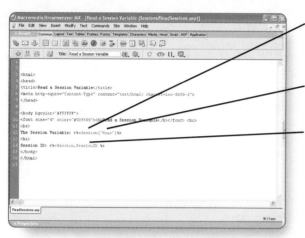

1. Type `Session` between the `<%=` and the `%>` delimiters. This writes the value stored in the `Session` variable to the Web page.

2. Pass the `Session` variable name to the `Session` object.

3. Type `Session.SessionID` between the `<%=` and the `%>` delimiters. This retrieves the unique session ID for the current user.

TIP

You can also use the Request Session Data Source from the Bindings tab to retrieve a `Session` variable and bind the value to a Web page.

Terminating a Session

A session is automatically terminated if no page requests have been made for 20 minutes. You can easily extend this period by setting the timeout property of the `Session` object.

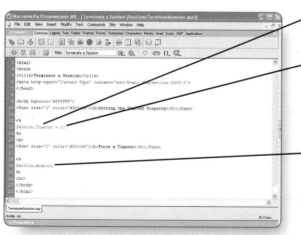

1. Type `Session.Timeout` between the `<%` and `%>` delimiters.

2. Assign the maximum amount of time in minutes that a session can remain inactive.

TIP

You can force a session to end by calling the `Abandon` method of the `Session` object.

17

Introducing ASP.NET

ASP.NET is not just an upgrade to ASP! In many respects, it is brand new technology developed to simplify the design and development of database-driven Web sites. ASP.NET delivers improved performance and scalability. It also changes the way Web applications are programmed by letting you process client-side events on the server. In this chapter, you'll learn how to do the following:

- Convert classic ASP applications to ASP.NET
- Use HTML server controls
- Create Web Forms in Dreamweaver MX

Building Your First ASP.NET Application

Microsoft designed ASP.NET to address numerous problems associated with Web development. ASP.NET changes the programming model for developing dynamic Web applications. ASP.NET has the following advantages over classic ASP:

- Programming logic is separated from page layout. This is particularly important when both programmers and designers need to work on the same file.

- ASP.NET has an enhanced feature set. You no longer need third-party components to send e-mail or upload files to a server. You can also validate data entry and cache page output with ease. This sort of in-built functionality is not available in classic ASP or traditional server-side scripting languages such as CGI (Common Gateway Interface) scripts written in Perl.

- Server-side code is compiled the first time a page is requested. All other requests are much faster because they are served from the cached version of the compiled code. The cached copy is deleted when the code gets updated.

- ASP.NET is not programmed with scripting languages. You can use compiled languages such as VB.NET, JScript.NET, and C#. While you are restricted to using one language per page, elements of your application can be programmed in different languages. Dreamweaver MX can generate either VB.NET or C# code depending on the server model that you choose. JScript.NET is not supported.

- ASP.NET applications can target multiple browsers as well as mobile devices.

- Server-side code can respond to events that occur in a Web browser. This eliminates the need to write client-side code in JavaScript. With ASP.NET, you can concentrate on the logic and not the information transfer between the browser and server.

The best way to understand and appreciate ASP.NET is to actually evaluate a simple page coded in classic ASP, and then look at how easy it is to build the same page in ASP.NET. The example that follows highlights the difficulties associated with building dynamic applications and provides a theoretical platform for the introduction to ASP.NET.

The example includes a form with a text box, drop-down list, and Submit button. The user must enter her name and favorite programming language, and then click on the Submit button to transfer the data to the server. Once the data is received by the server, the data entered by the user appears on the page. The form fields also retain the data previously entered by the user.

1. You must put ASP code between <% and %> delimiters. The code is VBScript, which is a scripting language. VBScript does not get compiled.

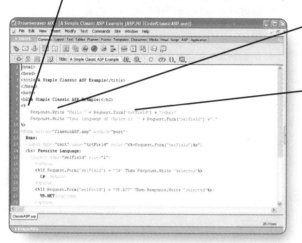

2. The `Response.Write` method prints data to the page. You use it to display the data entered by the user.

3. The `Request.Form` method retrieves the data entered into a form field. You must pass the name of the form field as a parameter to the `Request.Form` method. The data entered into the text box and the drop-down list is printed to the page with the `Response.Write` method.

4. The form includes an action attribute that posts the data entered back to the same page.

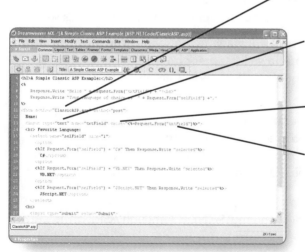

5. You use the `<input>` tag to insert a text box. The type attribute must be set to text.

6. The `value` attribute displays data in the text box.

7. The `Request.Form` method retrieves the data the user entered into a text box. The text box retains its state.

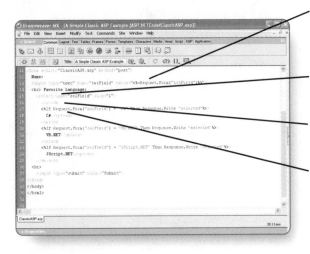

8. The <%= and %> delimiters print data to the page. This tag in effect replaces the Response.Write method.

9. You use the <select> tag to insert a drop-down list.

10. The <option> tags define the items in the drop-down list.

11. Retaining state in a drop-down list involves some programming. You must insert code in each option tag to decide which option is selected when the page reloads.

In general, you can spot the following shortcomings:

- ASP code is mixed with HTML. This mixture is hard to trace and does not let you easily change the layout without making some adjustments in the code as well.

- No state is retained when round trips are made to the server. You must manually program this aspect. Getting drop-down lists, check boxes, and radio buttons to remember their original value requires a lot of code. Can you imagine writing code to retain state on a larger form?

- The client (browser) and the server use different programming models. ASP renders HTML, which is displayed in a browser. The user enters data that is submitted back to the server for processing. You cannot respond to events that occur within the browser. You must use the Request.Form method to retrieve the posted form data.

Now for the exciting part—the conversion to ASP.NET. Although ASP.NET is different, it is not difficult.

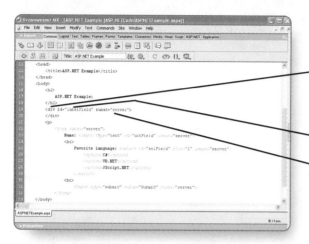

1. Change the file extension to .aspx. All ASP.NET pages must use this extension.

2. Insert opening and closing <div> tags. You use this tag to display the data entered by the user.

3. The <div> tag must have a unique ID.

4. You must place a runat attribute set to server within the opening <div> tag. The runat="server" means that server-side code can access the tag properties.

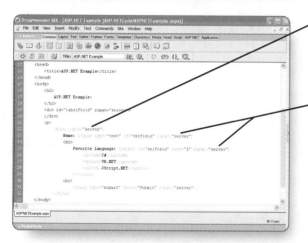

5. The <form> tag does not require action and method attributes any more. You just need to include runat="server" in the opening <form> tag.

6. Insert the runat="server" attribute in all form fields.

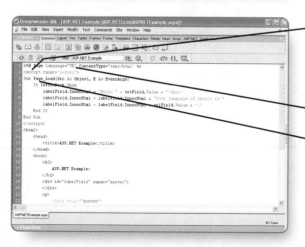

7. Insert opening and closing <script> tags. You must place all methods within these tags. This is known as a script declaration block.

8. Set the language attribute to VB.

9. Insert a Page_Load method. You place the void keyword in front of the method name because the method does not return any data. The Page_Load event occurs when ASP.NET loads the page.

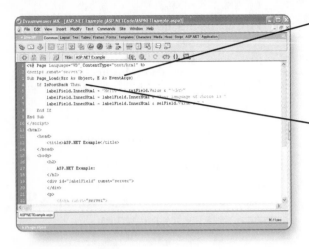

10. The `Page_Load` method takes two parameters. The first parameter, which must be type `Object`, contains the object that fired the event. The second parameter contains data associated with the object.

11. You don't want to execute the code within the `Page_Load` method unless the form is posted. The `IsPostBack` property returns `TRUE` if the form has been submitted back to the server.

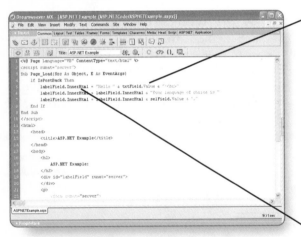

12. You can now access the data entered by typing the ID of the form element followed by a period and the name of the property that holds the data (value).

NOTE

You can use the same dot notation to change the data that is displayed in a form element.

13. The `<div>` tag has `label1` as its ID. A `<div>` tag has an `InnerHtml` property that contains the text and HTML formatting of the data displayed. You will assign some text that indicates what the user entered. When a page is displayed, the text will appear where the `<div>` tag is located on the page.

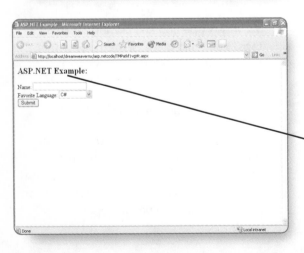

14. Preview the page in a Web browser. The form appears.

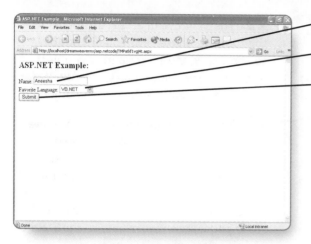

15. Enter your name.

16. Select your favorite language.

17. Click on the Submit button. The form data is sent to the server.

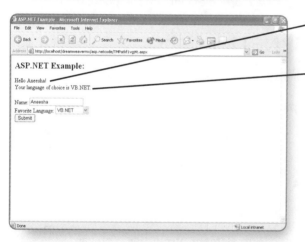

18. The data you entered appears in a sentence.

19. The form elements automatically retain their state during round trips to the server.

By looking at the source code that ASP.NET generated, you can get a better understanding of what it is doing behind the scenes.

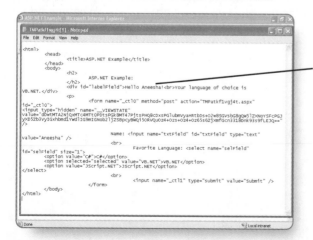

20. View the source code of the page that is generated.

21. The text appears within the <div> tags.

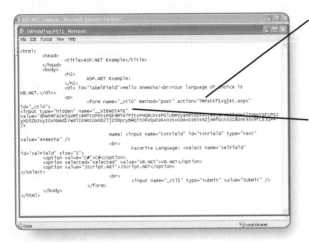

22. The method and action attributes for the form were inserted. You did not have to hand-code the action and method attributes. This allows you to change the file name without breaking the code.

23. You see a hidden form variable called _VIEWSTATE. This hidden form variable gets inserted by ASP.NET whenever a page is posted back to itself. The data it contains might look cryptic, but this is how ASP.NET stores data across multiple requests to the same page. VIEWSTATE maintains the state of all form elements on the page.

Converting ASP to ASP.NET

Migrating from ASP to ASP.NET is a simple five-step process.

1. Change the file extension to .aspx.

2. Insert a runat=server attribute in all form elements that you want to access from ASP.NET code.

3. Place methods in a special script block.

4. Set the language attribute on the script tag to VB.

5. Use dot notation to set and retrieve form element properties. You can manipulate any HTML tag that includes the runat="server" attribute from server-side code. You can dynamically set or retrieve these properties.

Working with the Dreamweaver MX ASP.NET Objects

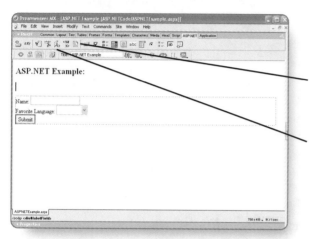

Dreamweaver MX includes a set of ASP.NET objects that will help you implement common ASP.NET functionality.

- The `Page_Load` object will insert the `Page_Load` method and server-side script tags.

- The `Runat_Server` object will insert the `runat="server"` attribute into the currently selected tag.

Using HTML Server Controls

In ASP.NET, code on the server can access any HTML element, provided that the element contains the `runat="server"` attribute. All HTML tag attributes become properties that can be accessed through dot notation.

You use the `<img>` tag to insert an image:

```
<img src="img1.gif">
```

You use the `src` attribute to specify the image that must be displayed. To convert this tag to an HTML server control, you give it a unique ID and insert the `runat="server"` attribute:

```
<img src="img1.gif" id="imgBannner" runat="server"/>
```

You must place the / before the closing > of the tag. You must use this notation when there is no matching closing tag.

You can now access the `src` attribute as a property on the server. From the server-side code, you can learn the name of the image as well as change the image displayed:

```
imgBannner.Src = "newimg.gif";
```

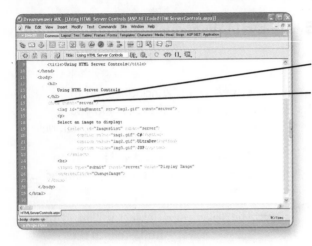

The code that follows uses a VB method to change the image that is displayed:

1. Insert opening and closing `<form>` tags.

2. Set the `runat` attribute to `server`.

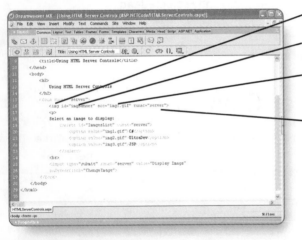

3. Insert an `<img>` tag.

4. Set the ID.

5. Assign an image to the `src` attribute. This image will initially be displayed.

6. Set the `runat` attribute to `server`.

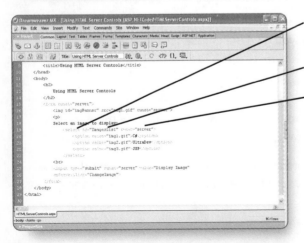

7. Insert opening and closing `<select>` tags.

8. Set the ID.

9. Set the `runat` attribute to `server`.

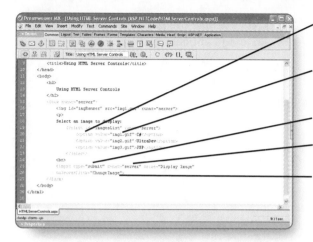

10. Insert opening and closing <option> tags for each image the user can select.

11. Set the value attribute to the image file name.

12. Insert a Submit button.

13. Set the runat attribute to server.

14. Set the onServerClick event to ChangeImage. The ChangeImage method executes on the server when the user clicks on the button.

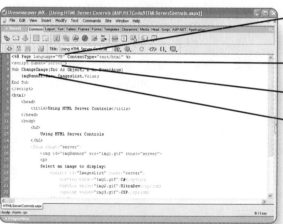

15. Insert opening and closing <script> tags.

16. Set the language attribute to VB.

17. Set the runat attribute to server.

18. Insert a void method named ChangeImage. A void method does not return a value.

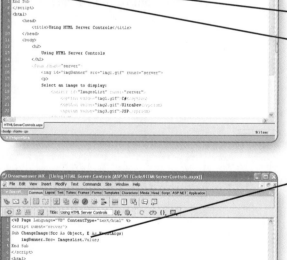

19. Assign the Value property of the drop-down list to the Src property of the image. This will replace the image that is currently displayed.

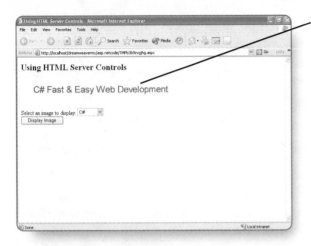

20. Preview the page in a Web browser. An image appears.

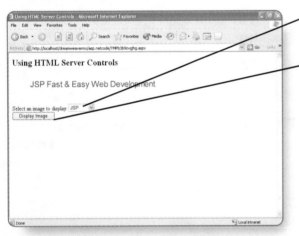

21. Select an image from the drop-down list. The option is selected.

22. Click on the Display Image button. Your selection is sent to the server.

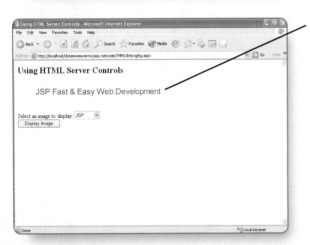

23. The selected image appears.

Creating Web Forms in Dreamweaver MX

Although HTML server controls introduced an innovative event-driven model for developing ASP.NET applications, the syntax used to access properties was not consistent across all controls. This was mainly due to the fact that HTML server controls mapped directly to their HTML counterpart tags. HTML tags don't exactly use a standard notation to describe their attributes. Web server controls address these issues. They provide a common set of properties that you can manipulate via C# code that reside on the server.

Dreamweaver MX enables you to build ASP.NET Web Forms in a visual and intuitive manner. The following ASP.NET WebForm server controls are available as objects:

- asp:button
- asp:checkbox
- asp:checkboxlist
- asp:dropdownlist
- asp:imagebutton

- asp:label
- asp:listbox
- asp:radiobutton
- asp:radiobuttonlist
- asp:textbox

You will now create a simple Web Form that uses the TextBox, Label, and Button server controls.

The TextBox control encompasses the two HTML free-form text-entry fields: the single-line input field and the multiline input field. The mode attribute allows you to specify whether a text box, multiline text box, or password entry field is displayed. The Text property retrieves the data that has been entered:

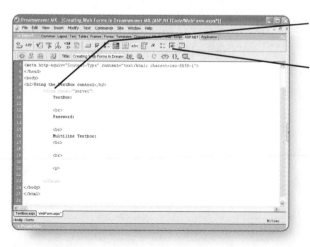

1. Insert opening and closing <form> tags. Set the runat attribute to server.

2. Click on the asp:textbox object. The Tag Editor dialog box opens.

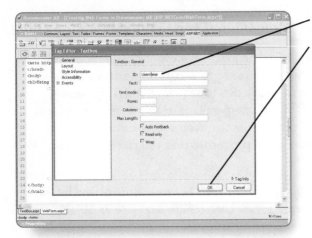

3. Set the ID.

4. Click on OK. The TextBox server control is inserted.

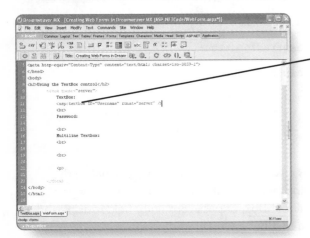

NOTE

The asp: prefix is placed in front of the control name.

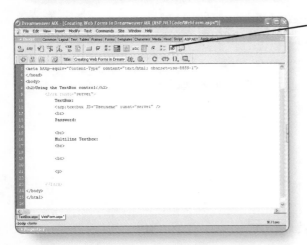

5. Click on the asp:textbox object. The Tag Editor dialog box opens.

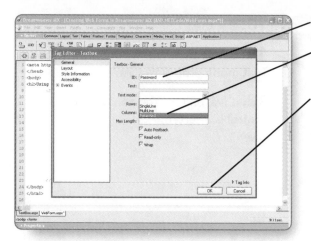

6. Set the ID.

7. Select the Password option from the Text mode drop-down list.

8. Click on OK. The TextBox server control is inserted.

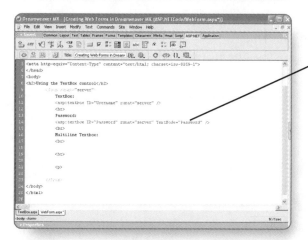

NOTE

The TextMode attribute is set to Password.

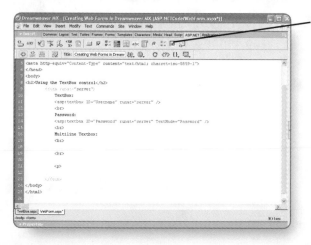

9. Click on the asp:textbox object. The Tag Editor dialog box opens.

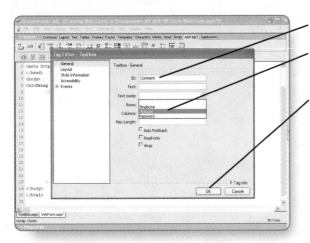

10. Set the ID.

11. Select the Multiline option from the Text mode drop-down list.

12. Click on OK. The TextBox server control is inserted.

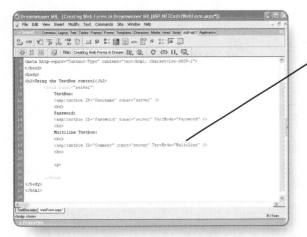

NOTE

The TextMode attribute is set to MultiLine.

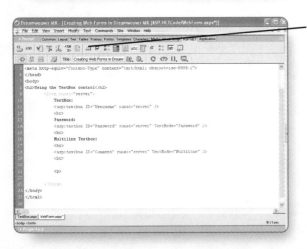

13. Click on the asp:button object. The Tag Editor dialog box opens.

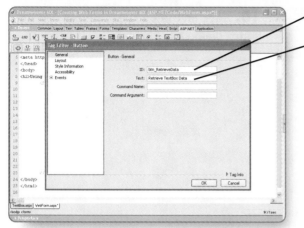

14. Set the ID.

15. Set the Text attribute. This text will appear as a label on the button.

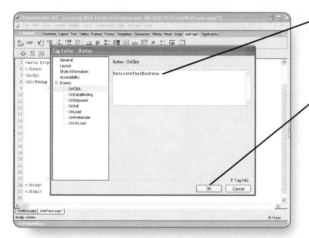

16. Set the OnClick event to RetrieveTextBoxData. When the user clicks on the button, the RetrieveTextBoxData method will execute.

17. Click on OK. The Button server control will be inserted.

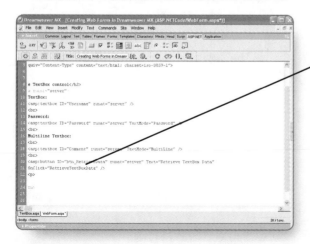

NOTE

The OnClick event is set to RetrieveTextBoxData.

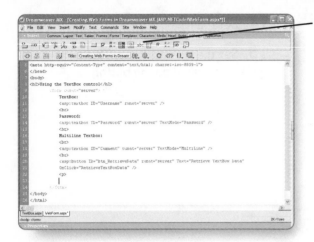

18. Click on the asp:label object. The Tag Editor dialog box opens.

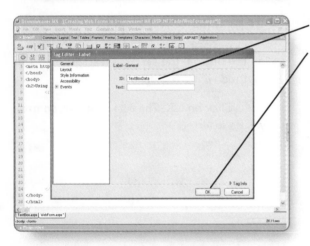

19. Set the ID.

20. Click on OK.

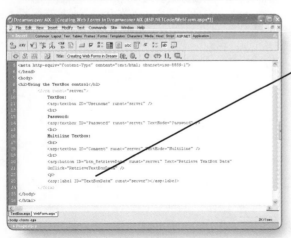

NOTE

The Label server control is inserted.

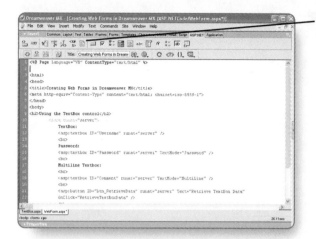

21. Click on the `asp:Page_Load` object. Opening and closing `<script>` tags are inserted.

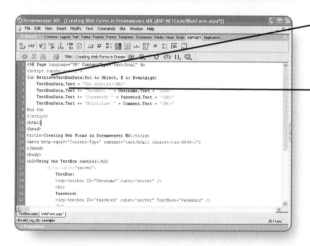

22. Insert a `RetrieveTextBoxData` method. The `RetrieveTextBoxData` method will execute when the user clicks on the button.

23. Assign data retrieved from the `TextBox` controls to the `Text` property of the `Label` control.

18

Writing Code to Enhance Your Web Site

Not all Web pages need to be linked to a database to be dynamic. You can use code to generate dynamic content as well. If used effectively, you can provide your site visitors with an interesting and interactive experience. In this chapter, you'll learn how to write ASP.NET code that does the following:

- Counts down to a date
- Randomizes the content on a Web page
- Redirects a user to another Web page
- Sends e-mail
- Uploads files
- Creates and appends data to a text file

Creating a Countdown

If you have ever wanted to count down to an important event such as the release of a new product or the New Year, you'll be amazed at how easy it is to do so using the `dateDiff` function.

NOTE

In this chapter, all of the examples are programmed for ASP.NET. VB.NET was chosen as the programming language because it was introduced in Chapter 17, "Introducing ASP.NET." Fully documented examples in C#, ASP, PHP, CFML and JSP can be downloaded from http://www.premierpressbooks.com/downloads.

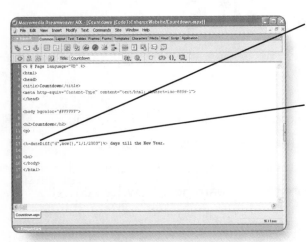

1. Type the `dateDiff` function between the `<%=` and the `%>` delimiters. Inserting the `dateDiff` function between these delimiters writes the result to the Web page.

2. Type `d` as the first parameter passed to the `dateDiff` function. This sets the countdown to be calculated in days.

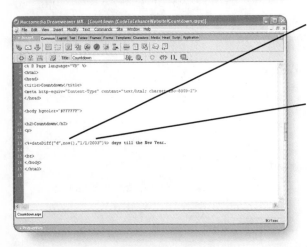

3. Type `now()` as the second parameter passed to the `dateDiff` function. The `now()` functions returns the current date, from where the countdown should be calculated.

4. Type the date that corresponds to the event that you are counting down to.

Displaying Random Content

Randomized content can provide your visitors with a unique experience each time they visit your Web site. You can display random messages or images.

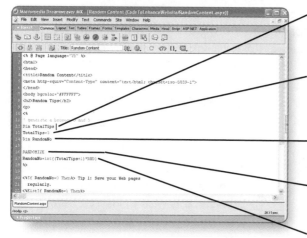

1. Create a variable that will be used to store the total number of items that you can randomly select.

2. Assign a numeric value to the variable that was created to store the number of random items available.

3. Create a variable that will be used to store the random number.

4. Call the RANDOMIZE function. This function re-seeds the random generator.

5. Multiply the variable that stores the number of items available by RND. RND is the random number returned by VB.NET. The result should be converted to an integer using the Int function and stored in a variable. Add a value of 1 to the random number to round it off to the nearest integer.

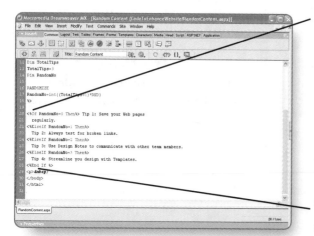

6. Use an If...Then...ElseIf statement to determine which random item should be displayed.

● Within the If and ElseIf statements, you need to test if the random number matches the item to be displayed.

● The random content could be text or an image. You may even include both as random content.

7. Close the If statement with an End If statement.

Redirecting

The `Redirect` method of the `Response` object enables you to redirect a user to a new Web page. You're probably wondering why you may ever need to use this functionality. It is handy when you restructure your Web site and don't want users who have bookmarked a page to get an error message. Rather than deleting the old page, redirect the user to the new page. Older browsers (below IE 4) don't handle redirecting very well, so you should always place a link to the new Web page as well.

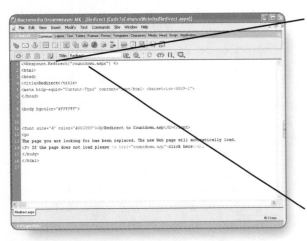

1. Type `Response.Redirect` within the `<%` and `%>` delimiters.

NOTE

The `Redirect` code must be inserted before any text is output to the browser. It is wise to insert it before the opening `<html>` tag.

2. Pass the name of the redirect Web page. Users are redirected to this page if they visit the current Web page.

3. Include a link to the redirect page because some old Web browsers don't support server side redirects.

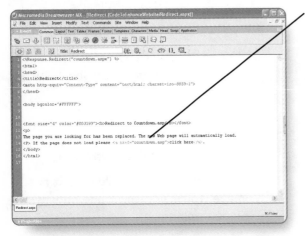

NOTE

You will receive an error message if you test a redirect in Live Data Mode. You must test the redirect within a Web browser.

Sending E-mail Messages

Enabling users to provide feedback is an important feature that all Web sites should have. In the past, this has usually been achieved with a `mailto` link, but that requires the user to have his or her browser correctly configured to send a message. Sending messages from a server is a much more reliable solution and is not as difficult as you might think. IIS (Internet Information Server) already has all the functionality required to easily send e-mail from a Web server. You can send messages in plain or HTML format and with or without attachments.

The `SmtpMail` object, which is located in the `System.Web.Mail` namespace, incorporates all the functionality required to send e-mail messages from an ASP.NET application. The `System.Web.Mail` namespace also contains other objects that enable you to model, encode, and format an e-mail message before it is actually sent via the Simple Mail Transfer Protocol (SMTP). Table 18.1 lists the classes contained in the `System.Web.Mail` namespace.

Table 18.1   The `System.Web.Mail` Namespace

Object	Purpose
SmtpMail	Models the messaging system
MailMessage	Models the structure of an e-mail message (To, From, Subject, and Body)
MailFormat	Sets the content type of the message to either text or HTML
MailPriority_enum	Sets the message priority. It can be high, low, or normal.
MailAttachment	Attaches a list of files to an e-mail message
MailEncoding	Encodes e-mail messages that have binary file attachments, such as images, sound files, and Word documents. Encoding methods include MIME, BinHex, and UUEncode.

Table 18.2   Using the `MailMessage` Object to Model a Message

Property	Description
To	The e-mail address of the receiver
From	The e-mail address of the sender
Subject	The subject of the message
Body	The body of the message
Cc	Additional recipients of the message that can be viewed by the main recipient
Bcc	Additional recipients of the message that can't be viewed by the main recipient
Priority	The priority of the message (high, low, or normal)
BodyEncoding	The encoding of the body message and file attachments
BodyFormat	Format of the message (HTML or text)
Attachments	A list of `MailAttachment` objects that represent files that must be attached to the e-mail message

This section provides a line-by-line explanation of the ASP.NET code used for sending an e-mail message. Use the sample code as a template. You only need to change the address, subject, and message properties of the `MailMessage` object and then call the `Send` method of the `SmtpMail` object to post the message (see Table 18.2).

NOTE

Before you can send e-mail, your server must have the SMTP (Simple Mail Transport Protocol) service installed. You should consult your server administrator.

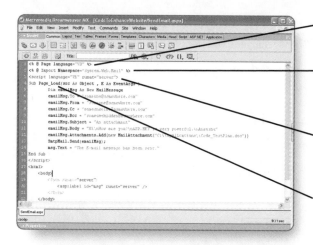

1. Use the Page directive to set the language to VB.

2. Import the System.Web.Mail namespace. This namespace includes the classes used to send e-mail.

3. Insert opening and closing <script> tags. Set the language attribute to VB and the runat attribute to server.

4. Insert a Page_Load method. This method sends the e-mail message after the page has loaded.

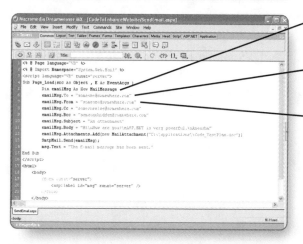

5. Create an instance of the MailMessage object.

6. Assign the recipient's e-mail address to the To property.

7. Assign the sender's e-mail address to the From property.

TIP

You can send the same message to multiple recipients by separating the e-mail address of each recipient with a semicolon (as in "email1@xyz.com; email2@xyz.com; email3@xyz.com").

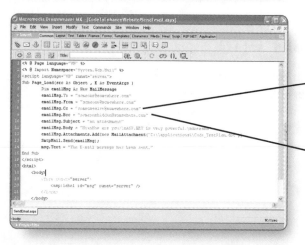

8. Assign additional recipients that the main recipient can view to the Cc property.

9. Assign additional recipients that the main recipient can't view to the Bcc property.

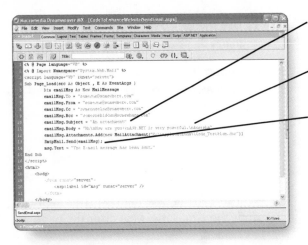

10. Assign the message subject to the Subject property.

11. Assign the message body to the Body property.

12. Pass the instance of the MailMessage object to the Send method of the SmtpMail object. Calling the Send method posts the e-mail.

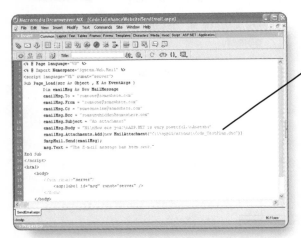

NOTE

Sometimes you may need to send e-mail and include a file attachment. This is easily achieved by creating a MailAttachment object from the path and filename and passing it to the Add method.

Creating an E-mail Form

Your next step is to create a form to collect information from a Web site visitor. The form must contain a text box that enables visitors to enter their e-mail address and a multiline Text Box field to allow for messages that span multiple lines. You can add as many fields as you like, but these two are essential.

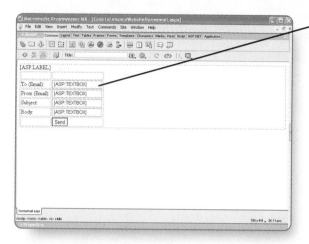

1. Create the e-mail form. You need to insert the following Web Form controls:

- A TextBox for the user to enter the recipient's e-mail address
- A TextBox for the user to enter his e-mail address
- A TextBox for the user to enter the subject of the message
- A multiline TextBox for the user to enter the body of the message
- A Submit button with an OnClick event that calls the Send_Mail method

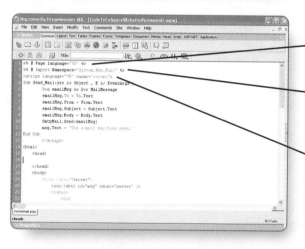

2. Use the Page directive to set the language to VB.

3. Import the System.Web.Mail namespace. This namespace includes the classes used to send e-mail.

4. Insert opening and closing <script> tags. Set the language attribute to VB and the runat attribute to server.

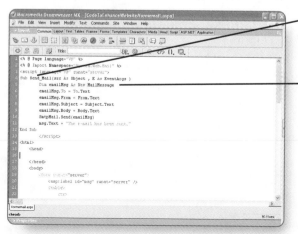

5. Insert a Send_Mail method. The Send_Mail method executes on the server when the user clicks on the Submit button.

6. Create an instance of the MailMessage object.

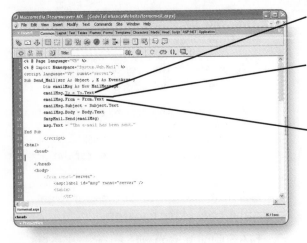

7. Retrieve the recipient's e-mail address from the form.

8. Assign the recipient's e-mail address to the `To` property of the `MailMessage` object instance.

9. Retrieve the sender's e-mail address from the form. The `Text` property of the `TextBox` stores the data entered by the user.

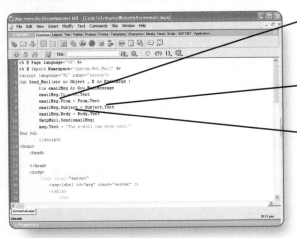

10. Assign the sender's e-mail address to the `From` property of the `MailMessage` object instance.

11. Retrieve the message subject from the form.

12. Assign the message subject to the `Subject` property of the `MailMessage` object instance.

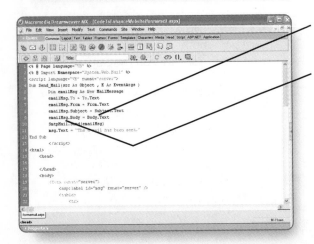

13. Retrieve the message body from the form.

14. Assign the message body to the `Body` property of the `MailMessage` object instance.

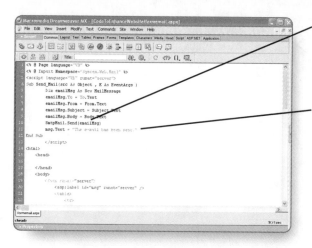

15. Pass the instance of the `MailMessage` object to the `Send` method of the `SmtpMail` object. Calling the `Send` method will post the e-mail.

16. Acknowledge that the e-mail has been sent successfully. You can use the `Text` property in a `Label` control to display the message.

Sending HTML-Formatted Messages

E-mail can look pretty bland sometimes because it is in plain text. If you want to apply formatting to your e-mail messages, you can send the message as HTML text. This will allow images and tables to be inserted in the message. Many e-mail clients already support HTML-formatted e-mail.

To send HTML-formatted messages, set the `BodyFormat` property of the `MailMessage` object to HTML.

1. Use a variable to store the HTML-formatted e-mail message and assign the message body to the `Body` property.

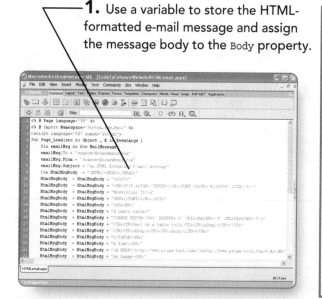

NOTE

You can

- Format text with the font, size, and color of your choice.
- Use tables to create complex layouts.
- Include links.
- Insert images in either GIF or JPEG format. You cannot use other image formats because they can't be displayed in HTML. Be sure to use absolute URLs when referencing images that reside on a Web server.

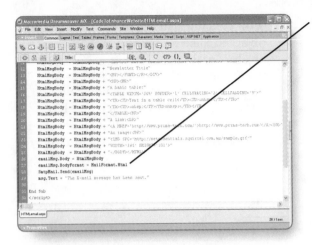

2. Set the `BodyFormat` property to `MailFormat.Html`.

Working with Files and Folders

Text files can sometimes be a handy replacement for databases. You should consider using text files when you only need to store a small amount of data that rarely gets updated.

Writing a File

With ASP, you have the power to create new text files and append data to existing files. This is achieved by creating a `StreamWriter` object. The `WriteLine` method writes text to a file.

> ### NOTE
> If your site is hosted on a Windows NT/2000 server, the folder that will contain the new file must have read/write access. Check with your system administrator if you are not sure.

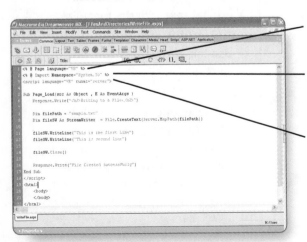

1. Set the `language` attribute of the `Page` directive to `VB`.

2. Import the `System.IO` namespace. The `System.IO` namespace contains the File class.

3. Insert opening and closing `<script>` tags. Set the `runat` attribute to `server` and the `language` attribute to `VB`.

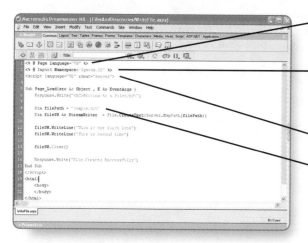

4. Insert a Page_Load method. This method executes when the page is loaded.

5. Declare the filePath variable as a string and assign the name of the file that must be created to the variable.

6. Create a StreamWriter object.

7. Pass the filePath variable to the CreateText method and assign the result to the StreamWriter object.

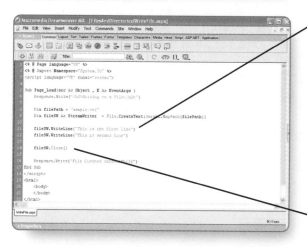

8. Use the WriteLine method of the StreamWriter object to print a line of text to the file. You must pass the text to the WriteLine method as a parameter.

NOTE

The WriteLine method prints a line break at the end of each line.

---

9. Call the Close method of the StreamWriter object. The stream closes.

Appending Data to a Text File

It is not very useful to overwrite the existing information each time you save data to a file. In fact, the ability to incrementally add data to a file lets you implement a number of practical applications. For instance, you could log user activity, store guestbook entries, and even save posted form data to a text file.

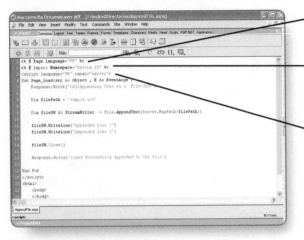

1. Set the `language` attribute of the `Page` directive to `VB`.

2. Import the `System.IO` namespace. The `System.IO` namespace contains the File class.

3. Insert opening and closing `<script>` tags. Set the `runat` attribute to `server` and the `language` attribute to `VB`.

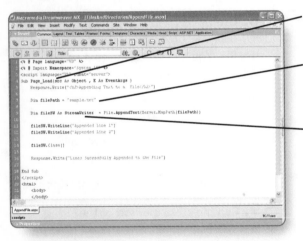

4. Insert a `Page_Load` method. This method executes when the page is loaded.

5. Declare the `filePath` variable as a string and assign the name of the file that must be created to the variable.

6. Create a `StreamWriter` object.

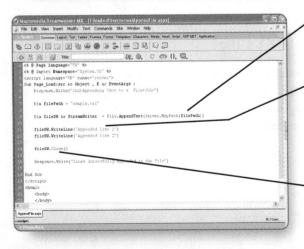

7. Pass the `filePath` variable to the `AppendText` method and assign the result to the `StreamWriter` object.

8. Use the `WriteLine` method of the `StreamWriter` object to add the text at the end of the existing file. You must pass the text to the `WriteLine` method as a parameter.

9. Call the `Close` method of the `StreamWriter` object. The stream closes.

Copying, Moving, and Deleting Files

The `FileSystem` object also has methods that enable you to copy, move, and delete files. You should always test these methods on your local machine before uploading them to a live server. If there are errors, you could accidentally delete your entire Web site!

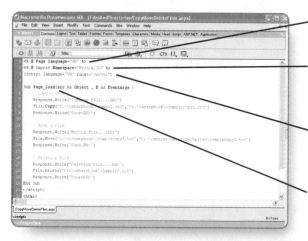

1. Set the `language` attribute of the `Page` directive to `VB`.

2. Import the `System.IO` namespace. The `System.IO` namespace contains the File class.

3. Insert opening and closing `<script>` tags. Set the `runat` attribute to `server` and the `language` attribute to `VB`.

4. Insert a `Page_Load` method. This method executes when the page is loaded.

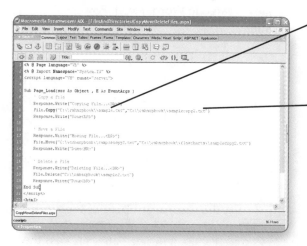

5. Pass the name and path of the source file as the first parameter to the `File.Copy` method. The source file is the file that will be copied.

6. Pass the name and path of the destination file as the second parameter to the `File.Copy` method. The destination file is a copy of the source file. It can be saved in another folder and have a different file name.

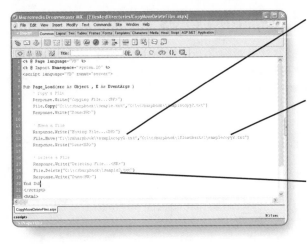

7. Pass the name and path of the source file as the first parameter to the `File.Move` method. The source file is the file that will be moved.

8. Pass the path to the file's new location as the second parameter to the `File.Move` method. The source file will move to this new location.

9. Pass the name and path of the file that must be deleted to the `File.Delete` method. The file will be deleted.

Uploading Files

ASP.NET is able to process file uploads. You can easily upload files of all types without the aid of a third-party component. You can save an uploaded file to a specified location. You can even determine the name, size, and content type of the uploaded file. Users will really appreciate the ability to update their content through a simple Web interface. You can upload files created in Word, Excel, PowerPoint, Acrobat, and just about any other application.

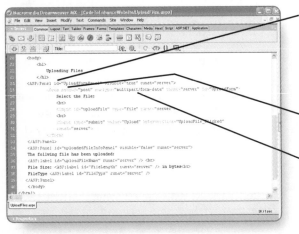

1. Insert a panel control called `UploadFormPanel`. Set the visible attribute to `true`. This panel will display when the page loads. The form that enables users to upload files appears on this panel.

2. Insert opening and closing `<form>` tags within `UploadFormPanel`.

3. Set the `enctype` attribute of the `<form>` tag to `multipart/form-data`. This step is required when a form sends a file to the server.

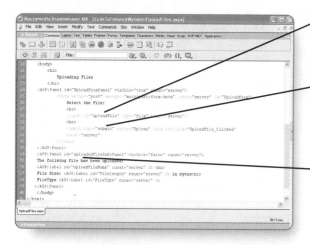

4. Insert an input field called `uploadFile`. Set the type attribute to `file`. This enables users to select the files they want to upload.

5. Insert a Submit button. Set the `OnServerClick` attribute to `UploadFile_Clicked`. `UploadFile_Clicked` is the method that will process the file upload.

6. Insert another panel called `uploadedFileInfoPanel`. Set the `visible` attribute to `false`. This panel will only appear when the file has been uploaded. It displays the properties of the uploaded file.

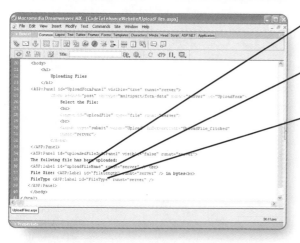

7. Insert a `Label` called `uploadFileName` that will display the name of the uploaded file.

8. Insert a `Label` called `FileLength` that will display the size of the file in bytes.

9. Insert a `Label` called `FileType` that will display the `mimetype` of the file.

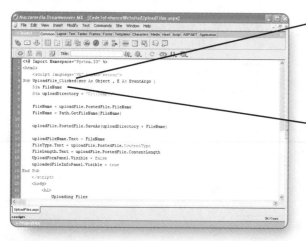

10. Insert the `UploadFile_Clicked` method. This method will execute when the user clicks on the Upload button. The method processes the file upload and displays information about the uploaded file.

11. Declare a variable called `FileName` that will store the name and path of the file specified by the user. The path maps to the user's hard drive. You need to extract the name of the file from the path.

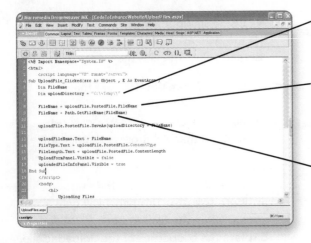

12. Declare a variable called `uploadDirectory`. This variable specifies where the file must be saved on the server.

13. Assign the `uploadFile.PostedFile.FileName` property to the `FileName` variable. The `uploadFile.PostedFile.FileName` property contains the path specified by the user.

14. Use the `GetFileName` method of the `Path` class to retrieve the file name. You don't require the existing path, which maps to the user's hard drive. The file is saved to a new folder that is specified by the `uploadDirectory` variable.

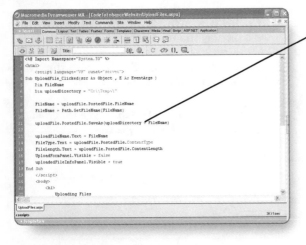

15. Concatenate the `FileName` and `uploadDirectory` variables and pass the result to the `SaveAs` method.

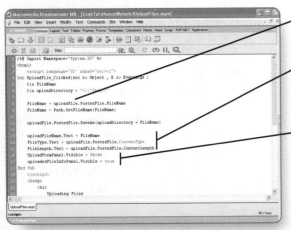

16. Use the `SaveAs` method to save the uploaded file to the server.

17. Print the `FileName`, `ContentType`, and `ContentLength` properties of the uploaded file to their respective labels.

18. Display `uploadedFileInfoPanel` by setting its `Visible` property to `true`. You must set the `Visible` property of `UploadFormPanel` to `false`.

19

Password-Protecting Your Web Site

You have thus far developed Web pages that can be viewed by all visitors to your Web site. There are many situations when you will need to password-protect certain areas of your site. Perhaps you would like to collect information from your visitors for marketing purposes or simply enable users who have paid a subscription fee access to your Web site. You also need to password-protect the areas that have been built solely for administration purposes. This chapter will help you implement a database-driven password-protection system with the Authentication server behaviors. In this chapter, you'll learn how to do the following:

- Design a database to store membership information
- Create a Login page and validate users against a database
- Display an Invalid Login error message
- Enable new users to register
- Password-protect individual pages in your site
- Log a user out

Designing the Authentication Database

The authentication database contains a list of all users who have access to the restricted areas. The database in the first instance only needs to contain a single table, which stores a unique ID for each user, their username, and password. You could also store other information such as a user's name, address, e-mail address, and phone number. This first table keeps things simple and only stores an e-mail address.

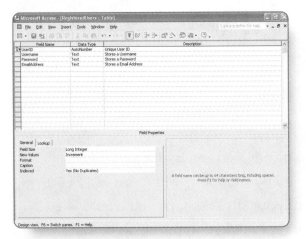

Creating a Login Page

The Login page contains a form that requires the user to enter their username and password. The Log In User server behavior must be applied to this page. It inserts code to check whether the user exists in the database and that the password is correct.

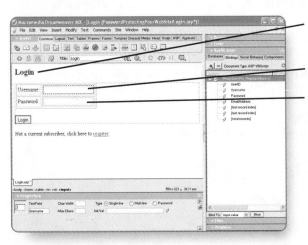

1. Create the Login form. You may use tables to help lay out the form.

2. Insert a Text field for the username.

3. Insert a Password field for the user to enter their password.

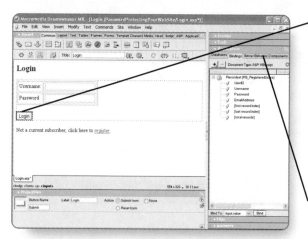

4. Insert a Submit button. The user will click on the button to send the login details to the server for processing.

> ### NOTE
> The label must indicate the purpose of the button.

5. Click on the Server Behaviors tab. The Server Behaviors tab is displayed.

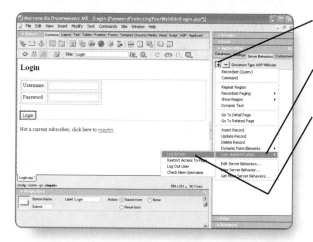

6. Click on the + sign. A submenu appears.

7. Click on User Authentication. A submenu appears.

8. Click on Log In User. The Log In User dialog box opens.

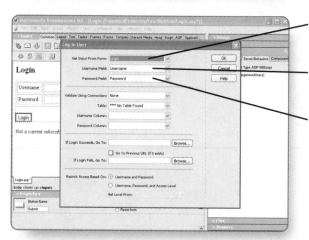

9. Select the form that contains the Username and Password fields.

10. Select the name assigned to the Username field.

11. Select the name assigned to the Password field.

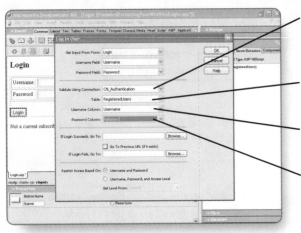

12. Select the database connection. The database must contain a list of registered users and their passwords.

13. Select the table where the details of registered users are stored.

14. Select the database column/field where the username is stored.

15. Select the database column/field where the password is stored.

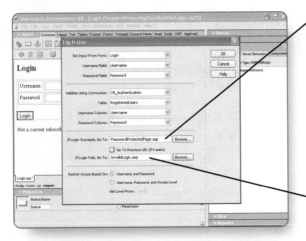

16. Type in the name of the Web page that will be displayed after the user has successfully logged in to the site.

NOTE

This will usually be a password-protected Web page.

17. Type in the name of the Web page that will be displayed if the login is unsuccessful.

18. Click on OK. The Log In User dialog box closes.

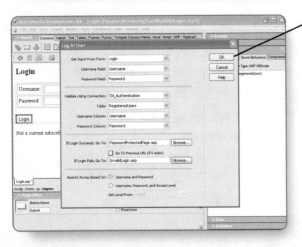

Creating the Invalid Login Page

The Invalid Login error message will be displayed if the user has accidentally entered the incorrect login details or simply does not exist in the database of valid users.

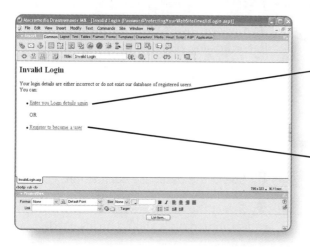

1. The Invalid Login page must link either to the

- Login page so that users can have another attempt at entering their login details.

OR

- Registration page so that new visitors wishing to access restricted areas can enter their details to register.

Registering New Users

You could also allow new users wishing to access restricted areas to add their details to the authentication database. The user will have to enter the information you require and a preferred username. The Check New User server behavior should be used to ensure that the username is not already taken.

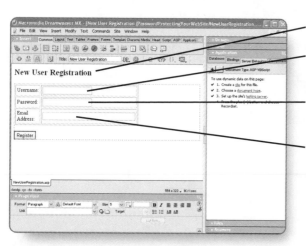

1. Create the New User Registration form.

2. Insert a Text field for the user to enter their preferred username.

3. Insert a Password field for the user to enter their password.

4. Insert any other fields that you require before a user can be registered. Sample fields include the user's first name, surname, address, and e-mail address.

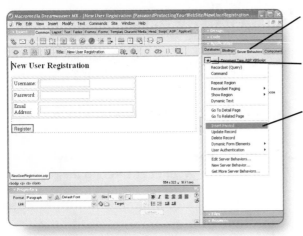

5. Click on the Server Behaviors tab, if it is not already selected. The tab is displayed.

6. Click on the + sign. A submenu appears.

7. Click on Insert Record. The Insert Record dialog box opens.

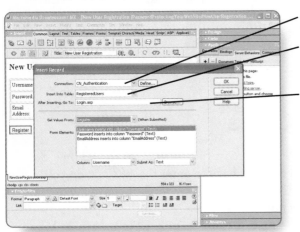

8. Select the database connection.

9. Select the database table where the registration details should be inserted.

10. Type in the name of the Web page that will be displayed after the user has registered.

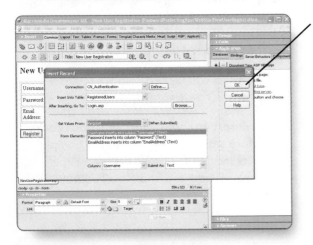

11. Click on OK. The Insert Record dialog box closes.

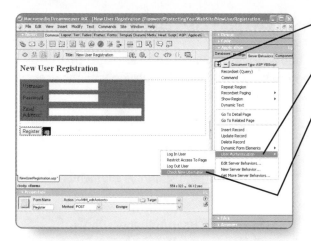

12. Click on the + sign. A submenu appears.

13. Click on User Authentication. A submenu appears.

14. Click on Check New Username. The Check New Username dialog box opens.

NOTE

The Check New Username server behavior will ensure that another user is not already using the same username.

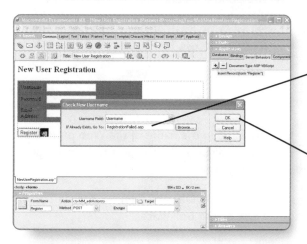

15. Type in the name of the Web page that will be displayed if the username is already in use. This page should display a Registration Failed error message.

16. Click on OK. The Check New Username dialog box closes.

Creating the Failed Registration Page

The Failed Registration page will only be displayed if a user's preferred username is already in use.

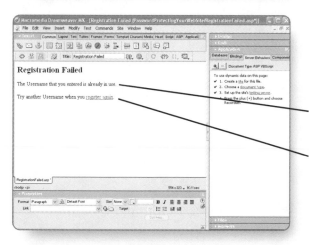

1. Inform the user that the username entered is already in use.

2. Insert a link back to the Registration page. This will enable the user to register again.

Creating a Password-Protected Page

The Restrict Access To Page server behavior must be applied to all pages that require password protection. These Web pages will not be displayed until the user has entered a valid username and password.

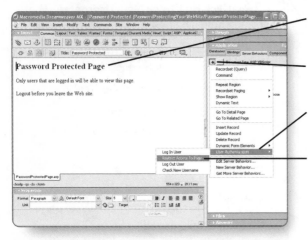

1. Open a Web page that you only want registered users to view.

2. Click on the + sign. A submenu appears.

3. Click on User Authentication. A submenu appears.

4. Click on Restrict Access To Page. The Restrict Access To Page dialog box opens.

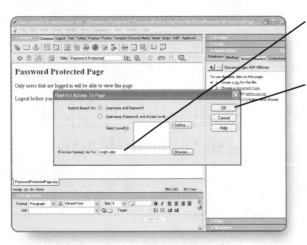

5. Type in the name of the Web page that will be displayed if the user has not logged into the site.

6. Click on OK. The Restrict Access To Page dialog box closes.

Creating a Logout Link

On each password-protected page, you should allow the user to log out of the Web site. This not only frees up valuable server resources but also provides additional security. This ensures that no other person can access the Web site within the same browser session.

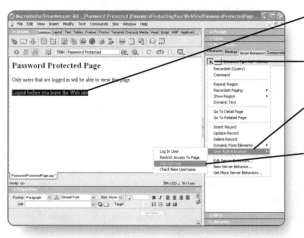

1. Select the text that the user must click on to log out of the site.

2. Click on the + sign. A submenu appears.

3. Click on User Authentication. A submenu appears.

4. Click on Log Out User. The Log Out User dialog box opens.

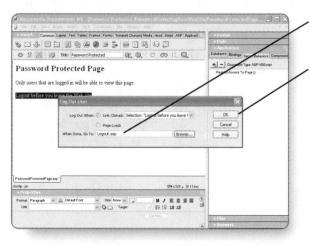

5. Type in the name of the page to display after the user has been logged out.

6. Click on OK. The Log Out User dialog box closes.

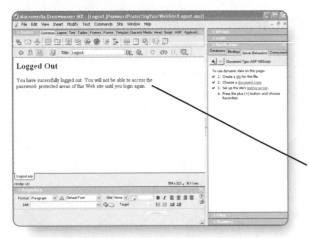

Creating the Logged Out Page

The Logged Out Web page simply displays any message you would like to display after the user has no access to restricted areas of the site.

● Inform the user that they have been successfully logged out and will not be able to access restricted areas of the site until they log in again.

Using Access Levels

We have only utilized a username and password to authenticate a user and allow access to restricted areas. This means that all users with a valid username and password can access your entire site. You may not want all your users to enjoy the same privileges. The User Authentication behaviors enable you to restrict access based upon levels. The authentication database needs an additional field to store the access level of each user.

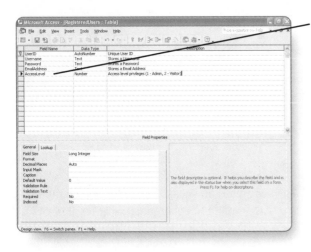

1. Add a field called AccessLevel to the RegisteredUsers table. This is a numeric field that stores the access level privileges for each user. An access level of 1 indicates the user is an administrator. A general user (Web site visitor) has an access level of 2.

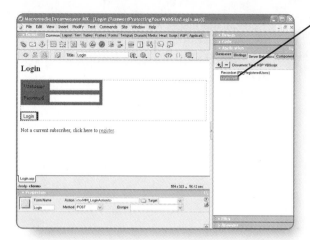

2. Open the Login page and click on the Log In User server behavior. The Log In User dialog box opens.

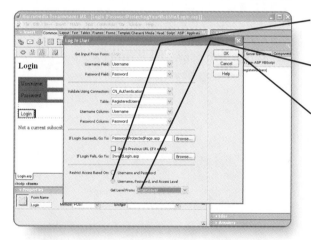

3. Restrict access based on the username, password, and access level.

4. Select the database field that stores the access level.

5. Click on OK. The Log In User dialog box closes.

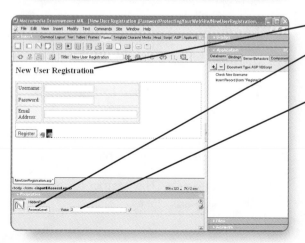

6. Open the New User Registration page.

7. Add a hidden form element called AccessLevel.

8. Set the value to 2. All new users will be assigned an access level of 2, which means they won't have administrator level rights.

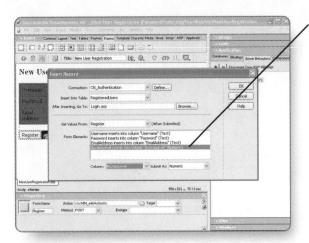

9. Edit the Insert Record server behavior. The data in the AccessLevel hidden form field needs to be inserted into the AccessLevel database field.

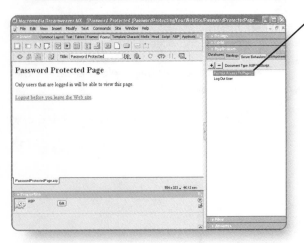

10. Open the Password-Protected page, and click on the Restrict Access To Page server behavior. The Restrict Access To Page dialog box opens.

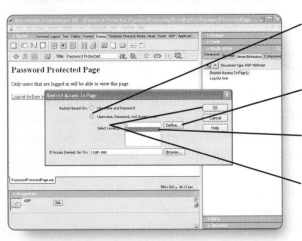

11. Restrict access to the Web page based upon a username, password, and access level.

12. Click on Define and enter the AccessLevel values.

13. Select the level that is required for a user to access the current page.

14. Click on OK. The Restrict Access To Page dialog box closes.

20

Customizing Dreamweaver MX

Dreamweaver MX is very versatile in terms of extensibility. The Server Behavior Builder has totally revolutionized the creation of simple but essential server behaviors that can easily be reused. With a basic knowledge of HTML and JavaScript, you will be able to customize the interface and build more complex extensions (objects, commands, and behaviors). The Dreamweaver MX Exchange Web site contains many extensions that are free to download and use. These will no doubt prevent you from having to hand-code that added bit of functionality that Dreamweaver MX is missing. In this chapter, you'll learn how to do the following:

- Utilize Dreamweaver MX Exchange
- Use the Server Behavior Builder
- Extend Dreamweaver MX with JavaScript

Using Dreamweaver MX Exchange

Dreamweaver MX Exchange is a Web site maintained by Macromedia that contains objects, behaviors, and commands created by other developers. These extensions are free to download and use after you register. Always check the Dreamweaver MX Exchange Web site before you create custom solutions because you could save valuable time by using existing extensions. You can also upload extensions that you have developed for others to use.

Dreamweaver MX Exchange groups extensions into categories. This makes it easy to locate and download the extensions that you require.

Using the Server Behavior Builder

You have probably developed a library of code to implement common functionality in your Web applications. With the help of the Server Behavior Builder, you can turn your code into reusable components. Building a server behavior used to be a complex task that required an understanding of XML, JavaScript, and the Dreamweaver MX API. The Server Behavior Builder enables you to concentrate your efforts on Web development while still enjoying the productivity rewards that customized behaviors bring.

Preparing your Server-Side Code

The Server Behavior Builder can be used to create server behaviors for your ASP (both VBScript and JScript), JSP, and ColdFusion scripts, but you have to create each separately. Creating a server behavior is very easy if you implement the process outlined as follows:

1. Divide your code into separate blocks. A server behavior can insert code at various positions in a Web page. These include

- Before/after the opening HTML tag
- Before/after the closing HTML tag
- Before/after the current selection
- Replacing the current selection

2. Decide where the separate code blocks should be inserted in the current document.

3. Determine the parameters that will be used to customize the script. There will usually be constants in your code that must be specifically set each time you insert the code. The Server Behavior Builder automatically creates a user-friendly interface for data entry.

Creating a Countdown Server Behavior

In Chapter 18, "Writing Code to Enhance Your Web Site," we discussed the code required to count down the days remaining before an event occurs. We now utilize the Server Behavior Builder to convert the Countdown script into a reusable and easily customizable component.

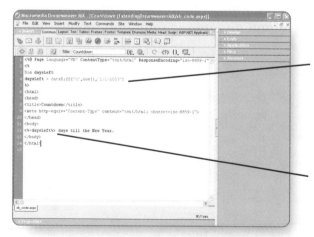

1. The code has been separated into two code blocks:

- The first code block uses the `dateDiff` method to calculate the number of days remaining and stores the result in the `daysLeft` variable. This code block needs to be inserted before the opening `<html>` tag.

- The second code block simply uses the `<%=` and `%>` delimiters to print the `daysLeft` variable to the Web page. This code block must replace the current selection. It could be inserted anywhere within the body of the Web page.

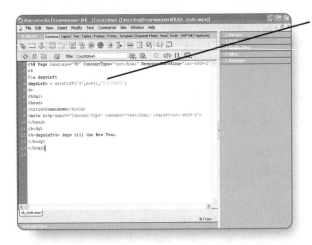

2. The date of the event needs to be a modifiable parameter. Each time you use the Countdown behavior you will be counting down to a different event.

We are now ready to create the Countdown server behavior.

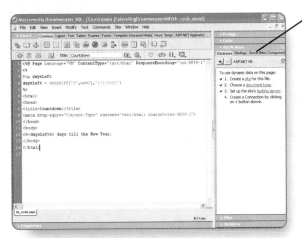

3. Expand the Application panel and click on the Server Behaviors tab. The Server Behaviors tab is displayed.

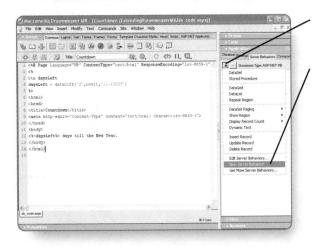

4. Click on the + sign. A submenu appears.

5. Click on New Server Behavior. The New Server Behavior dialog box opens.

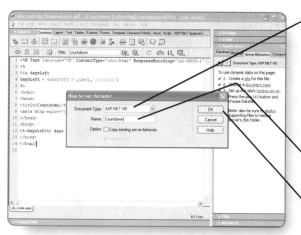

6. Select the server model under Document Type. The code that you want to implement as a server behavior must be written in the appropriate scripting language. The Countdown server behavior that we are creating is written for ASP.NET in VB.NET.

7. Type in the name of the server behavior.

8. Click on OK. The Server Behavior Builder dialog box opens.

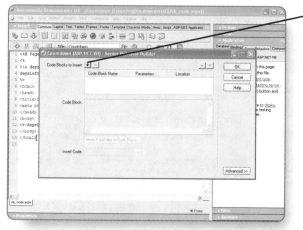

9. Click on the + sign to add the first code block. The Create a New Code Block dialog box appears.

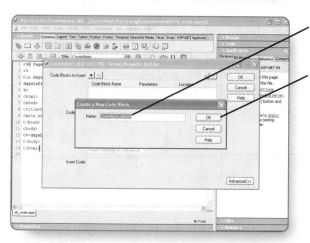

10. Type in the name of the code block. The default value is usually a safe bet.

11. Click on OK. The Create a New Code Block dialog box closes.

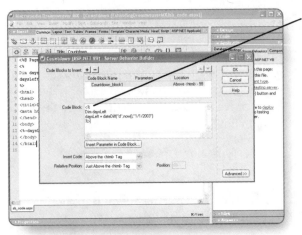

12. Paste the first code block into the Code Block field.

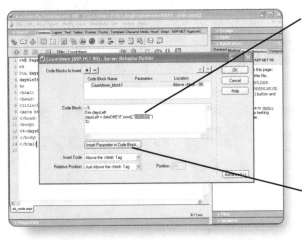

13. Select the hard-coded value that needs to be replaced by a parameter. The value is highlighted.

CAUTION

Don't include the surrounding quotation marks in the selection.

14. Click on Insert Parameter in Code Block. The Insert Parameter In Code Block dialog box opens.

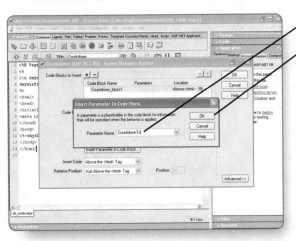

15. Type in a name for the parameter.

16. Click on OK. The parameter is inserted in the code block.

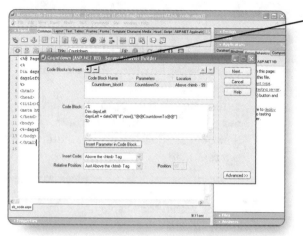

17. Click on the + sign to insert the second code block. The Create a New Code Block dialog box opens.

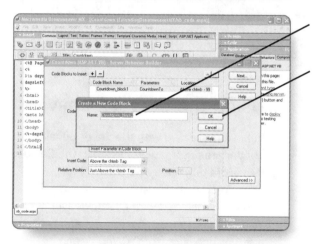

18. Type in a name for the second code block.

19. Click on OK. The Create a New Code Block dialog box closes.

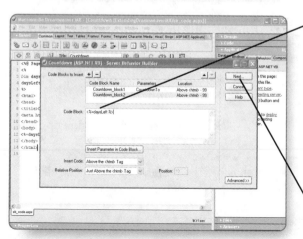

20. Paste the second code block into the Code Block field.

NOTE

When creating your own server behaviors, you will need to repeat steps 17–20 for each code block.

---

21. Click on Next. The Generate Behavior dialog box opens.

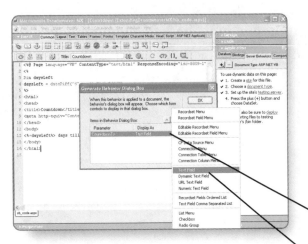

22. Click within the Display As column. A submenu appears.

23. Select the appropriate form control.

24. Click on OK. The Generate Behavior dialog box closes.

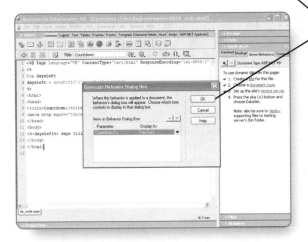

Using the Server Behavior

Behaviors created with the Sever Behavior Builder are automatically listed in the Server Behaviors tab. The generated server behaviors function just like the standard behaviors included with Dreamweaver MX. You can easily insert, customize, and remove a server behavior from a Web page.

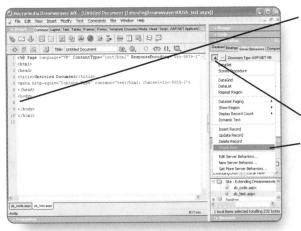

1. Select the placeholder text that must be replaced by the second Countdown code block. Remember that the second code block in the Countdown script simply prints the number of days left.

2. Click on the + sign. A submenu appears.

3. Click on the name of the server behavior. The dialog box for the behavior opens.

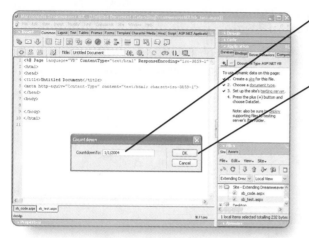

4. Type in a value for the parameter. In this case we enter the date of the event (New Year 2004).

5. Click on OK. The server behavior dialog box closes.

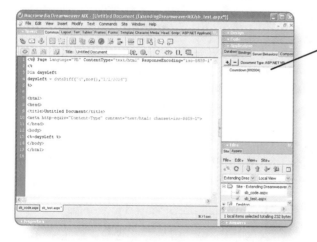

NOTE

The server behavior has been included in the Server Behaviors tab.

Creating Complex Extensions

With a working knowledge of JavaScript you can create new commands, server behaviors, objects, inspectors, and floating palettes. The Dreamweaver MX Document Object Model (DOM), a tree structure that describes the contents of HTML documents in terms of objects and properties, is fully programmable.

Viewing the Extending Dreamweaver Documentation

It is beyond the scope of this book to detail the Dreamweaver MX DOM and JavaScript API, but Extending Dreamweaver documentation is available.

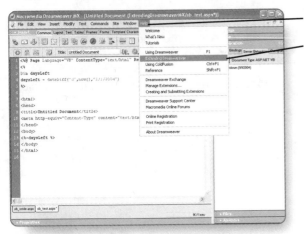

1. Click on Help. The Help menu appears.

2. Click on Extending Dreamweaver. The Extending Dreamweaver MX documentation is displayed in your default browser.

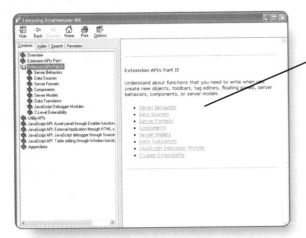

NOTE

The Extending Dreamweaver MX documentation serves as an excellent resource to get you started. The documentation contains detailed information about the Document Object Model, Dreamweaver JavaScript API, Design Notes API, File I/O API, HTTP API, and the Database API. You will also find well-documented examples of objects, Properties Inspectors, floating panels, and behaviors.

A

Using Keyboard Shortcuts

Keyboard shortcuts are a great way to increase the speed at which you build dynamic Web sites in Dreamweaver MX. A few shortcuts are mentioned within the book, but many more are listed here. In this appendix, you'll learn how to use shortcuts that do the following:

- Perform common tasks in Dreamweaver MX
- Open panels, windows, and inspectors

Keyboard Shortcuts to Perform Common Tasks

You will need to perform a number of common tasks, such as opening and closing a file, each time you work in Dreamweaver MX. While you can use menus, keyboard shortcuts offer a much quicker alternative.

Press This Key Combination	To Do This
Ctrl+n	Create a new file
Ctrl+o	Open a file
Ctrl+s	Save a file
Ctrl+w	Close a file
Ctrl+q	Quit Dreamweaver MX
Ctrl+Shift+S	Save all files
Ctrl+z	Undo your last step
Ctrl+x	Redo your last step
Ctrl+c	Copy the current selection
Ctrl+v	Paste the current selection
Ctrl+Shift+R	Enable Live Data Preview
Ctrl+Alt+I	Insert an image
Ctrl+Alt+t	Insert a table
Shift+F7	Check spelling
F1	Display Dreamweaver MX Help documentation
F12	Preview the current Web page in a Web browser

Keyboard Shortcuts to Open Panels, Windows, and Inspectors

Dreamweaver MX has many, many panels, windows, and inspectors. You can't display them all at the same time. You'll want to be able to open and close the panels you require quickly and easily. The Launcher provides a convenient way to do this, but it can only display a limited numbers of icons. The solution is to become familiar with the keyboard shortcuts that open panels, windows, and inspectors.

Press This Key Combination	To Open This
F8	Site window
Alt+F8	View Site Map
Ctrl+F2	Insert bar
Ctrl+F3	Properties Inspector
Ctrl+F9	Bindings panel
Ctrl+F10	Server Behaviors panel
Shift+F11	CSS Styles panel
Ctrl+F11	HTML Styles panel
Shift+F3	Behaviors panel
Shift+F10	History panel
F10	Code Inspector
F11	Assets panel
Ctrl+Shift+F1	Reference panel
Ctrl+Tab	Switch views

B

What's on
the Web Site?

The companion Web site for this book can be found at
http://www.premierpressbooks.com/downloads.asp

The Web site contains a variety of tools to help you get started
using Dreamweaver MX, including the following:

- Sample code from the book

- Three bonus Flash movies that will guide you step by step
  through using Dreamweaver MX to developing Web
  applications in JSP, PHP, and ColdFusion.

- Sample applications built with Dreamweaver MX including a
  Guestbook, Online Voting Booth, Job Board, and Content
  Management System.

- Examples from Chapter 18, "Writing Code to Enhance Your
  Web Site," written in ASP, PHP, JSP, and ColdFusion.

Index